# The Complete Book of
# United States History

## Grades 3-5

Acknowledgments:
School Specialty Publishing Editorial/Art & Design Team
Vincent F. Douglas, President
Tracey E. Dils, Publisher
Phyllis Armelie Sibbing, B.S. Ed., Project Editor
Rose Audette, Art Director
Allison Mohrman, Interior Design and Production
Brian Collins, Interior Production

Also Thanks to:
Victoria Cox Kaser, B.S. Ed., Writer
Caitlin Scott, Photo Researcher
Illustrated Alaskan Moose Inc., Cover Illustration

Photo Credits:
13, 251, 254: © Danny Lehman/CORBIS; 15, 19: b., 19: t., 20: t., 23, 137, 138: © Ohio Historical Society; 18, 31, 39, 55, 67, 89, 95, 98, 101, 112, 115, 119, 120, 121, 123, 126, 148, 149, 152, 156, 171, 183, 202, 205, 208, 221, 222, 223, 231, 233, 243, 278, 285, 287, 288, 294, 303, 306: b., 306: t., 307, 309, 316, 320, 330, 331: © Bettmann/CORBIS; 20: b. © Richard A. Cooke/CORBIS; 30: Alder Planetarium & Astronomy Museum, Chicago, IL.; 34: © Historical Picture Archive/ CORBIS; 40, 52: The Library of Congress; 44: Florida State Archives; 61: © David Muench/CORBIS. 61; 65: t., 142: The Granger Collection; 65: b. Plimoth Plantations; 68, 69, 70: The Library Company of Philadelphia; 79, 110, 116, 167, 181, 195, 210, 235, 264, 265, 271, 279, 296, 299: t., 312, 323: © CORBIS; 99: l., 129, 293: © Galyn C. Hammond; 99: r. © James M. Mejuto; 102: © Oscar White/CORBIS; 113: © Richard T. Nowitz/CORBIS; 114, 336: © Joseph Sohm/CORBIS; 128: © 1998 North Wind Pictures; 145: t. Francis Miller/Time Pix; 145: b. © 1974 Alex Webb/Magnum Photos, Inc.; 184: National Geographic Society; 203: © James L. Amos/CORBIS; 226: © Ted Spiegel/ CORBIS; 234: Tuskegee University Archives; 244: © Tykoff Collection/CORBIS; 249: © Museum of Flight/CORBIS; 275: © Arthur Rothstein/CORBIS; 308: World Wide Photos; 322: © Bob Rowan; Progressive Image/CORBIS; 326: © Eric and David Hosking/ CORBIS; 321: © Richard Howard/Black Star Publishing/Picture Quest.

Every effort has been made to credit all copyrighted material. Any errors or omissions are inadvertent and will be corrected in future printings.

School Specialty
Publishing

Send all inquiries to:
School Specialty Publishing
8720 Orion Place
Columbus, OH 43240-2111

ISBN 1-56189-679-9

10 11 12 13 14 15 WAL 11 10 09 08 07 06

# TABLE OF CONTENTS

# UNIT 4

## A NEW NATION IS BORN (1775-1810)

# UNIT 5

## THE U.S. FROM COAST TO COAST (1785-1860)

# UNIT 6

## AMERICA AGAINST AMERICA (1840-1870)

# UNIT 7

## THE UNITED STATES GROWS (1865-1900)

# UNIT 8

## A TIME OF CHANGE (1890-1920)

# UNIT 9

## A TIME OF TROUBLES (1914-1945)

# UNIT 10

## NEW FRONTIERS (1950-PRESENT)

# UNIT 1

*until early 1500s A.D.*

# THE FIRST AMERICANS

Some people think of America as a new land. That is probably because Christopher Columbus arrived on its shores only a little over 500 years ago. American history, however, stretches back much further than the European explorers such as Christopher Columbus. To know American history, we must start by reading about the first people who lived on this land. That means we must begin thousands and thousands of years ago.

**TIME LINE**

**About 70,000 years ago:** The Ice Age starts.

**About 15,000 years ago:** The first people arrived in North America.

**100 B.C.:** The Serpent Mound is built near Locust Grove, Ohio.

**1500:** Plains Indians start using horses to follow the buffalo herds.

**1325:** The Aztecs build Tenochtitlán

**1125:** The Hohokam use hundreds of miles of canals to farm the Sonora Desert.

| 68,000 B.C. | 14,000 B.C. | 250 B.C. | 0 | 250 A.D. | 500 A.D. | 750 A.D. | 1000 A.D. | 1250 | 1500 |
|---|---|---|---|---|---|---|---|---|---|

# PEOPLE ARRIVE IN THE AMERICAS

About 70,000 years ago, Earth's climate began to change. Our planet slowly started to cool. As temperatures dropped, water became ice. The ice formed into glaciers—great, thick, frozen sheets that covered the land. These glaciers, inch by inch and year by year, slowly blanketed northern lands. Scientists call this time the Ice Age. It was not Earth's first Ice Age, but it was the most recent.

*Ancestors of the earliest Americans hunted woolly mammoths.*

## The Sea Becomes Land

The amount of water on Earth always stays about the same. How, then, did the glaciers of the Ice Age form? They formed from water in oceans and lakes. This caused ocean levels to fall. In places where the oceans were shallow, land that was usually covered with water became exposed. One place where this happened is the Bering Strait.

Today, the Bering Strait is a shallow sea that separates Asia from North America. But during the Ice Age when the water levels dropped, a strip of land 1,000 miles long slowly emerged from beneath the shallow water. For most of the rest of this Ice Age—for thousands of more years—that strip of land connected the continents of Asia and North America.

*This map shows the location of the Bering Land Bridge and possible routes that early migrators followed.*

## The Land Becomes a Bridge

Before the last Ice Age, no humans lived in North America. But that changed. The new land connecting the continents dried out. Plants grew, and animals moved onto the new land to eat the plants. Other animals came to eat those animals.

*These are the types of shelters that might have been built by ancient Americans.*

Humans were living in Asia before the time of the Ice Age. These humans depended on animals for their food and clothing. So, as animals wandered onto the new land, some of these humans followed after them. Together, the animals and humans slowly moved eastward. After thousands and thousands of years, descendents of those early travelers became the first humans to reach North America. The land that had been at the bottom of the Bering Strait had become a bridge between continents.

9

Today, that bridge created by the Ice Age and known as the Bering Land Bridge is again beneath the sea.

## People Move Through the Americas

Slowly, groups of people spread down through North America, then into South America. These groups developed tools of stone and bone. They learned how to make fire. They first used spears, then spears hurled by atlatls (AT lat lz)—long, hooked sticks—to kill their prey. They also learned to weave plant fibers into clothing and baskets.

## How We Know What We Know

Scientists have many ways of learning about life in ancient times. Sometimes they use radiocarbon dating. Radiocarbon dating measures the amount of radiocarbon in an object. Everything that is or was once alive has radiocarbon in it. The smaller the amount of radiocarbon, the older the object. For example, scientists know that part of the Bering Land Bridge was still above the water as recently as 11,000 years ago. They know this because of radiocarbon dating of old plant material from the ocean floor there.

The plant material scientists dredged up from the bottom of the Bering Strait has told them other things, too. Scientists know that dwarf birch trees and certain kinds of grasses grew on the Land Bridge. This means that the climate there must have been cold, because cold climates are where those trees and grasses grow.

*An atlatl may have looked similar to this drawing. Atlatls were used to hurl spears.*

Scientists have learned, too, about those earliest Americans by studying the things they left behind. They know from old weapons and old campsites that these first Americans hunted animals like woolly mammoths, saber-toothed tigers, American lions, and giant beavers. Scientists also know that the people gathered wild plants and berries to add to their diets of meat.

The story of American history begins with these ancient peoples who spread throughout North and South America. But they were only the first of many peoples who came to settle this New World.

## Show What You Know

Here are pictures of three different animals that ancient Americans hunted. Go to the library or look on the Internet to find information about these animals. Next, draw a picture of each animal. Then, make a fact card for each animal. Write some interesting facts that you learned from your research.

until early 1500s A.D.

*Woolly mammoth*

*Sloth*

*Sabor-toothed tiger*

# THE PEOPLE OF THE OTHER AMERICAS

## The Maya

In 1841, American explorer John Lloyd Stephens was in the jungles of Honduras when he came upon the ruins of an ancient city. He later wrote, "It lay before us like a shattered bark [ship] in the midst of the ocean, her masts gone, her name effaced [erased], her crew perished, and none to tell whence she came, to whom she belonged, how long on her voyage, or what caused her destruction . . ."

What Stephens had found was the remains of a city built by an ancient people called the Maya. Most of the questions that Stephens asked would be answered as scientists studied that city and the other cities that marked the Maya civilization.

The Maya prospered from about 250 A.D. to 900 A.D. During those centuries, they built great limestone pyramids to honor their gods. The Maya influenced all the people of Central America's Yucatan Peninsula.

The Maya were great mathematicians. In fact, they are thought to be the first people in the world to use a zero. They also learned all about astronomy— the study of the stars. They used their math and astronomy skills to create two calendars. One calendar was to mark the important ceremonies of the Maya religion. This calendar was 260 days long. The other calendar

The Inca used knotted ropes as part of their numbering system.

## The Remembered Inca

Unlike the Maya, the Inca had no written language. Instead, they preserved their history by using people called rememberers. These rememberers would tell aloud the stories about the past of the Inca.

was 365 days long. This was more like the calendar we use today, because, like ours, that calendar was based on the length of time it takes for Earth to revolve around the Sun.

Part of the reason we know a lot about the Maya is because they developed a writing system. In their system, the Maya used little pictures to represent words and ideas. That kind of writing system is called hieroglyphics

*Above: This ancient Mayan marker is engraved with hieroglyphics.*

(high uh ruh GLIH fihks). The Maya carved hieroglyphics into many of the things they built. They also carved them on tall monuments. The writing on these monuments tells of important events in the lives of Maya rulers. As scientists figured out the meaning of these hieroglyphics, they were able to read all about the history and way of life of the Maya.

The Maya were among the first people known to cultivate corn. Cultivate means to grow on purpose. When the Maya first added corn to their diet, corn was not like it is today. Corn was a wild plant, and its little ears might have measured only an inch in length! But as the Maya farmed, they carefully chose the seeds to plant from the largest ears of corn. Gradually, the plants produced larger and larger ears, until finally they looked much like the corn we eat today.

Besides being a delicious addition to the diet of the Maya, corn was valuable for another reason. Unlike many other foods, corn did not spoil or rot quickly in the warm, moist climate of Central America. This meant that extra corn grown in one season could be stored to help feed the people until the next season's harvest.

Corn was so important to the Maya that it figured into their legends. For example, the Maya believed that the gods tried three times to create the first man. The first time, they made a man of clay. That man was destroyed by flood. The second time, they made a man of wood, but that man was destroyed by winds. The third man was made of corn. That man, according to the Maya, became the father of all people.

## The Aztec

Legend says that the Aztec spent centuries wandering the land, looking for a home. Finally, in 1325, they arrived at the edge of Lake Texcoco, an ancient lake in present-day Mexico. Then, one of their gods spoke. He told them to look in the swamps of Lake Texcoco. He said, "Go, go and look at the cactus, and on it . . . you shall see an eagle." The god said the eagle would be eating a snake.

The Aztec settled where they found the snake-eating eagle. On that place on an island in Lake Texcoco they built Tenochtitlán (teh nohch tee TLAHN). The Aztec decided that Tenochtitlán would be their capital city. From that center, the Aztec said, "We shall confront

AZTEC
MAYA
INCA

Pacific
Ocean

[face] all who surround us and . . . vanquish [conquer] them all . . . "

That is exactly what the Aztec did. During the 1400s, Aztec warriors conquered most of the peoples who lived in central Mexico. Those conquered groups paid tribute, or honor, to their conquerors by supplying the ruling Aztec with food, like corn, beans, and tomatoes. They also supplied the Aztec with valuable metals, such as gold, silver, and copper. And, they supplied the Aztec with people to sacrifice. The Aztec believed their gods needed human blood to stay strong. Only strong gods could guarantee that the crops would grow and the rains would come. So, they sacrificed people by the thousands.

Atlantic Ocean

The taxes and tribute paid by those conquered by the Aztec helped make the Aztec Empire rich. Tenochtitlán grew. It became one of the world's largest cities of the time, with thousands of stone buildings and huge stone pyramids. A network of

canals supplied water to the 300,000 people who lived in the city. The empire grew, too. Eventually, through conquest and war, the Aztec Empire ruled over 5 million people.

## The Inca

Much of South America along its Pacific coast is desert land. This desert continues inland for a short distance, and then ends where the Andes Mountains begin their climb into the sky. This is a dry, difficult region—the desert and the mountains. Yet it is here that, in the middle of the 1400s, the Inca created a great empire. At its strongest, the Inca Empire ran for 2,500 miles along South America's Pacific coastline.

The Inca were great builders. In fact, they could set the stones in a wall so closely together that cement was not needed to hold up the wall. They also built an extensive system of roads and bridges to connect the length of their empire. Parts of this transportation system are still in use today, 500 years after the Inca Empire ended.

## Show What You Know

Today, there are at least 300 kinds of corn grown and eaten by people all over the world. Look in a recipe book and find a recipe that uses corn as an ingredient. Then, with the help of an adult, follow the recipe to make the corn dish for your family or friends to enjoy.

# EARLY NORTH AMERICANS

Today, the southwest corner of the United States is mainly hot and dry. The land is broken by mountains and mesas (MAY suhz)—flat-topped hills. Great canyons mark the land like deep wounds. In fact, the Grand Canyon—almost a mile deep—runs through part of this region.

Thousands of years ago, the land in the Southwest was much the same as it is today. Yet, into this area came early Native American groups, who farmed and built villages and practiced their religions. They thrived for hundreds of years.

### The "Vanished Ones"

One of the early cultures that formed in the Southwest was the Hohokam (huh HOH kuhm). Scientists think the first Hohokam originally came up from Central America. Around 300 B.C., they settled in the valleys carved by the Gila (HEE luh) and Salt rivers.

The water of these rivers was the key to the Hohokam's success. Working together, the people built a complex canal system. The canals allowed the Hohokam to irrigate, or artificially water, their crops by bringing water from the rivers to the fields. Eventually, over 600 miles of canals delivered water to fields as far away as 16 miles!

## Hohokam Canals Discovered

*The city of Phoenix, Arizona, owes part of its success to the canal system of the Hohokam. In 1867, a man uncovered the old Hohokam canals and discovered that they still could bring water to the region! This encouraged people to settle in the valley, and eventually the city of Phoenix was born. It was named Phoenix because, like the mythical bird that rises out of its own ashes, this city arose on the ashes of the Hohokam civilization.*

For over 1,000 years, the Hohokam farmed and hunted and traded in the Southwest. Their civilization flourished. Then, around 1500 A.D., the Hohokam left their towns. No one is sure why. Some think the cause was a drought. Others think it might have been war. But whatever the reason, they were gone. This mysterious ending to their civilization is why this group is called the Hohokam. Hohokam is a Indian word for "vanished ones."

## The "Ancient Ones"

Look at a map of the United States. Find the place where the states of Utah, Colorado, Arizona, and New Mexico meet. This place is now called the Four Corners, but it was once home to the Anasazi (ah nuh SAH zee). Anasazi, or "ancient ones," is the name given to this region's early Native American groups by later Native Americans who lived in the region.

The first people to live in the Four Corners region hunted and gathered the food they needed. Then, corn was introduced to the area, and the people began to farm. Around 1 A.D., they also learned to use plant material like straw and vines to weave baskets. The baskets made it easier to collect and carry food. Perhaps 500 or 600 years later, they developed pottery. Pottery allowed them to cook and store their food.

Early Anasazi lived in pithouses—houses whose floors were dug several feet into the ground. Pithouses often had two rooms. In one room, the people worked, cooked, and slept. Another, smaller room probably was used for storage.

*The Cliff Palace of the Anasazi was one of the largest pueblos ever built.*

Around 750 A.D., Anasazi housing began to change. Houses now were built above the ground. Blocks of sandstone or adobe— sun-dried clay—were used to create tall buildings that were like apartments. In these buildings, people reached the higher floors by climbing up ladders. These early apartment buildings later became known as pueblos (PWEH blohz).

The Cliff Palace was one of the Anasazi's largest pueblos. Like many other pueblos, the Cliff Palace was perched on the ledge of a cliff, set into a canyon wall. This made it easy to defend against invaders. Perhaps 350 people lived in the 200 rooms that made up the Cliff Palace.

Like their neighbors, the Hohokam, the Anasazi suddenly left their homes. By about 1300, pueblos like the grand Cliff Palace stood empty. No one is sure what happened to the pueblo dwellers. Some scientists think, however, that the soil on the mesa tops the Anasazi farmed just gave out. When the farmers could not produce enough food, the people had to leave.

*These petroglyphs are Anasazi drawings found on stone walls.*

## Show What You Know

Some of what we know about the Anasazi comes from the thousands of petroglyphs (PEH truh glihfs) they left on the stone walls and cliffs in the Southwest. A petroglyph is a drawing on stone. The Anasazi drew petroglyphs of their hunters and their holy men. They drew the patterns of the stars and the routes they used to travel around their region.

The petroglyph pictured here shows a group of Anasazi along with an animal, possibly a deer. On a separate sheet of paper, draw a petroglyph that tells something about your everyday life. Share your petroglyph with a friend and challenge him or her to interpret it.

# THOSE MYSTERIOUS MOUND BUILDERS

Here is an example of clothing worn by the Mound Builders.

Between about 200 B.C. and 500 A.D., many different Native American groups lived along the Mississippi, the Missouri, the Ohio, and other rivers of the Midwest. These Native American groups were all different from each other. Yet, they had some things in common. The things they shared make scientists think of all the groups as part of one culture—the Hopewell culture.

## The Mound Builders

The name Hopewell comes from the name of one of the sites in southern Ohio where remains of that culture can be found. Those who shared that name also shared this: they all built mound-shaped earthen monuments for their dead.

This stone mask is believed to be that of a mound builder.

### The Adena Mound People

One of the most famous mounds in the world is The Great Serpent Mound in Adams County, Ohio. Scientists think the Adena built it. From the air, this mound looks like a serpent, or snake, uncoiling across the countryside for almost a quarter of a mile. The snake's open mouth seems ready to swallow the roundish mound in front of it. Some think this roundish mound looks like an egg. Both serpents and eggs have meaning in many different religions. Others, though, think the serpent is swallowing the sun, and this might show how the Adena thought eclipses occur.

This is how the mounds were built. First, Hopewell mourners put the ashes of those who died into log-lined tombs. Into the tombs also went jewelry, pipes, pots, knives, and other things the dead might need when their spirits moved to the next world. Then, the Hopewell piled ton after ton of dirt into a mound over the tombs. The mound might get bigger as more bodies—some in tombs, some not—were buried in its sides. Some of the thousands of mounds in this region were shaped like cones or cigars. Others were effigy (EH fuh jee) mounds— mounds shaped like living things. Sometimes the mounds are only 3 or 4 feet high. Sometimes they reach 50 feet or more!

Evidence shows that there had been mound builders before the Hopewell appeared. In fact, the Adena (uh DEE nuh) culture had thrived along the Ohio Valley, where the Ohio River runs, for 700 or 800 years before the Hopewell came to the region. Scientists think that the Adena hunted and gathered their food, while the Hopewell depended on farming to help meet their needs. This

*Top: This Wray figurine is from the Hopewell period.*
*Bottom: The Great Serpent Mound is almost a quarter of a mile long.*

allowed the Hopewell to stay in one place for longer periods of time than could the Adena, who had to follow the animals they hunted. Farming also allowed the Hopewell culture to grow, because it and hunting fed more people than hunting did alone.

## Trade Unites the Hopewell

The idea of mound building might have spread from one group to another as the groups met to trade. It was the rivers that allowed this to happen. The rivers gave the groups an easy way to travel through the region and beyond.

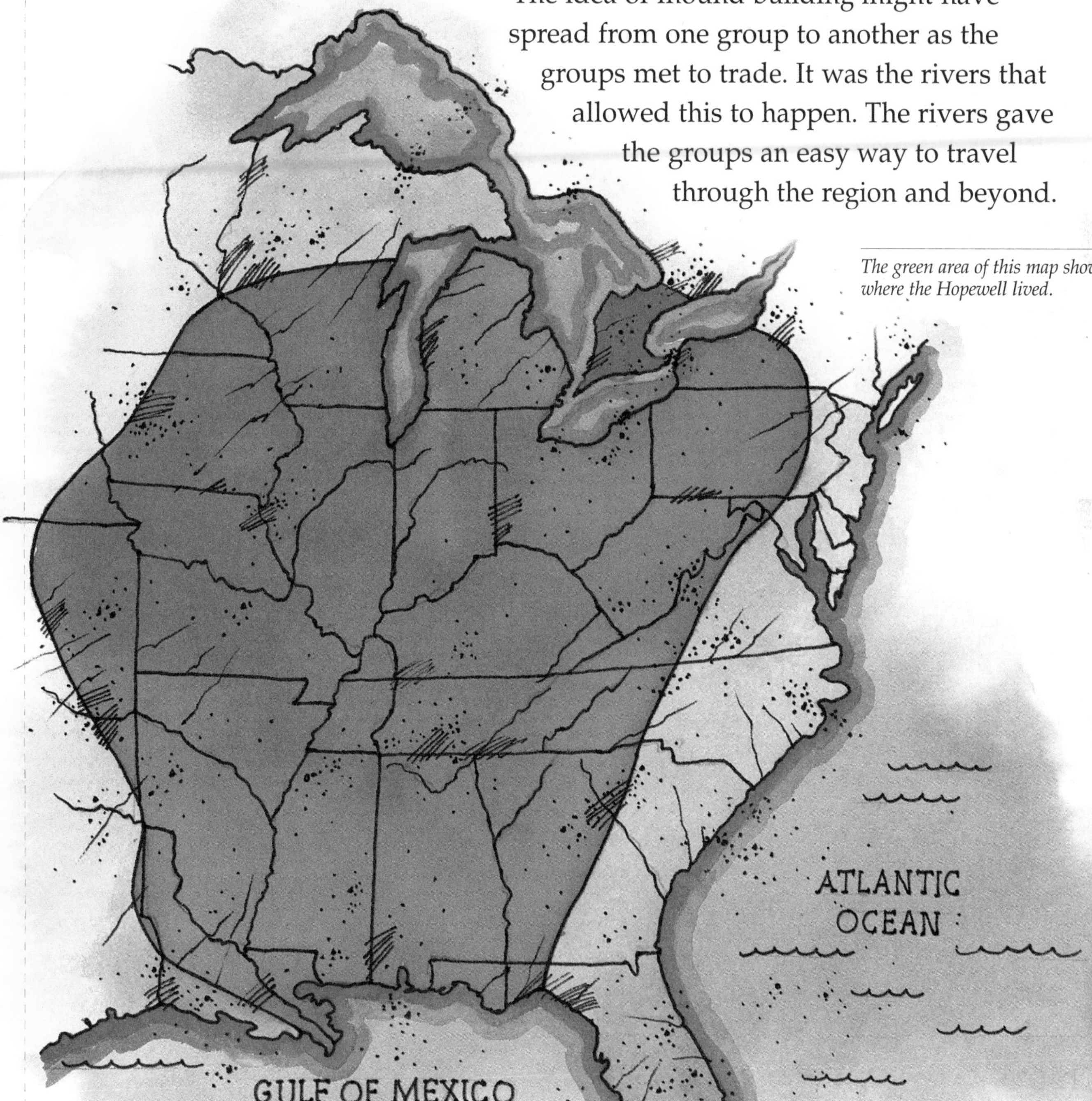

*The green area of this map shows where the Hopewell lived.*

ATLANTIC OCEAN

GULF OF MEXICO

The mounds themselves tell the story of trade and the Hopewell. Copper mined around the Great Lakes was used to make some of the bird effigies, rings, and bracelets found in the mounds. The mounds also contained necklaces carved from seashells from the Gulf of Mexico. The insides of the tombs sometimes were lined with mica, a shiny mineral that probably came from Tennessee.

## The End of the Mound Builders

Scientists do not know what caused the end of the Hopewell. But by around 500 A.D., the culture began to fail. Soon, all that remained of the Hopewell were thousands of mounds, which only hint at what the culture was like. Over a thousand years later, poet William Cullen Bryant said this about the land where the Hopewell had thrived:

> . . . The gopher mines the ground
> Where stood the swarming cities. All is gone;
> All—save the piles of earth that hold their bones . . .
>
> –from "The Prairies," by William Cullen Bryant

## Show What You Know

You have read how things found in Hopewell mounds tell about the Hopewell trade network. Use what you have learned to complete the table below.

| FOUND IN MOUNDS | CAME FROM |
|---|---|
| copper | |
| | Gulf of Mexico |
| silver | Canada |
| mica | |
| shark's teeth | Florida |

# LIFE IN THE IROQUOIS NATION

Northeast Woodlands does not describe just one group of Indians and one way of life. Instead, Northeast Woodlands is a term used to talk about all Native American groups that lived in the northeastern part of our country. This area extended from the Atlantic coast to the Mississippi River and from just below the Ohio River all the way into present-day Canada.

*Iroquois clothing was often elaborately decorated with embroidery and beadwork.*

The dozens of Native American groups living in the Northeast Woodlands were different from each other in many ways. But the groups of this region had one important thing in common—forests. These groups built their shelters and made their tools from the forests' trees. Animals that lived in the forests were important sources of food and clothing for all the groups of the Northeast.

## The Iroquois Nation Forms

Legend says that sometime in the 1500s, two Indian leaders began a journey. One, a holy man of the Huron tribe, was called Deganawida. The other was named Hiawatha, and he was a Mohawk shaman (SHAH muhn), or medicine man.

## The Five Nations' Ideas

*When George Washington, Thomas Jefferson, and the others were creating the new democracy of the United States, they looked to the Five Nations to see how the federation governed its members. Many of the Five Nations' ideas became part of our government. For example, the Iroquois chose sachems (SAY chuhmz), or chiefs, to represent the people in government. We choose senators and congressional representatives. Our president and cabinet (the president's official advisors) are like the Iroquois governing group called the Pine Tree Sachems. And like our capital of Washington, D.C., the Iroquois, too, had a city—Onondaga—that was the seat of their government.*

With this journey, the men hoped to unite several of the tribes living in the area we know today as New York State. These two leaders thought that united, the tribes could better defend their lands.

Deganawida and Hiawatha suggested that all the groups share one government. That common government would decide when the groups would go to war and would try to settle differences among member groups.

Eventually, five groups united. The Mohawk, the Oneida, the Onondaga, the Cayuga, and the Seneca became the Iroquois federation called Five Nations. (Iroquois comes from the word for the language the groups spoke.) Two centuries later, the Tuscarora joined the federation, and the Five

Nations became Six Nations. Sadly for Deganawida, the Huron never joined the Iroquois federation. In fact, in the middle of the 1600s, the Five Nations attacked the Huron, killing thousands, forcing the rest to flee.

## The Life of the Iroquois

Iroquois boys began early to learn the weapons of war. They practiced with bows and arrows, with war clubs, and with knives. They knew that one way to earn respect in their group was to become a skilled and fearless warrior. Men, too, practiced their warring skills.

*The Iroquois, as well as other Native Americans, played lacrosse. Some played the game as training for combat.*

They also taught their sons how to hunt and fish. In addition, they made the things they needed, such as their weapons and the canoes they used for travel.

Iroquois women were the farmers in the family. After the fields were planted, the women and children spent part of each day caring for the corn, beans, and squash they grew. The women taught their daughters everything they knew about farming. Daughters also learned how to cook and how to sew the clothing their families wore.

Iroquois families lived in long, narrow, bark-covered shelters called longhouses. Several families might share one longhouse, which could be up to 100 feet long. In fact, the Iroquois considered their federation to be one gigantic longhouse shared by five nations. They even called themselves the "People of the Longhouse." The Mohawks stood guard at the longhouse's eastern door. The Seneca watched over the western door.

## The Success of the League

Together, the Five Nations were almost unstoppable. They waged war on neighbors in every direction. Those they captured often were made to run the gauntlet (GAWNT luht). This means they had to run between two lines of Iroquois warriors, who struck the prisoners with sticks and branches. Prisoners who lived through the gauntlet might be adopted by the Iroquois, or they might still be killed. Until the Five Nations broke apart, their warriors made the Iroquois such feared rulers of the region that they were called the "poisonous snakes" by others.

### Show What You Know

Imagine that you are Hiawatha. You want to persuade one of the Indian nations to become part of the Iroquois Five Nations. Think of what you might say to convince them. On a separate sheet of paper, write down two reasons why your nation would benefit from being part of the Five Nations.

# THE HORSE CHANGES LIFE ON THE PLAINS

Most Native American groups began as hunters and gatherers. Over time, as they learned about many different plants and animals, they became farmers. The opposite was true for Indians of the Plains, however.

The Great Plains is a vast, treeless grassland. It comprises the middle of our nation, from the Mississippi River to the Rocky Mountains. For thousands of years, bears, wolves, deer, rabbits, and other animals large and small made the Plains their home. So did millions upon millions of shaggy-maned, hump-shouldered, grass-eating American buffalo.

## How Indians Used the Buffalo

*The Indians of the Plains used almost all parts of the buffaloes they killed. Some buffalo meat was eaten on the spot, either roasted or raw. Women cut extra meat into strips, which they dried and smoked. This dried meat lasted a long time and could help feed the group through the winter months. The Indians also ate buffalo tongue, liver, and kidney.*

*Buffalo skins were very valuable to the Indians. The hides were stretched and scraped clean. Then, the women worked into the skins a mixture that softened the hides. They could then be worked into clothing and blankets. Ten or 12 hides sewed together became the sides of a tepee.*

*Other parts of the buffalo also were used. Parts of the muscle became thread, rope, and the strings of bows. And bones were carved into tools and sled runners.*

Indians, too, lived on the Plains. Many were farmers, tilling the rich soil of the Plains' river valleys. They made their shelters of earth or grass. But then something happened that changed the way of life of the Plains Indians forever. That something was the coming of the horse.

## The Horse Returns to North America

In ancient times, prehistoric horses roamed every continent on Earth. No one knows why they died off on the American continents. But there were no modern horses in the New World until the Spaniards brought them when they came exploring in the 1500s.

The Plains people had always hunted buffalo. But buffalo hunts could happen only when a herd wandered close to a village. Thanks to the horse, hunters no longer had to wait for the buffalo to come to them. Instead, they could use horses to follow after the buffalo herds.

Slowly, the river-valley villages emptied. People packed up their belongings

and loaded them onto their horses. They traded their permanent valley houses for more portable tepees. The Plains Indians became nomads, or wanderers, always searching for and following the great buffalo herds.

## Indians—Master Riders

At first, Indians tamed horses they captured wild. Soon, though, they started to raise horses themselves. They became expert breeders, and their horses were strong and swift.

The Indians of the Great Plains were perhaps the greatest riders who ever lived. With his horse at a full gallop,

*This map shows possible routes in which horses came north from the Spanish settlements in New Mexico.*

28

an accomplished rider could swing himself to the animal's side and fire arrows under the horse's neck. He also could, holding onto his horse with just with his legs, reach down and pull up a fallen friend.

### Life Changes for the Plains Indians

With the help of their horses, the Indians of the Plains—the Blackfeet, the Cheyenne, the Crow, the Sioux, and dozens of other separate groups—lived their lives around the ever-moving buffalo. But that changed. White men began to come to the Plains. They used guns to kill off—both for profit and for fun—the great buffalo herds. By 1890, the herds were gone. The way of life of the Plains Indian was over.

## Show What You Know

The horse made it easier for different groups of Plains Indians to meet and trade. These different groups often spoke different languages. As a result, Plains Indians developed a kind of sign language. Like the sign language of the hearing impaired, the sign language of the Plains Indians was based on hand signals. Each hand signal stood for a different word or thought.

These pictures show several of the hand movements used in the sign language of the Plains Indians. Practice making the same signals with your hands. Next, think of two or three other words for which the Indians would have needed hand signals. Make up a hand signal to represent each word you chose. Then, teach the signals you practiced and the signals you created to a friend.

TRADE     FRIEND

HORSE     TEPEE

BUFFALO     PEACE

# UNIT 2 1492-1700
# EUROPEANS EXPLORE AMERICA

Europeans had developed a taste for the spices, sugar, silks, and other exotic goods from the Far East. They sailed across the ocean looking for a new route that would make those goods cheaper. They discovered the New World instead. So, they looked for riches there.

*Left: An astrolabe was an instrument that helped early sailors to use the stars to guide them. Right: Columbus and his three ships—the Niña, the Pinta, and the Santa Maria— sailed to the New World in 1492.*

**TIME LINE**

**1492:** Christopher Columbus sails to the New World.

**1497:** John Cabot's voyage gives England a claim to the New World.

**1513:** Ponce de León claims Florida for Spain.

**1523–1524:** Giovanni da Verrazano establishes a French claim in North America.

1400  1435  1470  1505  1540  1575  1610  1645  1680  1715

# COLUMBUS SAILS TO A NEW WORLD

Cristoforo Colombo—the real name of the man we call Christopher Columbus—was born in 1451 in Genoa, on Italy's northwest coast. His father was a wool weaver. His mother was the child of a wool weaver. Christopher, however, would not be a weaver of wool. Instead, Christopher would go to sea.

## Christopher Columbus, the Sailor

Christopher Columbus worked on ships that traveled to places like the Canary Islands and western Africa. The crews of these ships traded the goods they brought with them for the goods of the places they visited. But Christopher had bigger dreams. He wanted to trade with China.

*In this painting, Columbus is shown getting ready to sail to the Indies.*

## Christopher's Ships

*Improvements in shipbuilding played a big role in Christopher Columbus reaching the New World. Around 1450, Mediterranean shipbuilders developed a new kind of ship that could sail against the wind. The new ships were smaller, lighter, and easier to maneuver than earlier ships. They also did not have to use oars when sailing into the wind. These ships had three masts, or poles, that carried both square and triangular sails. This combination of sail shapes allowed the ships to take advantage of winds blowing from any direction.*

*The Niña, Pinta, and Santa Maria had few comforts. Only the highest officers had bunks to sleep in. Other crew members slept on the deck in good weather and below the deck in bad weather. Columbus had a total of about 90 crew members to sail the three ships. He had few navigational instruments. He relied mostly on a compass and the stars to navigate the ships.*

Europeans loved the gold, jewels, silk, and spices that trade with China brought. The trip to China—a journey over land for thousands of miles—was long, expensive, and filled with danger. Because of this, explorers searched for a sea route to the Indies. The Indies is the name they gave China, Japan, and other countries of the Asian continent. A sea route, they hoped, would be quicker, cheaper, and safer.

Most explorers thought the best sea route would take them around the continent of Africa, then on to China. Christopher Columbus thought he had a better way. Like others of his time, he knew nothing of the Americas. He believed the world had only three continents—Europe, Africa, and Asia. Christopher reasoned that if he sailed west, across what we call the Atlantic Ocean, he would come to the coast of Asia.

First, Christopher asked Portugal's King John II to pay for the journey westward. But the king turned him down. Then, he asked Spain's king and queen—Ferdinand and Isabella—if they would finance the exploration. For seven years, again and again, he asked them. Finally, in 1491, they agreed. They would pay for Columbus to try to reach the Far East by going across the Atlantic Ocean. In return, if Columbus succeeded, the Spanish crown would get nine-tenths of all the jewels, gold, pearls, silver, and spices he brought back.

*Below: This map shows the four routes Columbus took to the New World.*

NORTH AMERICA

ATLANTIC OCEAN

PACIFIC OCEAN

SOUTH AMERICA

## The Journey Begins

On August 3, 1492, Columbus and his three ships—the *Niña*, the *Pinta*, and the *Santa Maria*—began their momentous voyage. For the next couple of weeks, they followed along Africa's coast until they reached the Canary Islands. There they resupplied their ships with more food and water for the journey.

Finally, on September 6, Columbus gave the order for the ships to head out into the unknown sea: "West; nothing to the north, nothing to the south."

A week passed. Two weeks passed. Then, three. Then, four. Still, they saw no land. By this time, some of the men were getting very nervous. Supplies were running low, and the crews faced a four-week trip back, with no place to restock before they reached home.

Columbus was worried his crews would turn against him so he kept two logs, or travel diaries. In one log, Columbus recorded the distances he really thought the ships had gone. In the other, he recorded lesser distances, so the crews would not get upset about their true distance from any shore.

EUROPE
FRANCE
PORTUGAL SPAIN
ASIA
AFRICA
ATLANTIC OCEAN

*This painting shows Columbus meeting the Native Americans in the New World.*

## The Far East or a New World?

Christopher Columbus thought he had landed on an island in the Indies. In fact, for many years, Native Americans have been called Indians because that is who Christopher thought they were—people of the Indies. However, Christopher was wrong. The island on which he landed actually was in the Caribbean Sea, off the coast of North America, thousands of miles away from China.

On October 9, Columbus told the crews that if they did not come to land in three days, they would head home. Two days passed, with the ships still surrounded by the ocean. On the third day, early in the morning, the cry came for which everyone had been waiting. "Tierra! Tierra!" cried the lookout. "Land! Land!" he said. The three ships had found a shore.

Christopher Columbus made three more trips to the Americas. Despite all those trips, and the trips of others who followed his course, he said that he had found a new route to Asia. In fact, until the end of his life, Christopher Columbus did not believe he had connected Europe to a New World.

## Show What You Know

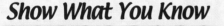

The map to the right shows how Europeans viewed the world before Columbus's voyage. Find a present-day map of the world. Then, on a separate sheet of paper, list three ways in which the 1490 map is wrong.

# PONCE DE LEÓN SEARCHES FOR THE FOUNTAIN OF YOUTH

Christopher Columbus was only the first in a long line of Spanish explorers who set their sights on the New World. Those who came, came for several reasons. One reason was to claim land for Spain. Another reason was to find gold, silver, and other riches.

The dark green on this map shows the parts of the New World that were claimed by Spain.

## The Gulf Stream

As Juan Ponce de León's ships traveled down Florida's eastern coast, something amazing happened. The ships encountered waters that would not let them move forward, even with the help of the winds in their sails. Juan and his sailors did not know their ships had run into the Gulf Stream. The Gulf Stream is an Atlantic Ocean current. It is like a great river in the ocean, running fast to the northeast, along the coast of North America. Two of Juan's ships made it safely through the Gulf Stream. But the current swept the third away.

35

Some came to bring Christianity, their nation's religion, to the people who lived in the Americas. And others wanted the fame and glory that came at the end of a successful voyage.

## Ponce de León Finds Florida

One who followed Columbus west across the ocean was Juan Ponce de León. Actually, historians think Juan might have sailed with Columbus on his second trip. Juan served as a soldier for Spain, helping to conquer the Native Americans of first Hispaniola (the island now home to Haiti and the Dominican Republic), then San Juan (the island now called Puerto Rico).

In 1512, the Spanish King Ferdinand told Juan "to discover and settle the island of Bimini." Bimini was a name of legend, an island where there was a spring of water said to make the old young again.

In 1513, Juan set sail. He left Puerto Rico and headed north, toward where Bimini was believed to be, hoping to find land, riches, fame, glory—and the Fountain of Youth. Juan and his three ships sailed through the islands of the Bahamas. Then, Juan saw the great, wide shoreline of what he thought was another island. Juan named this new discovery La Florida. On April 2, 1513, Juan claimed La Florida and all the land it touched for Spain.

Juan wanted to see how big this "island" was. So he sailed south, following Florida's eastern coast. He rounded Florida's tip, then started north again, following Florida's western coast. Partway up the coast, near present-day Fort Myers, Juan decided to turn back. In seven weeks of travel, Juan could not determine the size of the "island" of La Florida. Nor had he found the riches and magic waters he sought.

## Juan's Last Voyage

In 1521, Juan returned to Florida. By now he was 61 years old. Finding the Fountain of Youth became even more important to him.

On this voyage, Juan brought 200 men with him to settle a colony. When they landed on Florida's western shore, they were met by warriors from the region's fierce Calusa tribe. In the battle that followed, many Spaniards were killed. Juan himself was wounded. His ships returned to Cuba, where Juan died a few days later.

*Hernando Cortés and his army marched on and conquered the Aztec civilization. After destroying the Aztec capital, Tenochtitlán, Cortés built Mexico City.*

## Spain Creates an American Empire

Juan Ponce de León probably never realized it, but he gave Spain a great gift. When he placed a Spanish flag into Florida's soil, he actually claimed for Spain a whole new continent!

Those who came after Juan Ponce de León also brought Spain wealth from the New World. In 1519, for example, Hernando Cortés sailed to present-day Mexico in the name of Spain. There, he crushed the 200-year-old Aztec civilization. In 1532,

Francisco Pizarro traveled to Peru to conquer the Inca Empire. The treasures Cortés, Pizarro, and others took from the Americas and sent back to Spain helped Spain become one of Europe's most powerful nations.

### Show What You Know

On the map below, orange circles mark places along the route Juan Ponce de León followed on his 1513 voyage. Use what you learned in the reading to connect the circles and recreate part of Juan's trip.

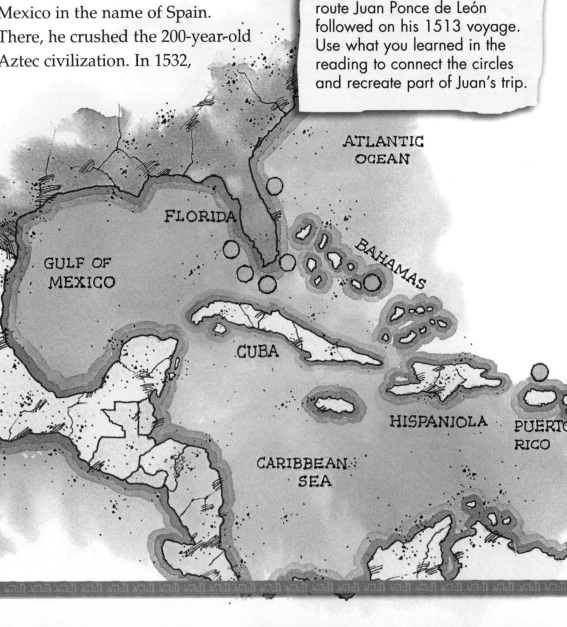

# THE SEARCH FOR A NORTHWEST PASSAGE

Giovanni da Verrazzano was an Italian who explored the New World for the French king.

S ome explorers to the New World took a southerly route. Others went to the north. They, too, hoped to find a new, faster route to Asia. They searched for a water route that would cut through the continent. If one did not exist, they wanted to see whether they could sail around the top of the New World. Even before explorers found a route, they had a name for it. They called it the Northwest Passage.

## Verrazzano Explores for France

Giovanni da Verrazzano was one of the first explorers to turn north once he reached the mainland of the New World. Giovanni was born in Italy, but he sailed under the French flag. In 1523, he left for America with orders from France's king to find a Northwest Passage.

Giovanni landed, historians think, near the shores of the Carolinas. Then, he turned north, sailing along the coast. He sailed past the Chesapeake Bay, the Delaware Bay, and the mouth of the great Hudson River.

## What Did Sailors Eat?

There were two foods on which many sailors of exploration days relied. One was pickled beef and pork, which lasted a long time and which sailors called "salt horse." The other was a dry, tooth-breaking kind of bread called a "bisket." The bisket supply was stored in the driest part of the ship. Still, as the days passed, the bisket became moldy and filled with maggots—the wormlike larva that turn into flies. Sometimes the sailors ate their bisket at night, so they couldn't see what was in it.

All appeared big enough to encourage exploration—the possibility of a Northwest Passage. Yet, for reasons not known, Giovanni explored none of them. Still, by the time he sailed past present-day Maine and turned toward Europe and home, his voyage signaled to other nations that France was interested in the Americas.

## Hudson Sails for a Dutch Company

The costs of exploring were great, so most explorers' journeys were paid for by a country. Sometimes, though, a single company hired an explorer. The Dutch East India Company is one example.

The Dutch East India Company was the only company allowed to trade between Asia and the Netherlands. It grew rich supplying the people of the Netherlands with East Indies goods, such as cinnamon and nutmeg. Its profits would only grow larger if a shortcut to Asia could be found.

In 1609, the Dutch East India Company hired English explorer Henry Hudson. His assignment was to find a Northwest Passage.

*European explorers and Native Americans were curious about each other.*

Henry already had captained one trip for another company. On that trip, as he searched for a Northwest Passage, he sailed so far north that the ice of the North Pole forced him to turn back.

With a company-supplied ship—the *Half Moon*—and 20 men to crew it, Henry set off. Unlike other explorers, Henry approached the continent from the north, starting at Canada's northern shore and sailing south along the coast to the Carolinas. Then, he headed back up north, retracing his route.

The *Half Moon* sailed into what is now New York Harbor. From there, to the north, Henry saw the mouth of a great river. He hoped it would prove to be the beginning of the sought-for Northwest Passage. Eleven days later, as the *Half Moon* reached the place where Albany, New York, is today, Henry realized the river was getting narrow and shallow. Now he knew this was not the passage of which he dreamed. Soon he turned back.

The journey made by the *Half Moon* led the Netherlands to claim the land Henry had explored. It came to be called New Netherland, and it included parts of present-day Connecticut, New York, New Jersey, and Delaware. The great river he had traveled was named the Hudson River, in his honor. At its mouth, Dutch settlers started the colony of New Amsterdam. In time, that little colony became New York City.

## Hudson Sails for English Businessmen

The search for a Northwest Passage also meant the exploration of parts of Canada. Henry became part of Canada's history when he was hired by English businessmen to continue his search for a Northwest Passage. In 1610, he and his crew sailed their ship, the *Discovery*, far to the north, along the coasts of Greenland and Baffin Island, and into a giant, northern bay. This bay later became known as Hudson Bay.

Hudson Bay is so big that, for a while, Henry thought he had sailed into the Pacific Ocean. By the time he realized his mistake, winter began to set in. The crew was forced to spend the next months freezing and starving through the cold Canadian winter. One crew member later wrote that the men were so hungry, they "searched the woods, hills, and valleys for anything that might serve for food . . . the frogs . . . were not spared, nor the moss that grew on the ground."

When spring came, Henry planned to continue his search for a Northwest Passage. However, his exhausted crew mutinied, or turned against him. They put Henry, his son, and seven others into a small boat without food or supplies, and set the boat adrift in the bay. Then, the mutineers sailed the *Discovery* back to England.

We know what happened to the mutineers. Some were killed by Eskimos, but the rest made it back to England alive. Once home, some were tried for the crime of mutiny, though none were found guilty.

We do not know what happened to Henry and the eight with him after the *Discovery* sailed away. No trace of them has ever been found.

## Show What You Know

Below is a map that shows routes followed by Verrazzano and Hudson as they searched for a Northwest Passage through the New World. Use what you have learned to complete the map key by writing the explorer's name next to the line representing the route he took. Here are the three answers you will use to complete the key:

### HUDSON (1610)    VERRAZZANO (1523)    HUDSON (1609)

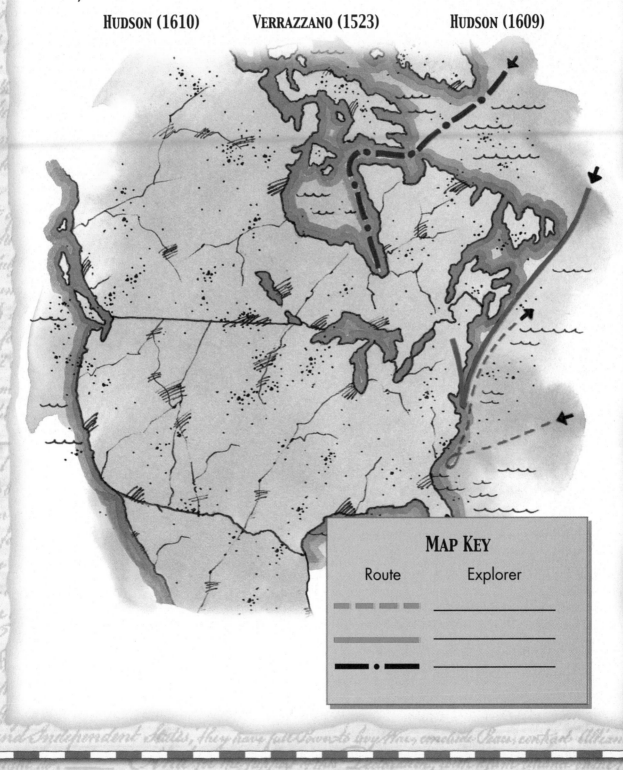

### MAP KEY

| Route | Explorer |
|-------|----------|
| – – – | _____ |
| ——— | _____ |
| —•— | _____ |

# ESTEVANICO EXPLORES THE SOUTHWEST

## The Shipwrecked Men

*Alvar Núñez Cabeza De Vaca was one of the men who, with Estevanico, walked into Mexico City that June day in 1536. Alvar is the reason we know so much about the ill-fated voyage of Pánfilo de Narváez. That is because Alvar wrote a book about the eight years he and the others spent on their journey from Florida to Mexico. He called his book* Los Naufragios—The Shipwrecked Men.

*Alvar's book also teaches us a lot about the Native American groups with whom he came in contact. For example, Alvar learned that the prickly pear cactus was an important food for the tribes of dry, barren, southern Texas. Here is what he wrote about the prickly pear: "The happiest part of the year is the season of eating prickly pears; they [the Indians] have hunger then no longer, pass all the time in dancing and eat day and night."*

I n 1528, five Spanish ships landed at Tampa Bay, on Florida's Gulf Coast. The ships were commanded by Pánfilo de Narváez, who wanted to take control of land given to him by Spain. He brought with him 400 people—both slaves and freemen—to help.

*Pánfilo de Narváez led an unsuccessful exploration of Florida and the Gulf Coast.*

### Narváez Makes a Mistake

Narváez decided that 300 of the men and the 40 horses they had brought with them should get off the ships at Tampa Bay. Then, for some unknown reason, he ordered the ships, still loaded with most of the food and supplies, to go ahead north, along Florida's coast, to a place where the land party would again meet up with them.

CULIACÁ

The ships sailed north, pulled into a harbor, and waited. But the land party never came. For almost a year, without success, the ships searched for Narváez and his men. Finally, the ships turned away from Florida and sailed toward Spanish-held Mexico.

While the ships were sailing and searching, the land party was struggling north. On the trip, sickness, starvation, and the arrows from Native Americans cost many their lives. After a month of misery, the survivors decided to build rafts and float to the safety of Mexico.

Then, after weeks at sea, a terrible storm blew in and wrecked the rafts. Only 80 of Narváez's 300 men survived the storm.

A year later, just four people remained to tell the tale of Narváez's mistake. Three were white soldiers. The other was a black slave named Estevanico. Some history books call him Estevan the Moor. That is because he was originally kidnapped from his home in the African nation of Morocco.

NUEVA ESPAÑA

FLORIDA

CABEZA DE VACA

† NARVÁEZ SHIPWRECKED

CUBA

SANTIAGO DE CUBA

NARVÁEZ

## A Journey for Survival

The four who survived had to save themselves. They decided they would walk to Mexico City.

Year after year, they wandered through North America's southwest corner. On their long journey, they met many different Native American tribes. Sometimes they served the tribes as healers. Other times, the tribes enslaved them.

Finally, in June 1536, Estevanico and the others entered Mexico City. They had spent eight years walking 3,000 miles to reach their destination.

## Estevanico Takes Another Trip

On their journey, the survivors heard rumors of rich Native American cities to the north. These seven cities, it was said, were made of gold. According to the rumor, the cities could be found in the land Spaniards called Cibola—the land of the buffalo.

The survivors told these rumors to the Spaniards in Mexico City. In 1539, some of these Spaniards decided to go north in search of the Seven Cities of Cibola. Estevanico, with his knowledge of Native American languages and cultures, joined the group to lead the way.

As the group approached the Zuni pueblo thought to be one of the Seven Cities, the Zuni, who thought they were invading, attacked. Estevanico was killed. Others in the party turned back. On their return, they reported that they had seen one of the fabled cities. This might be because, from a distance in the sun, the reddish-brown adobe buildings must have shown like gold. It was not until a year later that another Spanish explorer discovered the golden Cities of Cibola were really pueblos made of clay.

*The golden Cities of Cibola were really pueblos made of clay.*

## Show What You Know

When Pánfilo de Narváez and his men built rafts, they used what their surroundings provided. They cut down pine trees and split them into planks. They used the hair of their horses' manes and tails to make rope. Then, they used knots to tie together the planks with the ropes they had made. Pictured below are two of the knots Narváez's men might have tied as they built their rafts. These knots have been used by sailors for centuries.

Use two pieces of rope or string (even shoestrings will work). Then, follow the directions to see if you can tie these knots, as Narváez's men did so long ago.

A                                              B                                          A

B

### FIGURE-OF-EIGHT KNOT

This knot is called a figure-of-eight knot, because it looks like the number 8. This knot is good for keeping the end of a rope from pulling out. To make this knot, study the picture and follow these steps:

1. Make a loop in a piece of rope or string. Notice how one end of the rope is behind the other end. This is end A.

2. Bring end A around the top of the loop's tail.

3. Put end A through the loop, from the bottom up.

4. As you pull the rope tight, you can see the 8. Keep pulling the rope until the knot is tight.

### SQUARE KNOT

This knot is called a square knot. It often is used to join together two pieces of rope. To make this knot, study the picture and follow these steps:

1. Use two pieces of rope or string, A and B, as in the picture. Hold A in your right hand and B in your left.

2. Put A over B. Bring A under and up. Now A is in your left hand, and B is in your right hand.

3. Put A over B. Bring A through the loop, from the bottom up.

4. Pull the two ropes tight.

# LA SALLE TRAVELS THE MISSISSIPPI RIVER

Like Spain, France, too, wanted to explore the New World. Spain went to the Americas to conquer. France went to the Americas to trade.

## La Salle Tries His Luck

By the time he was 23 years old, Frenchman René-Robert Cavelier, Sieur de La Salle, had already been rich and then poor. He was determined to be rich again. He decided that the best place to make his fortune was in the New World. So, in 1666, he went to Canada, the land called New France. There, he began a life of exploring.

## The Upper Country

Traveling with René-Robert was a man named Henry de Tonty. Tonty already knew that the Mississippi River region offered up pelts for clothing and wood for ship-building. But he thought that the rich land of the area could provide food as well. He said, "If wheat will not grow at the lower part of the river, the upper country could furnish it; and the islands [of the Caribbean] might be supplied with everything they need, such as planks, vegetables, grain and salt beef. . . ."

This is a scene along the Mississippi Rivers as La Salle might have seen it.

Like others, René-Robert had heard of the river the Native Americans called the Mississippi—the Great River. He also heard reports of white men who had traveled part of the fabled river. These included the French explorers Jolliet and Marquette, who had traveled farther south on the Mississippi than had any white person.

René-Robert knew there was money to be made on the Mississippi River. He decided that he would claim the fur trade along the river's route. In 1674, he went to France and was granted by King Louis XIV the fur rights to the region. That meant that René-Robert was the only New World explorer who could profit from the furs of the animals in the region of the Mississippi River.

René-Robert returned to the New World and went right to work. By 1680, he had built a ship and begun exploring the region. He started the settlement of Fort Crêve Coeur near the present-day city of Peoria on the Illinois River, which feeds into the Mississippi River.

René-Robert had to overcome many obstacles. For one, the ship he filled with his first furs disappeared with its load. That also meant that there was no ship to return to the fort with supplies. René-Robert was forced to return north and get the supplies himself. While he was gone, some of the men he left at Fort Crêve Coeur stole everything and ran away. Plus, two of his scouts were taken by Indians, though they were later rescued.

## René-Robert Paddles the Mississippi

René-Robert did not give up. In 1681, with the king's permission, he began exploring the Mississippi River. About 40 others, both French and Indian, accompanied him. Together, they used canoes to travel south down the river. They paddled past the mouths of the Ohio, the Arkansas, and the other rivers that flow into the Mississippi. They also paddled past the point where Jolliet and Marquette had turned back, fearing the Spaniards who had settled to the south.

For almost two months, René-Robert and his party paddled south. Finally, they reached the mouth of the river—the place where the fresh water of the Mississippi meets the salt water of the Gulf of Mexico. There, René-Robert placed a cross and France's coat of arms. Then he said: "In the name of the most high, mighty, invincible, and victorious Prince, Louis the Great, by the Grace of God, King of France and of Navarre, Fourteenth of that name, this ninth day of April one thousand six hundred and eighty-two, I . . . do now take, in the name of his Majesty and of his successors to the crown, possession of this country of Louisiana, the seas, harbors, ports, bays, adjacent straits; and all the nations, people, provinces, cities, towns, villages, mines, minerals, fisheries, streams, and rivers, comprised in the extent of the said Louisiana."

With these words, René-Robert Cavelier, Sieur de La Salle, claimed for France the Mississippi River and all the land it drained for France. With these words, he also named this vast region. He called it Louisiana, in honor of King Louis XIV.

At first, France's king was not impressed that René-Robert had claimed for him half a continent. It would have saddened René-Robert to learn that the king wrote this to his financial advisor: "I am convinced, like you, that the discovery of the Sieur de La Salle is very useless."

The king soon changed his mind. In addition to the land, René-Robert's claim gave France use of the continent's greatest river. France now controlled both ends of the Mississippi.

*La Salle might have explored in a boat similar to this one.*

That meant that in winter, when the northern ports froze over, furs and other goods still could be shipped south to the Gulf of Mexico, where the water never freezes. From there, they could reach markets in the Caribbean and in Europe.

## La Salle Starts a Colony

René-Robert went back to France. He gathered together almost 400 colonists, put them on four ships, and set sail for the Gulf of Mexico. His goal was to start a colony at the mouth of the Mississippi River. The colony would help France keep control of the river.

Avantures mal-heureuses du Sieur de La Salle

When he reached the Gulf of Mexico, René-Robert became lost. By accident, he and his colonists ended up on the coast of present-day Texas, over 400 miles west of the mouth of the Mississippi. They also lost their ships. Two sank. One was captured by Spaniards. And one, along with its mutinous men, sailed away.

Food and supplies ran low in the new Texas colony. Starvation and disease killed colonists by the hundreds. Finally, René-Robert took 17 others on an overland trek toward the Mississippi. There he could get more supplies. However, on this trip, some of his men turned against him, and René-Robert was killed. There is no grave for René-Robert, for his body was left to the wolves in the wilderness of east Texas. Two years later, Spaniards burned to the ground what was left of the colony René-Robert began.

René-Robert was gone. His colony was destroyed. Yet because of this explorer, France now had a firm grip on the vast middle of the present-day United States. France held onto this land for over 100 years.

*This drawing shows La Salle landing with his colonists in Matagorda Bay, Texas, in 1685, after he became lost.*

## Show What You Know

Did you notice that France's king was named Louis XIV? The letters at the end of Louis's name are Roman numerals. That is, they are some of the symbols the ancient Romans used to represent their numbers.

Here are the seven symbols that together make up all Roman numerals:

> I = 1     V = 5     X = 10
>
> L = 50     C = 100     D = 500     M = 1,000

Instead of using place values like units, tens, and hundreds like we do, Romans strung their numerals in a row and then added them together. So, VI is 6 (V+I, or 5+1) in Arabic, the name of the numbering system we use. XV stands for 15 (X+V, or 10+5). And CI stands for 101 (C+I, or 100+1).

Roman numerals are subtracted if a numeral of a lesser value comes before a numeral of a greater value. For example, IV meant 4 (V – I, or 5 – 1). So, the Roman numerals at the end of King Louis's name stand for 14 (X + IV, or 10 + 4). He was called Louis XIV because he was the fourteenth French king with the name Louis.

Read the sentences below. In each sentence, translate the Roman numeral into the Arabic number that is the same value.

1. René-Robert spent almost II _____ months canoeing down the Mississippi River.

2. René-Robert was XXIII _____ years old when he came to the New World.

3. René-Robert used IV _____ ships to bring his colonists to the Gulf of Mexico.

4. In Texas, René-Robert took XVII _____ colonists overland to get supplies.

5. France held on to Louisiana for more than C _____ years.

Write the following in Roman numerals:

Your age _____        The current year _____

# UNIT 3  1550-1775
# COLONIAL TIMES

In 1607, Virginia became the first English colony in America. By 1732, the colonies numbered 13. The colonists were ruled by England. However, England was 3,000 miles and months of travel away. Because of this, the colonies pretty much ruled themselves as the colonists carved new lives in the New World.

*Ships sailing in the harbor in Charleston.*

TIME LINE

**1590:** Sir Walter Raleigh returns to find the colonists of Roanoke have vanished.

**1607:** Virginia becomes England's first colony in the New World.

**1620:** The Pilgrims sign the Mayflower Compact, which describes how they will be governed in Massachusetts.

**1732:** Georgia becomes the 13th colony.

**1769:** Daniel Boone explores Kentucky.

| 1550 | 1575 | 1600 | 1625 | 1650 | 1675 | 1700 | 1725 | 1750 | 1775 |

# THE LOST COLONY OF ROANOKE

In 1584, England's Queen Elizabeth granted Sir Walter Raleigh the right to build colonies in the New World. He chose Roanoke Island, off the coast of present-day North Carolina, as the spot for his first colony. There actually were two tries at building a colony on Roanoke Island. The first colony was abandoned. The second was lost.

## Roanoke's First Colony

In August 1585, 107 settlers arrived in the New World. Sir Walter Raleigh had instructed them to start a colony on the island of Roanoke.

Things did not go well for these first colonists. Many came looking for gold and silver, which the Spaniards had found farther south in the lands of the Aztec and Inca. These colonists were not interested in farming the land.

## Those Sent to Roanoke

Most of the people Sir Walter first sent to Roanoke were soldiers. Two, though, were scientists. They were sent to determine whether there was wealth to be had in the New World. Joachim Gans was a specialist in metals. Thomas Hariot was a surveyor, an astronomer (studier of the skies), and an oceanographer (studier of the seas). In 1586, the scientists returned to England with the others. Thomas's descriptions of the New World helped inspire the group that headed to Roanoke the next year to start another colony.

Sir Walter Raleigh was the first to try to start a colony in the New World.

At first, the Indians of the region helped the colonists by giving them corn and other foods. In spite of their neighbors' generous aid, the colonists fought with the Indians. Then, the colonists had to rely only on the supplies they brought with them. By the summer of 1586, after 10 long months, their supplies were almost gone.

In June, the colonists finally saw English ships approaching. They hoped they were Sir Walter's ships, returning with supplies. However, they were the ships of another explorer, Sir Francis Drake. He was the first Englishman to sail around the world. Sir Francis agreed to take the discouraged colonists back to England.

A few weeks later, Sir Walter's supply ships landed at an empty colony. The ships sailed away, leaving 15 men to guard the post. The men were also left to guard England's claim to the region. Unfortunately, the 15 men were never seen again.

## The Mystery of Roanoke's Second Colony

In May 1587, Sir Walter Raleigh tried again to build a colony at Roanoke. This time, his ships carried 117 men, women, and children to the New World. When the ships left the new colonists at Roanoke, the crews promised to return soon with more supplies.

When the ships got back to England, Sir Walter loaded them with the promised supplies. Before he could send them back to Roanoke, war broke out. Spain's navy attacked England's navy, and England needed Sir Walter's ships to help in the fight.

England won the battle, but Sir Walter's ships were not able to get back to America until 1590. By the time they again reached Roanoke, not one person remained.

*Colonists arrived on the Roanoke Island in August 1585.*

COLONIAL TIMES • 1550–1775

The colonists had disappeared. The only clue to what happened was that someone had carved the name of a nearby Native American group into a tree: "CROATOAN."

John White was a member of both the Roanoke colonies. In fact, it was John White's daughter who gave birth to the first English child born in the New World—a little girl named Virginia Dare. John had returned to England on a ship picking up more supplies for the colony. This is what he saw when he returned:

*"We came to the place where I left our colony . . . . We found the houses taken downe. . . . in fayre [closely joined] Capitall letters was graven [carved] CROATAN. . . . Wee found five chests. . . . three were my owne, and about the place many of my things spoyled [spoiled] and broken, and my bookes torn from the covers, the frames of some of my pictures and Mappes rotten and spoyled with rayne [rain], and my armour almost eaten through with rust."* *

---

* This is a direct quote from John White. The misspelled words are just the way he wrote them. The words in brackets have been inserted to help you understand the words he used.

To this day, no one knows what happened to the people of the Lost Colony of Roanoke.

## Show What You Know

A time line shows the order in which events happened. It also can help you see how events are connected to each other. Time lines can cover centuries, or they can show just a few years.

Write each of the four entries in the correct boxes on the time line.

- A second group of colonists come to Roanoke.
- Colonists return defeated to England.
- Supply ships arrive to find no one left at Roanoke.
- The first settlers arrive at Roanoke.

## HISTORY OF ROANOKE

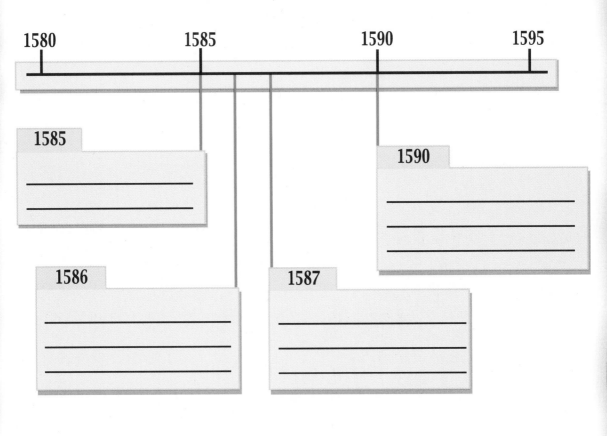

58

# ONE MAN AND ONE CROP HELP JAMESTOWN SUCCEED

In 1607, three ships—the *Susan Constant*, the *Godspeed*, and the *Discovery*—arrived at the Virginia shore. The ships and the 105 men aboard had been hired by the London Company to start a colony in the New World. The spot they chose was about 60 miles up the James River, a river they named for their king. There, on a little jut of land, they began to build the colony of Jamestown, also named for their king.

## Problems in the New Colony

Jamestown was plagued with problems from the start. In 1608, less than nine months after the men had arrived, a fire swept through the colony.

This drawing shows a Powhatan dressed in traditional clothing.

### Pocahontas Saves John Smith

John Smith wrote several books about his Jamestown experiences. In one, he tells the story of how his life was saved by the daughter of the great Powhatan. Powhatan was the chief who ruled the Indians of the region. His daughter's real name was Matoaka, but white people called her Pocahontas—"the playful one."

According to the story, John had been captured by Powhatan. Powhatan was just about to kill him when "the king's dearest daughter . . . got his head in her arms, and laid her own [head] upon his to save him from death. Whereat the emperor [Powhatan] was contented he should live . . ."

Pocahontas was only 12 years old when she saved John Smith's life. Later, she went to live with the white people. She fell in love and married John Rolfe, a tobacco farmer. That marriage helped keep peace between the colonists and the Indians.

One colonist wrote that almost everything was lost to the flames: ". . . our fort was burned, and the most of our apparel [clothes], lodging and private provision." Also that year, rats ate most of the corn supply.

There were also problems with the London Company. The London Company wanted to make money from its colony as soon as possible. So, twice in 1608, it sent ships to Jamestown. Whenever this happened, the colonists had to stop working on the colony and fill up the ships with cedar wood, lumber, and sassafras, a root used to make tea. The ships then sailed, full of goods to sell in Europe and other markets far away.

Other problems were caused by the colonists themselves. Many of the men considered themselves

"gentlemen." As gentlemen, they did not want to do any hard work. Some wanted, instead, to look for silver and gold. Others wanted to do nothing at all.

## John Smith Becomes Leader

John Smith finally took control of the colony in 1608. This blue-eyed, bushy-bearded explorer was also a soldier who had fought in several wars. And, John loved to brag about his adventures.

John Smith wasn't very well liked by the other colonists. In fact, he had arrived at Jamestown in chains, because others feared he meant to take over the colony. However, John proved himself a good leader. He kept order in the new colony. He also made the gentlemen get to work. He told others to pour cold water on anyone who complained about the chores.

*Above: This statue of Pocahontas shows one artist's idea of what she looked like.*
*Below: In 1619, the first women arrived in Jamestown.*

John believed that only people willing to work hard should come to the colony.

The people worked harder. Also, the London Company sent supplies. Still, it was not enough. In the winter of 1609–1610, so many men starved to death that the season became known as the "starving time." John Smith ordered the colonists to go out and gather anything that could be eaten. Later, he wrote that if he had not forced them to look for food, they would have all starved.

Under John Smith, the colony did a little better, but his role as leader of Jamestown ended in 1609. In that year, John was burned when a bag of gunpowder he had hung on his hip blew up. He had to go back to England to recover.

### One Crop Saves Jamestown

One crop brought success to the colony of Jamestown. That crop was tobacco. Tobacco was an American crop, first grown by the Indians. The Europeans had never seen tobacco until it was brought back with early explorers.

Around 1612, a Jamestown farmer named John Rolfe discovered a kind of tobacco that Europeans really liked. (This was a time when no one knew that tobacco could hurt the human body.) Soon, people all over Europe were demanding the tobacco grown in Jamestown.

Tobacco also encouraged thousands to sail to Jamestown. Jamestown grew and prospered. Tobacco farms dotted the James River. By 1630, ships regularly sailed down the James River to drop off supplies and settlers and to pick up tobacco. That one crop had helped Jamestown succeed when many other New World colonies failed.

THE
DISCOVERY
OF
New Brittaine.

Began August 27, Anno Dom. 1650.

By
Edward Bland, Merchant
Abraham Mowder, Captaine
Sackford Brewster,
Elim Pennant,
Gentlemen

From Fort Henrey, at the head of Appamattuc River in Virginia, to the Fals of Blandina, first River in New Britaine, which runneth West; being 120. Mile South-west, between 25. & 37. degrees, (a pleasant Country,) of temperate Ayre, and Fertile Soyle.

LONDON.

Printed by Thomas Harper for John Stephenson, at the Sun below Ludgate. M.D.C.L.I.

### Show What You Know

To help their colonies grow, companies created pamphlets and brochures to encourage people to go to the New World. Imagine you work for one of those companies. On a separate sheet of paper, write an advertisement that you think would help people decide to seek their fortunes in America.

# SQUANTO HELPS THE PILGRIMS

The Pilgrims were the second group to build a permanent, English-speaking colony in the Americas. The Pilgrims were persecuted in England for their religious beliefs. Now, they came to the New World seeking religious freedom. Can you imagine the Pilgrims' surprise when out of the woods came two Indians who spoke to them in English?

One of the Indians was named Samoset. Samoset probably learned the language from English fishermen he met along the coast. He was the first to greet the Pilgrims.

The other was Tisquantum. The colonists called him Squanto. It was Squanto who helped the Pilgrims learn how to live in the New World. And, it was he who helped bring peace between the Pilgrims and their Indian neighbors.

## Squanto Dies of Smallpox

In 1622, Squanto died from "Indian fever." "Indian fever" was another name for the deadly disease we call smallpox. Smallpox was one of many illnesses unknown in the New World before the Europeans came.

Most Native American groups were not killed off by Europeans' guns. Instead, they died of Europeans' diseases. Smallpox, measles, typhus, and other illnesses swept through the land. These diseases killed entire tribes. In fact, historians think that most of the members of Squanto's Pawtuxet tribe died during a smallpox epidemic (eh puh DEH mihk), or time of sweeping sickness.

## Squanto Is Kidnapped

The Pilgrims were not the first white people Squanto met. In 1615, he was kidnapped by an English trader. The trader took him to Spain and sold him into slavery. There, another Englishman saw him, bought him, and took him to England. In 1619, Squanto was able to get passage on a ship bound for America. He arrived in New England to find that his own tribe, the Pawtuxet, had been wiped out. So, he became a member of the nearby Wampanoag, where the few other Pawtuxet survivors had gone.

Squanto could have been bitter about his experiences at the hands of the English. Instead, he decided to help the white people who had landed at Plymouth Rock. During his travels, he had learned to speak English. He now used that skill to talk to the Pilgrims.

## The First Winter at Plymouth

The Pilgrims arrived at Plymouth, in present-day Massachusetts, in December. It was far too late to plant fields and hope for a harvest. So, they spent their first winter living on the *Mayflower*, the ship that brought them to America, using up what was left of their supplies. They hunted the woods for anything they could eat. And, they stole corn from the Indians.

Sickness, cold, and hunger killed half the colonists before the winter was over. In fact, the winter was so awful that, at one point, only seven Pilgrims still were strong enough to tend to the sick and bury the dead.

The Pilgrims, however, had been through tough times before. When the *Mayflower* and its crew returned to England the next spring, none of the surviving Pilgrims went back with the ship. As one Pilgrim wrote, "It is not with us as with other men, whom small things can discourage." In other words, they weren't going to give up because of a difficult winter.

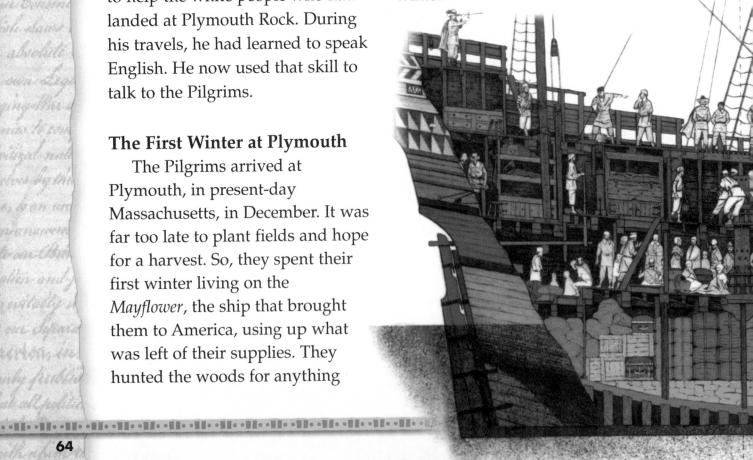

*This painting shows the suffering of the Pilgrims during their first winter.*

## Squanto Offers Aid

It was that first spring when Squanto and Samoset came walking out of the woods. As the Pilgrims cleared their first fields, Squanto showed them how to plant corn, pumpkins, and beans. He showed them how to use a certain fish to fertilize, or feed, their crops. He also showed them where to hunt and fish.

With Squanto's help, the Pilgrims grew enough food for the colony that very first year. To give thanks for a good corn harvest, the Pilgrims held a three-day celebration. Their Indian friends joined them for a feast that included corn bread, duck, goose, turkeys, and shellfish.

*This is a cut-away view of the Mayflower with passengers and cargo.*

The Pilgrims and the Indians celebrated the first Thanksgiving together.

## Show What You Know

On board the *Mayflower*, each person had about 18 square feet of space. This means that, if you were traveling on the ship, a piece of floor perhaps 6 feet long by 3 feet wide would belong to you.

Imagine that you and your family are traveling on the *Mayflower* to the New World. You are allowed to bring only a backpack full of things from your old life. Lay out the things you want to take with you. Then get a backpack, or any small bag or suitcase, and actually pack your things into it, to make sure everything will fit. If you have too much, you will have to make choices about what to leave behind. Make a list of things that would be most important for you to take.

We have come to call that early celebration Thanksgiving, and that Pilgrim Thanksgiving was the start of a tradition that continues today. On the fourth Thursday of every November, all over the United States, many families gather to share a big Thanksgiving meal. Thanksgiving is a chance to be grateful for our many blessings. It also is a day to remember the story of Squanto and how he helped the colonists at Plymouth succeed.

# WILLIAM PENN'S GREAT EXPERIMENT

In England, during the days of William Penn, it was against the law to practice any religion except the country's official religion. William Penn thought that was wrong. He thought people should be able to worship the way they chose. In fact, William was expelled from school for saying aloud what he believed.

William Penn was the founder of the colony called Pennsylvania.

When he was a young man, William discovered a religion that agreed with him. It was the religion of the Society of Friends. The Friends, or Quakers, as they are also called, felt people should follow their own spiritual paths. They also did not believe in war, and they thought prisoners and mentally ill people should be treated with mercy and kindness. At the age of 22, William became a Quaker.

## Delaware Becomes Part of Pennsylvania

Pennsylvania was a land that provided almost everything its colonists needed. William Penn, however, wished it had one more thing; he wished it had a shoreline on the Atlantic Ocean.

In 1682, William Penn got his wish. James, Duke of York, was the brother of King Charles, and the king had given him vast tracts of land in America. The Duke of York honored William's request and granted to him the land that later became the state of Delaware.

William Penn gave the people who lived in this Delaware region equal say in Pennsylvania's government. In 1704, the people of the region began holding their own government meetings, though they were still part of Pennsylvania. The region did not become a separate state until 1776, after the Revolutionary War had begun.

William was sent to prison several times for his religious beliefs. In fact, there were times when England's jails seemed full of Quakers. William realized that the Quakers could never live in peace in England.

## William Penn Starts a Colony

When William Penn's father died, King Charles of England was in debt to him. So, the king repaid the debt to the son. In 1681, King Charles gave William land in America. The land was named Pennsylvania, or Penn's Woods.

William Penn saw Pennsylvania as a place for Quakers—and others—to live in peace, according to their beliefs. William immediately began to advertise for settlers. He said that those who came to Pennsylvania could practice the religion of their choice. He also said they could take part in their own government.

In the first two years, over 3,000 settlers came to live in Pennsylvania. Quakers came. Mennonites and Jews and Baptists came. People came from Ireland and Germany and Scotland and England. All wanted what William Penn offered—to live in a land of religious freedom and self-government.

## William Penn Plans Philadelphia

One of the first things William Penn did when he arrived in Pennsylvania was to plan a capital city. It would sit on high land

*This painting shows part of the city of Philadelphia in about 1720.*

between the Delaware and Schuylkill rivers. He would call it Philadelphia—a combination of the Greek words for love and friend. The city Penn planned would have straight streets that formed a grid. Its houses would be brick, to keep fires from roaring through the town. And, each house would have its own garden.

People flocked to the new city of Philadelphia. By 1700, its population grew to 4,500. The city also became an early, important center of trade, with ships from far-off places crowding the Delaware River. By 1710, Philadelphia was the largest city in North America.

*The map from 1682 shows how the streets of Philadelphia were laid out.*

## William Penn Respects the Native Americans

This was a terrible time for the Native Americans of North America. Many Europeans had come, with their diseases and their distrust. They had taken over the land and hunted down the animals of the land. The colonists killed the Indians, and the Indians killed the colonists. Places like Massachusetts even offered a reward for Indian scalps.

William Penn wanted a different kind of relationship with the Indians who already lived in Pennsylvania. Even before he sailed for America, he wrote a letter to the Indians. He said that, according to the God of the Quakers, people should "love and help, and do good to one another, and not to do harm and mischief one unto another." He explained that he and others "of the same mind" were going to come and live on the land, and he asked for their permission to do so. He hoped "that we may always live together as neighbors and friends. . . ."

*William Penn insisted on treating the Indians fairly in his dealings with them.*

LITH. & PUB. BY N.CURRIER.                                             152 NASSAU ST. COR. OF SPRUCE N.Y.

Wᵐ PENN'S TREATY with the INDIANS when he founded the PROVINCE of PENNSYᵃ 1661.
THE ONLY TREATY THAT NEVER WAS BROKEN.

William Penn was true to his word. He bought the land from the Indians. He promised that the treaty, or pact, of friendship they made together would be honored "as long as water flows, and the sun shines and grass grows."

Some say that William Penn's treaty was the only treaty made with the Indians that was not broken. For more than 50 years, peace reigned between Pennsylvania's colonists and Indians.

## More Trouble in England

William Penn left Pennsylvania in 1684. He returned to find that things had changed in England. William lost the trust of England's king. He was put in prison again, and his colony was, for a while, taken from him.

Eventually, though, William Penn regained control of Pennsylvania. William died in 1718. After his death, his family held onto Pennsylvania until it became a state of the United States. No other Penn, though, proved to be the fair, just, and wise leader that William Penn was.

## Show What You Know

You have read about some of the traits, or qualities, that made William Penn a great leader. Honest, respectful, and fair all are words that could be used to describe William Penn.

Here is a list of traits you might look for in a leader. Decide which, in your opinion, is most important for a leader to have. Write a 1 by that trait. Then, number the other traits in order of importance. Cross out any traits you think are not important. Add other traits you would like to include on the lines at the bottom.

**BRAVE**

**CURIOUS**

**PATIENT**

**RELIGIOUS**

**HONEST**

**RESPECTFUL**

**FAIR**

**SMART**

_____

_____

_____

# LIFE IN COLONIAL TIMES

The American colonists had many different life experiences in the New World. Some lived in crowded cities, others lived on farms, and still others manned outposts on the frontier. Some lived where winters were bitter and frozen, while others had summers so long they could harvest crops twice. There are, however, some general things we can say about life in colonial times. Here is a look at the lives of farmers and townspeople during the days before America became a nation.

## The Life of a Colonial Farmer

The American farmer and his family had to do just about everything for themselves.

### The Importance of Pigs

*Pigs were important to farming colonists. One reason is because pigs could roam the forests and find their own food. Another reason is that the male hogs, with their short, razor-sharp tusks, offered some protection against the wolves that often preyed on farm animals. Maybe the most important reason is that the meat from four big pigs could feed a family for an entire winter!*

The nearest neighbor might be a day's walk away. First, the farmer had to clear the land. Then, he had to build a house for his family and fences for his animals. With only his oxen and his plow, he farmed the fields. If he needed a chair, he made it. If his wagon broke, he fixed it.

## The Life of a Colonial Farmer's Wife

The women of colonial times had many chores, too. Women took care of the children. They spun thread or yarn and sewed cloth into clothes for their family. They prepared and cooked the food, much of which grew in gardens they tended. They also helped in the fields, for there were never enough hands during planting and harvesting times.

These chores are chores many people still do today. In colonial times, though, they were all done by hand. For example, to wash clothes, a woman had to boil water. Then, she beat the clothes in the hot water to force the dirt from them. She hung the clothes to dry. When they were dry, she heated her iron with hot coals and pressed everything. Washing the clothes for a family could take two or three days!

*Here are some typical scenes from colonial life on a farm. Part of the house has been removed to show the inside.*

## Life in a Colonial Town

Living in town was very different from living on a farm. First, there were neighbors close by. Then, there were blacksmiths and carpenters and chimney sweeps. There were rope-makers and wheel-makers and barrel-makers. There were butchers' shops and bakers' shops and other stores. All this meant that the people in town did not have to do everything themselves, as farm families did. Instead, in town, there were workers they could hire and goods they could buy.

## Life for Children on Farms and in Towns

The children of colonial times were well-loved, but they had to grow up faster than children of today do. Their chores started at an early age. By the time they were three or so, many were given simple tasks to do. As children grew older, fathers taught their sons and mothers taught their daughters the skills they would need as grownups.

Many children were sent to live with skilled workers as apprentices. A contract promised that the skilled worker would teach the child his skill. In return, the child provided faithful service to the worker for a certain amount of time. That amount of time usually was from four to seven years, but it could be longer. Becoming an apprentice was one way for a child to learn a skill with which to make a living.

School buildings often were one room, with a stove in the middle. All grades learned in that one room, with older children helping younger children with their reading, writing, and religion studies.

*Here are some colonial children playing outside their one-room school. All grades were in the same room.*

schools cost money to attend. Free schools were not common for another hundred years.

## Death in Colonial Times

Childhood was a dangerous time in the colonies. One reason was because colonists did not have the medicines we have today. Because of sickness and disease, one of every four children did not live to be one year old. In some colonies, half the children didn't live to adulthood.

Disease did not just strike the young. Grownups, too, got sick and died. About one-third of the children in the colonies lost a parent before reaching the age of ten.

Not all children could go to school. In farm regions, there sometimes was no school. Or, the children were needed at home to help work the farm. In those homes, fathers and mothers became teachers, too. Plus, early

## Show What You Know

People in colonial times didn't have the modern conveniences you have today. Think about machines such as vacuum cleaners, dishwashers, microwave ovens, and washing machines that help people do work today. If you could have only one modern machine, what would it be? Write about why that machine is important to you.

# MARY JOHNSON, EX-SLAVE

The first African slaves arrived to work the land of the New World almost with the first colonists. In 1619, a group of 20 slaves was delivered to Jamestown. Just three years later, Mary Johnson joined a growing number of Africans who were brought to America against their will.

## Mary Johnson: From Slavery to Freedom

In 1622, the ship *Margrett and John* landed at Virginia. Part of the "cargo" the ship carried was an African woman. The records call her Mary. No one knows her true African name.

Mary was one of a group of Africans who had been kidnapped, chained, branded, and packed into the *Margrett and John* for delivery to the New World. Mary was to be a slave, bound for life to work on a tobacco plantation in Virginia.

Something wonderful happened to Mary. Somehow, she and her husband Anthony, a slave from another plantation, gained their freedom. They took the last name Johnson

## The Start of Slavery

*Slavery did not start with American colonists and captured Africans. Slavery has been around for thousands of years. Slaves often were prisoners of war, criminals, and those who owed money. Even in America, long before the colonists came, Indians often made slaves of other Indians captured in battle.*

and settled on the Pungoteague River. Together with their four children, they built a 250-acre farm. There, at peace with their neighbors, they raised cattle and pigs.

Later in life, Mary and Anthony moved to a farm in Somerset County, Maryland. Their grown children farmed the land around them. After 40 years of marriage Anthony died. No one is sure when Mary passed away.

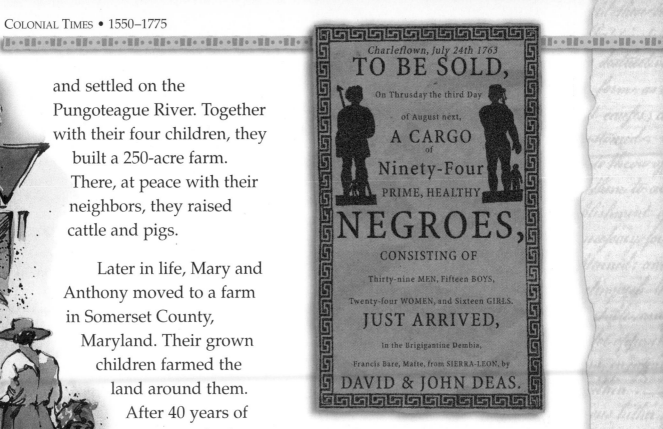

*This advertisement announced an upcoming slave auction.*

*Many slaves worked on tobacco plantations.*

Mary's story really wasn't as unusual as it sounds. In the early days of slavery in the colonies, slaves were treated more like indentured servants. That is, if they worked for a certain number of years, they were able to earn their freedom. Plus, the line between black skin and white skin that later divided this country had not been drawn yet. For example, Mary and her husband lived in an area that had both black families and white families. Blacks worked for whites, and whites worked for blacks. All were members of the community. When a fire almost burned down the Johnson farm, Mary's neighbors offered to help.

In fact, to help the Johnsons rebuild, the local government declared that Mary didn't have to pay local taxes for the rest of her life!

## Laws Change African Lives

In her lifetime, Mary saw things change. New laws began to squeeze out free blacks. Some laws said that black farmers could no longer hire white help. There were few free blacks to hire, so those laws limited the size of black-owned farms to the land the family alone could plant and harvest.

Laws also made it illegal for blacks to carry guns. Laws kept blacks from holding office or testifying in court. Laws said blacks could not hit whites, even in self-defense. And still other laws allowed slavery to last for the life of the slave. By the 1660s, laws in Maryland and Virginia let the condition of slavery pass from the slave to the slave's children and to the children's children.

All these new laws meant that few black people had the opportunities Mary Johnson had in the New World. Instead, in the colonies of America, where so many white settlers found great opportunities, most Africans found only a life of slavery.

## Show What You Know

Think about the lesson you just read. Then, put a 1 by the sentence that describes the first thing that happened to Mary. Put a 2 by the second thing, and so on, until all the sentences, in order, tell the story of Mary's life.

_____ Mary and Anthony move to Maryland.

_____ Mary is kidnapped and taken to America.

_____ Anthony dies.

_____ Mary marries Anthony.

_____ Mary goes to work on a Virginia farm.

_____ Mary is born in Africa.

_____ Mary and Anthony start a farm.

_____ Mary and Anthony gain their freedom.

_____ Mary dies.

Now, use the sentences, in order, to create a storybook of Mary Johnson's life. Draw a picture to illustrate each sentence. Use the sentences as captions for your pictures. Look in other books to see how people dressed during the time Mary lived. After you have finished, use your pictures and captions to tell the story of Mary's life to a family member.

# DANIEL BOONE BUILDS A ROAD

Through the 1600s and into the 1700s, thousands upon thousands of Europeans arrived in America. These people began to fill up the East Coast, clearing and farming land between the Atlantic Ocean and the Appalachian Mountains. Few tried to go farther west.

There are a couple of reasons why most people stayed east of the mountains. One reason is that it was against the law to settle on the other side of the Appalachians. The law was made in 1763 to keep white settlers and Native Americans apart. Another reason is that the mountains themselves made western travel difficult. Any trail across them had to be cut through great forests. In these forests, some trees reached heights of 150 feet or more. Their trunks were thicker than the average human is tall. In addition, few white settlers had traveled west. So, they knew little of that vast, wild region.

*Daniel Boone was an important explorer of the land west of the Appalachian Mountains.*

## Daniel Boone Runs the Gauntlet

One time Daniel Boone was captured by the Shawnee. They made Daniel run the gauntlet. Many prisoners died running the gauntlet. But Daniel was barely injured. That is because he ran in a zigzag pattern, back and forth, instead of in a straight line. Eventually the chief adopted Daniel, and he became a member of the Shawnee group.

Some called the land west of the Appalachians the "back of beyond."

## Daniel Boone Heads West

Daniel Boone was one person with a desire to see the West. He had heard of a western land called Kentucky. It was a land that no Native Americans claimed but where many Native Americans hunted. It was a land of great buffalo herds. It was a land where giant flocks of wild turkeys darkened the skies with their flight. It was a land of good soil and sweet, pure water.

For someone like Daniel Boone, Kentucky must have sounded like heaven. That is because Daniel Boone was an adventurer. He had little school learning. But he learned everything he could about the world around him. He became an expert hunter and trailblazer, that is, he was a man who loved to explore new places.

In 1769, Daniel Boone left his wife and children behind to go on a hunting trip. This trip was different from the many other trips he had taken. On this trip, Daniel followed Native American trails through the Cumberland Gap. The Cumberland Gap is one of just a few natural passageways in the long Appalachian Mountain chain. Daniel used the Cumberland Gap to finally get to Kentucky.

*Daniel Boone leads pioneers through the Cumberland Gap to Kentucky.*

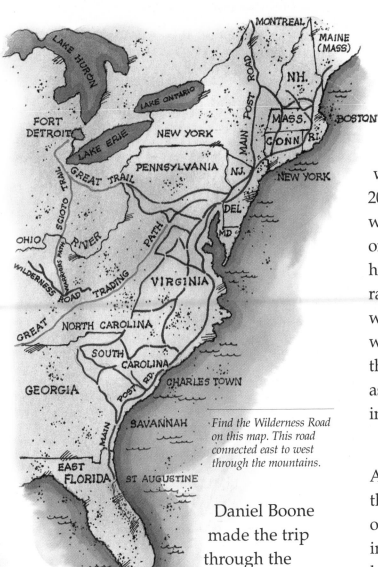

Find the Wilderness Road on this map. This road connected east to west through the mountains.

## Dangers on the Wilderness Road

The trip west was a dangerous one, and life in the West was dangerous, too. The Wilderness Road itself was perilous. It really was just a narrow, winding, walking path. (In fact, it would be 20 years before the path was made wide enough for wagons to travel on.) Sometimes, the path climbed high ridges. Other times, it crossed raging waters. In addition, the wolves, panthers, bears, and other wild beasts that filled the forests threatened the small pioneer parties as they traveled through and settled in this untamed land.

It was perhaps Native Americans who were the greatest threat. They often tried to capture or kill the newcomers who were invading their land. Daniel Boone himself was captured by Native Americans three times! Daniel's 13-year-old daughter, Jemima, also was kidnapped by Native Americans. Daniel rescued her by following the bits of torn clothing she and the two friends captured with her left along the trail. In addition, two of Daniel's sons, James and Israel, were killed in conflicts with Native Americans.

Daniel Boone made the trip through the Cumberland Gap several more times. Then, a North Carolina judge hired Daniel to build a road to Kentucky. In 1775, he and 30 others started work on what became known as the Wilderness Road. Together, they cut down trees and cut back undergrowth, slowly clearing a path through the Cumberland Gap. When they finished, the Wilderness Road they built connected east to west.

## Kentucky Gets "Too Crowded"

Despite the difficulties and dangers, many Americans decided to make the journey through the Appalachians. By 1800, over 75,000 people had followed the Wilderness Road to a new life in what they thought of as the back of beyond.

Daniel Boone, too, settled in Kentucky. But as thousands joined him there, he eventually found Kentucky "Too crowded! Too crowded!" Daniel moved farther west, into the scarcely settled land of Missouri. He died there in 1820. He was 85 years old.

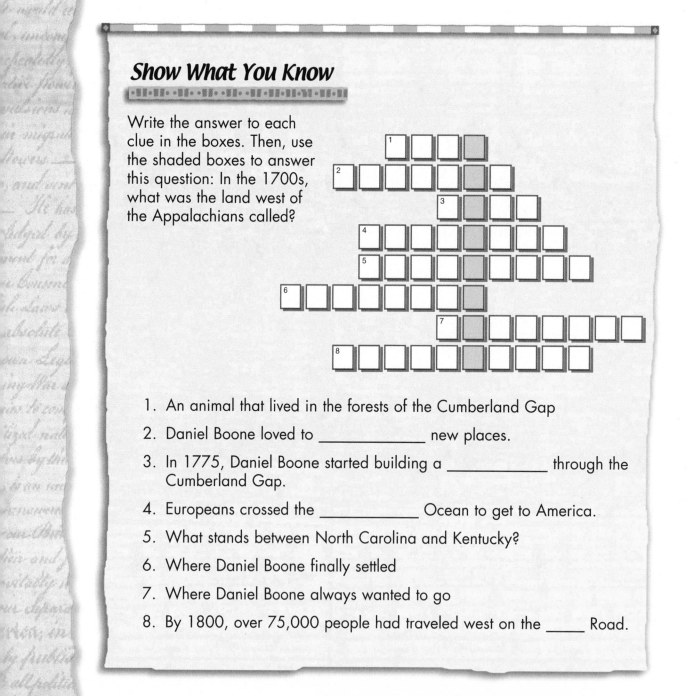

## Show What You Know

Write the answer to each clue in the boxes. Then, use the shaded boxes to answer this question: In the 1700s, what was the land west of the Appalachians called?

1. An animal that lived in the forests of the Cumberland Gap

2. Daniel Boone loved to _____ new places.

3. In 1775, Daniel Boone started building a _____ through the Cumberland Gap.

4. Europeans crossed the _____ Ocean to get to America.

5. What stands between North Carolina and Kentucky?

6. Where Daniel Boone finally settled

7. Where Daniel Boone always wanted to go

8. By 1800, over 75,000 people had traveled west on the _____ Road.

# SPANISH MISSIONS IN NORTH AMERICA

By the middle of the 1500s, Spanish explorers had trekked over much of this country's South and Southwest. They did not find the gold and silver they sought. Most turned back, disappointed.

Soon, though, a different kind of Spaniard came to this area. These Spaniards were Catholic priests. Their goal was not to find riches. Instead, they served as missionaries. Missionaries are people who bring their own religion to other groups. In the case of the Catholic priests, they brought their religion to the people who already lived in the Americas.

## A Pueblo Story

*The following story is part of the belief system the Pueblo people created long before the Spaniards came and built their New Mexico missions:*

*At first, everyone lived 'Below'—under the ground. One, however, escaped to Cloud land, the land above. There, he proved his bravery to the Cloud chiefs. When he explained that there were many others in the Below, one Cloud chief said, 'It is well, you are brave and deathless; your heart and those of your people must be good; go tell them to come, and all this land shall be theirs.' And that is how the first people came to live on Earth.*

## Spanish Priests Build Missions

To reach their goal of bringing Christianity to the Indians, the missionaries decided to live among the Native American groups. But they did not live in the Indian villages. Instead, they established settlements they called missions, where the Indians were welcome.

Spain's first missions in what would be the United States actually were to the south, in Florida. In 1565, near St. Augustine, Spaniards built their very first mission. They called it Nombre de Dios, Name of God.

By 1650, nearly 26,000 Florida Indians had become Christians as they worked at over 30 Florida missions. Many of the missions formed a rough line across northern Florida. Each mission was about a day's travel from the next.

As the 1600s ended and the 1700s began, Spanish missions began to dot the Southwest, too. Soon, New Mexico, Arizona, and Texas all had a Spanish presence.

In 1769, Spain built its first mission in California. In fact, the city that grew up at that site still bears the mission's name—San Diego. Over the next 30 years, 20 more missions were built to bring Christianity to California's Indians.

## A Typical Mission

Missions were made up of several buildings, with an open courtyard in the middle. Usually, there was a place for the missionaries to live. There was also a place for the Indians to live.

*Spanish missions were built in the Southeast and Southwest areas of what is now the United States. Missions were places where missionaries and Indians lived and worked together.*

85

There were schools, workshops, and a church—often with a mission bell. Adobe or stone was usually used to make the buildings and also the surrounding walls that protected the settlement.

Outside the mission walls lay farms. Indians did the farm work for the missionaries. They also helped with mission building. In return, the missionaries provided the Indians with food and clothing. The missionaries schooled the Indians in the Catholic religion. Many Indians also learned to read and write in Spanish.

## Indians and the Missionaries

Sometimes, Indian groups welcomed the Spanish missionaries. One reason for this was that the Spanish soldiers who came with the missionaries could help them protect their land from other Indian groups. Another reason was that for some, belief in their own religion had faltered, for many were dying from European diseases, and the Indian holy men seemed powerless to help.

Sometimes, though, the Indians did not welcome Spanish priests. In Texas, for example, Indian anger at these trespassing Spaniards eventually led early priests to bury their mission bells and abandon the first missions.

## What Happened to the Missions?

Spain never had a really good hold on its settlements in North America. The region Spain claimed was just too big. In fact, Spain considered the Southwest as only a buffer between the more important Mexico and its potential enemies.

Eventually, Spain's missions began to close. One reason for this was sickness. So many Indians died of European diseases that some missions ran out of workers. Other missions were seized, and their lands given to others. By the middle of the 1800s, most of the missions were gone.

## Show What You Know

Missions of the Southwest often were made of adobe or stone. In Florida, though, the walls of many mission buildings were made from wattle and daub. First, Indians built a wooden latticework, or wattle. Then, the wattle was covered with clay, called daub.

To build your own wattle-and-daub house, you'll need toothpicks, glue, and modeling clay. First, use the toothpicks and the glue to build a wattle, as shown. Then, cover the wattle you have built with a layer of clay, or daub. Repeat the process four times to make your house's four walls. Create a doorway in one of the walls. Finish by forming the walls into a square, using more daub to hold the walls together.

*These Indians are using the wattle and daub method of building.*

# UNIT 4

# A NEW NATION IS BORN

## 1775–1810

For over 200 years, colonists built a new life in America. They were far from the rules and regulations of the nations that had once been their homes. So, they made their own rules, and they developed their own ways of doing things. They enjoyed the freedom they found in the New World.

Then, Great Britain decided to tighten its grip on its American colonies. However, the colonists would not give up their freedom. Instead, they went to war. When the war was over, a new nation was born. That nation is the United States of America.

*This was the original U.S. flag which showed only 13 stars for 13 states.*

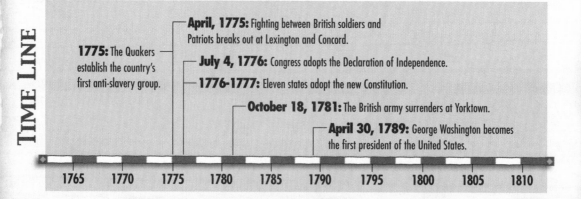

**TIME LINE**

**1775:** The Quakers establish the country's first anti-slavery group.

**April, 1775:** Fighting between British soldiers and Patriots breaks out at Lexington and Concord.

**July 4, 1776:** Congress adopts the Declaration of Independence.

**1776-1777:** Eleven states adopt the new Constitution.

**October 18, 1781:** The British army surrenders at Yorktown.

**April 30, 1789:** George Washington becomes the first president of the United States.

1765  1770  1775  1780  1785  1790  1795  1800  1805  1810

# THE SHOT HEARD ROUND THE WORLD

*Paul Revere was a silversmith and a Patriot.*

By 1775, Britain had declared the colonies in "open rebellion" of its rule. The British soldiers stationed in the colonies were ordered to put down the uprising. Their leaders decided to march on Concord, near Boston. Concord was a natural target, because the town was a major supply center for the Patriots. The British would try to take or destroy the supplies they found there.

## Colonists Sound the Alarm

The Massachusetts colonists discovered that British troops were on their way to Concord. The colonists also feared that the British meant to arrest John Hancock and Samuel Adams, two great Patriots who were in Lexington, a town near Concord.

Patriot leaders sent several riders to warn the people of the countryside and of both towns that the British were coming. Paul Revere, a silversmith, and William Dawes, a tanner, were two who rode. By different routes, they reached Lexington, where Paul alerted Hancock and Adams of the danger on the way. Along the way, they cried out the news to the countryside, alerting the minutemen of trouble. Minutemen were Patriot soldiers who could be ready to fight at a minute's notice.

### Paul Revere's Ride

*Paul Revere's role in the start of the American Revolution was written into a poem. The poem is called "Paul Revere's Ride," and was written by American Henry Wadsworth Longfellow. Although not all the facts of the poem are correct, the poem has made Paul Revere the best-known of the Patriots who rode to warn of a British attack that night. Two stanzas of the poem appear on page 92.*

Dr. Samuel Prescott also rode with the news. The doctor reached Concord only after he escaped British troops that had captured both him and Paul Revere. Paul was later released, but the British kept his horse. William Dawes escaped capture but had to turn back.

## A Killing at Lexington

At dawn, 700 British troops came to the common, or town green, in Lexington. Waiting for them there were only 70 minutemen. At a British command, the minutemen, who were overwhelmingly outnumbered, began to leave the common. Suddenly, someone shouted, "Fire! By God, fire!" and one shot, then more shots, rang out. When the smoke cleared, eight Patriots lay dead on Lexington Common.

## A Fight at Concord

The British marched on, turning their attention toward Concord. By now, more Patriots were coming. As word spread, the Patriots started toward Concord, too. They came from Lincoln. They came from Chelmsford. They came from Carlisle. They came from Acton.

Together, the Patriots marched toward Concord's North Bridge.

There, the British opened fire, and Patriots fired back. Very few were killed on either side, but this action signaled something bigger than the deaths they caused. British subjects were firing on British soldiers. This was war. The American Revolution had begun.

## The British Retreat

For some unknown reason, the British decided to turn back. The soldiers retreated in the stiff, straight lines that marked the style of the British army. But the Patriots were shadows to their right and their left, in front of them and behind them, shooting and running, hounding them as they marched for the next 20 hours, until they reached Charlestown and the safety of the British-controlled harbor. One British soldier wrote, "We were fired on from Houses and behind Trees . . . the Country was . . . full of Hills, Woods, stone Walls . . . which the Rebels did not fail to take advantage of. . . ."

Thousands of Patriot bullets were fired. Yet only about 150 found their mark. That is because most of the Patriots were not highly trained soldiers. Instead, they were just ordinary men who had left their towns and farms by the thousands to fight together for a cause. And this is what is important about that day—that so many felt strongly enough to fight. One Patriot named Thomas Paine spoke for many when he explained why Americans would go to war: "It is not a field of a few acres of ground, but a cause, that we are defending. . . ." The cause was freedom from an unfair government. The cause was self-rule.

*Here are the routes taken by Paul Revere, William Dawes, and Dr. Samuel Prescott as they try to warn the colonists that the British are coming. The Revolutionary War begins when the British and the Patriots fire at each other on Concord's North Bridge.*

## Show What You Know

Henry Wadsworth Longfellow's poem about the famous ride of Paul Revere is not exactly accurate. For example, signal lanterns were placed in the steeple of Boston's North Church. But they were signals for Patriots in Charlestown. Paul Revere already knew which way the British were coming.

Read the first two stanzas of "Paul Revere's Ride." Then, circle the correct answers to questions 1–3 and follow the directions for number 4.

### PAUL REVERE'S RIDE

*By Henry Wadsworth Longfellow*

*Listen, my children, and you shall hear*
*Of the midnight ride of Paul Revere,*
*On the eighteenth of April, in Seventy-five;*
*Hardly a man is now alive*
*Who remembers that famous day and year.*
*He said to his friend, "If the British march*
*By land or sea from the town to-night,*
*Hang a lantern aloft in the belfry arch*
*Of the North Church tower as a signal light,--*
*One, if by land, and two, if by sea;*
*And I on the opposite shore will be,*
*Ready to ride and spread the alarm*
*Through every Middlesex village and farm,*
*For the country folk to be up and to arm. . . ."*

1. According to the poem, at what time did Paul Revere's ride start?
   a. in the afternoon
   b. at midnight
   c. at noon

2. According to Paul, what should his friend do if the British come by sea?
   a. Hang one lantern in the North Church tower.
   b. Hang two lanterns in the North Church tower.
   c. Ride through Middlesex.

3. Why was Paul Revere going to ride through the countryside?
   a. to get home to his family
   b. to warn the British that the Americans were coming
   c. to warn the Americans that the British were coming

4. Underline the part of the poem that shows that it was written long after Paul Revere took his midnight ride.

# Washington Winters at Valley Forge

The fall of 1777 found General George Washington and his men fighting in southeastern Pennsylvania. On September 11, 1777, they lost the battle of Brandywine. On October 4, they lost the Battle of Germantown. Now, the British had a firm grip on the city of Philadelphia.

Winter was approaching fast. Washington marched his ragtag troops to a place about 20 miles northwest of Philadelphia, along the Schuylkill River. There, he and his soldiers spent a terrible winter.

## The Winter at Valley Forge

The new government of the United States had very little money. Only a little of that money ever made it to the fighting troops. Even as American soldiers limped into Valley Forge for the winter, they were already hungry—their clothes already tattered and worn. General Washington observed that "you might have tracked the army . . . to Valley Forge by the blood of their feet."

Conditions at Valley Forge were almost unbearable. Drafty, hastily built huts provided little protection from winter's snow and cold. Clothing wore out, and there was none to be found or bought, even for cash. One observer described the soldiers suffering there: "They had neither coats, hats, shirts, nor shoes; their feet and legs froze until they became black. . . ." One guard stood his watch while standing on his hat, to keep his bare feet out of the snow. There was not enough water, and there was not enough food. In fact, there was so little food that for Thanksgiving, each man received some rice and a tablespoon of vinegar.

General Washington was so worried about conditions that he wrote to Congress. In the letter, he said, that if the men did not receive supplies, the army would either "starve, dissolve, or disperse."

Still, few supplies came. Many—almost a quarter of the men—died, killed by hunger or smallpox or typhoid fever. Some of the survivors mutinied, or turned against their leaders. Others ran home. But most—thousands and thousands—stayed. Together, they tried to live through that awful winter at Valley Forge.

## A Fighting Army Emerges

On February 23, 1778, a Prussian soldier arrived at Valley Forge. (Prussia was a region which is now part of Germany.) He had a very long name—Baron Friedrich Wilhelm Ludolf Gerhard Augustin von Steuben—and he had been an officer in the Prussian army. Baron von Steuben spoke little English. But he liked the men, and the men liked him. He convinced George Washington that he knew how to turn those men into fighters.

Immediately, the Baron began to train a group of Patriots in proper soldiering. When he was done, he sent that trained group out to train other groups, while he trained a new group of men. He repeated this process again and again, working from dawn until dusk. By the end of spring, he had changed the men from farmers and townsmen huddled around Valley Forge campfires into a true, tough, trained army ready to fight for the United States of America.

*Above: Baron von Steuben helped train the soldiers at Valley Forge.*
*Left: George Washington and his troops suffered a terrible winter at Valley Forge.*

## Show What You Know

Baron von Steuben did something else for the U.S. Army. He wrote the first army manual. He spoke so little English that he had to write the manual in French and then have it translated. The manual spelled out everything a man needed to know to be a good soldier.

Baron von Steuben's contribution did not end at Valley Forge. He also helped command troops in Virginia, Carolina, and Pennsylvania. He became an American citizen in 1783. In 1784, he was discharged from the army.

The Baron was never paid for his service to the country. To thank him, Congress gave him a pension for life, and New York State gave him a farm. He died on that farm in 1794.

In this very long sentence, the Baron explains how a soldier should stand at attention:

> *"He is to stand straight and firm upon his legs, with his head turned to the right so far as to bring the left eye over the waistcoat [vest] buttons; the heels two inches apart; the toes turned out; the belly drawn in a little, but without constraint; the [chest] a little projected; the shoulders square to the front and kept back; the hands hanging down at the sides with the palms close to the thighs."*

1. Practice standing at attention by following the Baron's instructions. Then, have a relative or friend check the way you are standing against the instructions the Baron wrote down.

2. Now, rewrite the Baron's instructions in your own words as if you are writing a manual for a soldier. Make sure to number the steps. Then, make your own drawing of a soldier standing at attention.

# HEROINES OF THE REVOLUTION

American women, too, helped in the struggle to win the Revolutionary War. Some of them were adults, with husbands and children. Others were just girls, not much older than you are right now.

At that time, women were not allowed to serve in the armed forces, as they are today. However, many women went along with their husbands when they signed up to fight in the army. These women cooked and washed and mended. They cared for the sick and wounded. Some even went onto the battlefields, to bring water to thirsty soldiers. The water they brought also cooled down the cannons, which became hot as they were fired. Because of the water pitchers they sometimes carried, these women often were called by a common name–"Molly Pitcher."

## The Everyday Heroines

*Many nameless women helped win the Revolutionary War. They took over the farms and stores when their husbands and fathers and brothers went off to fight. In New England, one observer described the support of the women in this way: ". . . at every house Women and Children [were] making Cartridges, running Bullets, making Wallets, baking Biscuit, crying and bemoaning & at the same time animating [encouraging] their Husbands & Sons to fight for their liberties, tho not knowing whether they should ever see them again."*

*Women brought water for the soldiers to drink. Water was also used to cool down the cannons.*

## Margaret Corbin, Fighter for Freedom

One of the women who followed her husband into battle was Margaret Corbin. Margaret was born in 1751 in the frontier land of western Pennsylvania. Her parents were killed by Indians, and Margaret was raised by relatives. In 1772, Margaret married John Corbin. When John went east to fight in the Revolution, Margaret went, too.

On November 16, 1776, John and Margaret Corbin were at a battle site near Fort Washington, New York. John was manning a gun, firing at the approaching enemy. As Margaret watched in horror, John was killed. Margaret did not stop to mourn. Instead, she took her dead husband's place. She ran to the gun, and she began to fire. She stayed there until she, herself, was too wounded to continue.

Margaret lived, but she never recovered from her wounds. To honor Margaret's heroic deeds, Congress gave her a soldier's pension. In 1783, Congress officially discharged her from the army she had never officially joined.

*Some women even loaded cannons to help the soldiers.*

## Sybil Ludington's Call to Arms

Sybil Ludington lived with her family in Patterson, New York. Patterson was a small town near the New York-Connecticut border. Sybil's family was a family of Patriots. Her father, Henry, was a colonel in charge of hundreds of minutemen who lived in the surrounding area.

On April 26, 1777, when Sybil was 16 years old, word came that the British had reached Danbury, Connecticut, only a few miles away from Patterson.

This stamp honors the brave girl who rode to gather the minutemen for battle.

Sybil Ludington is honored by this statue in Carmel, New York.

Sybil mounted Star, her horse. Then, she galloped across the countryside through the rain to tell the minutemen of the invasion. "The British are burning Danbury!" Sybil shouted again and again as she rode. "Muster [gather] at Ludington's!"

Four hundred minutemen answered Sybil's call. Together, they forced the British out of Danbury and back to their ships.

Paul Revere is the Revolutionary rider who usually is remembered by Americans. But Sybil, too, has been honored. A statue of her astride Star stands in Carmel, New York. In 1975, the nation she served remembered her by putting a picture of Sybil on her ride on an eight-cent stamp.

## Women Spy on British Troops

Several women became successful spies during the Revolutionary War. One was Dicey Langston. Dicey lived in South Carolina. She was 15 years old when British troops set up camp next to her father's farm. As Dicey went about her farm chores, she carefully counted the number of soldiers. She also took note of the supplies they had. Then, she passed what she had learned about the enemy on to American soldiers.

Lydia Darragh was also a Patriot. She had to serve dinner to British officers stationed in Philadelphia. The officers paid no attention to Lydia as they planned their next military moves over their meals. But Lydia paid attention to them. She wrote down what they said. Then, she sewed her notes into the linings of her clothes and smuggled the papers to General George Washington.

## Show What You Know

You have just read about the adventures of some of the American women who helped win the Revolutionary War. Choose one of the women mentioned in this reading. Then, on a separate sheet of paper, draw a picture showing how that woman helped the war effort. For example, you could draw a picture of Margaret Corbin at a battle site. Or, you could draw a picture of Sybil Ludington riding through the countryside. When you have finished, think of a title for your drawing. Make sure the title uses the heroine's name. Then, write a paragraph below describing your picture.

_____

_____

_____

_____

_____

_____

# John Paul Jones, Hero of the Seas

*John Paul Jones is considered the father of the U.S. Navy.*

The colonies had made their living with ships, sending goods to England and shipping goods back to America for sale. However, when the Revolutionary War began, the new nation had no navy. Eleven of the new states had their own navies, but these navies mainly patrolled the states' rivers and harbors. Plus, these state navies were like the minutemen. Just as the minutemen assembled when called to arms, crews manned the ships only when trouble loomed.

Congress had little money for shipbuilding. It mainly hired privately owned gunboats to help defend America's shores. During the war, these gunboats captured hundreds of British ships.

Congress did, though, add about 60 ships to its new navy. Several of these ships were piloted by a man whom some call the father of the American Navy. His name was John Paul Jones.

## John Paul Becomes John Paul Jones

John Paul Jones began life in Scotland with the name John Paul. At the age of 12, he went to sea. Ten years later, he was in command of his own ship.

### The Grave of John Paul Jones

*John Paul Jones died in Paris on July 18, 1792. For over 100 years, his body lay in an unmarked French grave. Then, in 1905, a body believed to be John's was dug up. U.S. Navy ships brought John Paul Jones back to the United States, and he was laid to rest in the chapel of the U.S. Naval Academy in Maryland.*

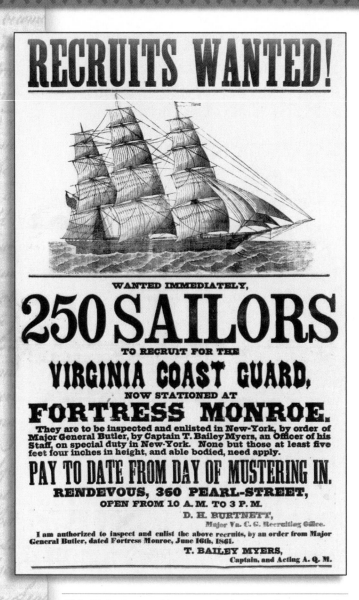

# RECRUITS WANTED!

WANTED IMMEDIATELY,

# 250 SAILORS

TO RECRUIT FOR THE

## VIRGINIA COAST GUARD,

NOW STATIONED AT

## FORTRESS MONROE.

They are to be inspected and enlisted in New-York, by order of Major General Butler, by Captain T. Bailey Myers, an Officer of his Staff, on special duty in New-York. None but those at least five feet four inches in height, and able bodied, need apply.

## PAY TO DATE FROM DAY OF MUSTERING IN.

RENDEVOUS, 360 PEARL-STREET,

OPEN FROM 10 A.M. TO 3 P.M.

D. H. BURTNETT,

Major Va. C. G. Recruiting Office.

I am authorized to inspect and enlist the above recruits, by an order from Major General Butler, dated Fortress Monroe, June 16th, 1861.

T. BAILEY MYERS,

Captain, and Acting A. Q. M.

*This Civil War recruiting poster is similar to those produced in the late 1700s.*

On a trip to the West Indies, John punished a sailor. The sailor later died. Then, on another ship, John killed a sailor who was taking part in a mutiny. Both times, John was accused of murder. The second time he fled, sailing to the colonies. At that time, he also changed his name. From then on, he was known as John Paul Jones.

When the Revolutionary War began, John Paul Jones immediately joined the new navy. Within nine months, he had been promoted to captain. As captain, he commanded several ships in the name of the United States.

## John Paul and the *Bonhomme Richard*

In August 1779, John was given command of an old merchant ship. He renamed it the *Bonhomme Richard*—Poor Richard—and fitted it with guns. Then, aboard the *Bonhomme Richard* and in the company of four other ships, John sailed the waters around Britain, causing trouble wherever he could.

In September 1779, John's little fleet came upon a group of trading ships. The ships were sailing under the protection of two British gun ships—the 40-gun *Serapis* and the *Countess of Scarborough*. One of John's ships attacked the *Countess*. The *Bonhomme Richard* went after the *Serapis*.

John knew that the *Richard* was outgunned by the bigger *Serapis*. The only chance for an American win, he decided, was close combat. So, John sailed up beside the enemy and tied his ship to the *Serapis*.

Thus began one of the fiercest battles ever to take place on the sea. For more than three hours, the men of the *Richard* fought the men of the *Serapis*. Then, the old *Richard* began to take on water, even with all its pumps pumping. The British commander demanded that the crew of the *Bonhomme Richard* surrender. But John refused.

According to legend, this was John's response: "I have not yet begun to fight!" John himself later wrote that he said no "in the most determined negative."

Against all odds, the Americans won the battle. Some historians say the Americans won just because they would not quit. The *Richard* was so badly damaged that John moved his crew to the *Serapis*. Two days later, the *Richard* sank. John was scheduled to take command of another big, new ship. Before that could happen, the war ended. Congress disbanded the navy, and John Paul Jones went to sail for other nations.

## Show What You Know

Imagine that you are a sailor during the Revolutionary War. You have just fought for the country and for John Paul Jones aboard the *Bonhomme Richard*. On a separate sheet of paper, write a diary entry describing the battle between the *Bonhomme Richard* and the *Serapis*. Make sure your entry tells how you felt about the battle. Also, tell what you think the battle meant to the United States' war effort.

# A New Flag for a New Nation

*John Paul Jones raised a flag like this one over the* Serapis *after his ship, the* Bonhomme Richard, *defeated it in the battle.*

## Red, White, and Blue Stripes?

*In 1778, Benjamin Franklin and John Adams were asked to describe America's new flag for the King of Naples. The flag they described was not quite the same as the flag described by Congress. Here is what Benjamin and John said:*

*"It is with pleasure that we acquaint your Excellency that the flag of the United States of America consists of 13 stripes, alternately red, white and blue; a small square in the upper angle, next the flag staff, is a blue field, with 13 white stars, denoting a new Constellation."*

*This actually comes close to describing the flag that John Paul Jones raised over the* Serapis *after it surrendered to the* Bonhomme Richard.

As you have learned, French flags, Dutch flags, Spanish flags, and English flags all flew over America. It was not until the Revolutionary War that the United States needed its own flag. There are legends about who designed and sewed the first American flag. There are also some facts of which we are sure.

## The Legend of Betsy Ross

When Betsy Ross was an old woman, she told her grandson a story. She said that in June 1776, three men came to her house in Philadelphia. One was her husband's uncle, George Ross. One was a man named Robert Morris. And, one was General George Washington.

*Betsy Ross is often given credit for creating this flag design.*

These men knew that Betsy was a seamstress. She made her living sewing flags and upholstering furniture. They asked her to use her skills to sew a flag for the new nation.

Betsy agreed to try. She looked at the rough sketch the men had drawn. Then, she went to work. When she finished the flag, General Washington presented it to Congress.

There is no evidence to prove that the story about Betsy Ross is true.

There is no evidence to prove it untrue, either. The making of a flag probably would have been a secret affair, which might explain why no record of the visit to Betsy's house exists. In addition, General Washington was indeed in Philadelphia at that time. However, that was before the Declaration of Independence had been adopted. So, there would not yet have been a need for a new flag, since there was not yet a new country.

## The Nation's First Flags

In the first two years of the Revolutionary War, American soldiers fought under many flags. For example, South Carolina Patriots carried a yellow flag, on which was curled a rattlesnake ready to strike. Below the snake appeared these words: "DON'T TREAD ON ME." Ships sailing for the state of Massachusetts often sailed under a flag on which a pine tree appeared.

At that time, there was no recognized national flag. The closest one was a flag that had red and white stripes. But instead of stars, the upper left-hand corner had a smaller version of Britain's flag. This version of the flag often was called the Grand Union flag.

On June 14, 1777, Congress made its first official mention of a flag for the nation. In the journal Congress kept was this entry: "RESOLVED: that the flag of the United States be made of thirteen stripes, alternate red and white; that the union be thirteen stars, white in a blue field, representing a new constellation." The 13 stripes and the 13 stars both represented the original 13 colonies.

## The Flag Changes Again

By 1794, the Revolutionary War was long over. The United States had grown larger by two states. To show this change, Congress ordered that the nation's flag have 15 stripes and 15 stars.

That remained our nation's flag for the next 23 years.

More states continued to join the Union. Congress realized that the number of stripes on our flag could not continue to grow. So, in 1818, it set the number of stripes again at 13, for the 13 original colonies. At the same time, Congress declared that each state would be represented on the flag by a white star. Ever since, every time a new state has joined the Union, a new star has been added to the flag.

## Show What You Know

It is important to treat the American flag with respect. So, there are rules about how to handle the flag. For example, if you are not flying your flag, you should fold it into a triangle. To do this, you first fold the flag in half twice, lengthwise. Then, starting at the star end, fold one corner over, to make a little triangle. Fold over the triangle again, then again and again, until you reach the end of the flag. Tuck leftover material into the fold. Now, the flag can be stored in a neat triangle until you are ready to fly it once more.

Use a bathroom or kitchen towel. Imagine that it is an American flag. Follow the instructions above to fold your "flag" into a triangle for storage.

# Planning Washington, D.C.

On October 17, 1781, at 10:00 in the morning, a sudden hush fell over the Yorktown battlefield. In the air over the British side, a white cloth appeared. It signaled the surrender of over 7,000 British soldiers. All the paperwork would take another two years to complete. But, on that day—October 17, 1781—the Revolutionary War ended. The work of building a new nation began.

### The White House

*Abigail Adams, wife of John Adams, became the first wife of a president to live in the White House. Here is how she described her new home:*

*"The house is on a grand and superb scale, requiring about thirty servants to attend and keep the apartments in proper order, and perform the ordinary business of the house and stables. . . . The house is made habitable [livable], but there is not a single apartment finished. . . . it is a beautiful spot, capable of every improvement, and the more I view it, the more I am delighted with it."*

## A National Constitution

First, in 1787, Congress created a constitution. It had seven parts, called articles. Together, these articles spelled out how the United States government would work. Then, Congress sent the Constitution out to the states to get their approval. After all, the Constitution would be the supreme law of the land. This means that no state law can go against the nation's Constitution.

By June 1788, nine states had approved the Constitution. According to the Constitution itself, nine state approvals meant the Constitution was adopted. The next year, the people followed the Constitution's guidelines to elect the nation's first president. The man they chose was General George Washington.

## A New Capital for a New Nation

The adoption of the Constitution put a new national government into place. Now, the United States needed a place for that government to meet. Philadelphia had served as a temporary capital for the nation. It was time to find the government a permanent home.

*Top: The British surrender at Yorktown on or around October 17, 1781. Middle: This illustration shows the White House as it looked in 1807. Bottom: This illustration shows the Capitol as it looked in 1824.*

Everyone disagreed about the location of the new capital. Northern states wanted the capital in the North. Southern states wanted it built in the South. In addition, each state clamored to have the capital built within its own borders. The states were sure that the capital city would become an important trade center. That would bring money to the lucky state in which it was built.

Finally, in 1790, an agreement was reached. The new city would be located where the Potomac and the Anacostia rivers meet. Both Maryland and Virginia agreed to give up a little land to the national government. That way, the new city would be on national soil, not on the soil of any one state.

## L'Enfant Plans a City

President George Washington hired Pierre Charles L'Enfant (lahn FAHN) to plan the new capital city. Pierre was a French engineer who had served with the Patriots in the Revolutionary War.

In the design Pierre created, he focused on two buildings. One was the "Congress house." The other was the "president's house." According to Pierre's plan, these two "houses" would be like hubs in a wheel. The wheel's spokes would be long, wide roads going out in all directions from each "house."

*This sketch shows Charles L'Enfant's original plan of Washington, D.C.*

In 1791, Pierre began to build the city he had designed. However, Pierre made many enemies as he worked. He didn't like to listen to anyone else, and he often ignored the advice of others. He spent more money than was in the budget. Once, he found that a home stood in the path of a street he had proposed. Without anyone's permission, he tore the house down and kept building.

Because of his attitude, in February 1792—not even a year after he began building Washington—Pierre was fired. Others took over building the capital city. These new planners ignored most of Pierre's plans as they built.

## The Government Moves to Washington

In 1800, the government officially moved to Washington, D.C. The city was only partly finished. The Capitol, where Congress would meet, and the White House, where the president would live, were incomplete. In fact, it took decades for all the work to get done.

Washington did not become the trade center everyone expected. It just could not compete with the other, old East Coast cities, like New York and Philadelphia and Baltimore. Instead, it stayed a small city for the next 50 years.

### Show What You Know

Many of the streets in Washington, D.C., are named after states. Here is a map showing the area around the U.S. Capitol. Look carefully at the map. Then, on a separate sheet of paper, list all the streets you see that share their names with states.

# THOMAS JEFFERSON, OUR THIRD PRESIDENT

*This painting is a portrait of Thomas Jefferson, our third President.*

## Thomas Jefferson's Epitaph

*Before he died, Thomas Jefferson wrote his own epitaph, or words for his gravestone. Here is what it says:*

*"Here was buried Thomas Jefferson, author of the Declaration of American Independence, of the statute [law] of Virginia for religious freedom, and father of the University of Virginia."*

*His gravestone does not say that Thomas Jefferson was the third president of the United States.*

Many words can describe Thomas Jefferson. He was an inventor. He was a farmer. He was an architect. He was a lawyer. And, he was a Patriot. Let's take a look at who Thomas Jefferson was and what he did for our nation.

## Jefferson, the Man

Thomas Jefferson was born on his father's plantation in Virginia. When Thomas was 14 years old, his father died. That meant that Thomas, as oldest son, inherited the family land.

Thomas was a serious student. In fact, he finished college in only two years by studying 15 hours a day! He continued his schooling to become a lawyer. He took law cases all over Virginia.

When Thomas was in his 20s, he fell in love with Martha Skelton. When they were courting (an old-fashioned word for "dating"), they played music together. He played the violin. She played the harpsichord. One story goes that two other men were interested in Martha. However, both gave up after they heard the lovely music Martha and Thomas made together.

Thomas and Martha married on New Year's Day, 1772. They lived in a one-room house for a couple of years, until Thomas finished building the wonderful house he had designed. He built it on a hilltop near Charlottesville, Virginia. He called the new house Monticello (mahn tih CHEHL oh)—"little mountain."

Over the next ten years, Thomas and Martha had six children. Three children did not live to see their first birthday. A fourth child died when she was only 3-1/2 years old.

Martha herself died soon after her sixth child was born. Thomas never remarried. In fact, he was the first widower to be elected President of the United States.

## Jefferson's Political Life

Thomas Jefferson spent many years serving the state of Virginia. In Thomas' opinion, one of the most important things he did as a state representative was to write a certain bill. That bill guaranteed religious freedom in Virginia. In part, it said, "no man shall be compelled to frequent or support any religious worship, place, or ministry whatsoever. . . ." The bill also made sure that the people of Virginia could not be punished for their religious beliefs.

*Monticello, Thomas Jefferson's home in Virginia, is shown in this photograph.*

Thomas Jefferson also served in the nation's government. In 1776, for example, Thomas was given an assignment. He was asked to write a document for the government. That document was to declare our nation's independence from Great Britain. From June 11 to June 28, Thomas wrote and wrote and wrote. Then, he presented the finished document to Congress. Congress then made changes to the Declaration of Independence. On July 4, 1776, it was adopted.

*This is an illustration of the original Declaration of Independence.*

The Declaration of Independence stated that the United States wanted to be free. It declared "these United Colonies are, and of Right ought to be, Free and Independent States."

The Declaration of Independence did more than declare America's freedom. It also spelled out the human rights that should be protected by our government. "We hold these Truths to be self-evident," it said, "that all Men are created equal, that they are endowed [gifted] by their Creator with certain unalienable rights [rights that can't be taken away], that among these are Life, Liberty, and the Pursuit of Happiness . . ." In addition, the Declaration of Independence explained that a government must protect these rights. If it does not, the people can get rid of that government and put in its place a new government. That belief explains why the Revolutionary War was fought.

*The signers of the Declaration of Independence are shown in this painting.*

In 1800, Thomas Jefferson was elected President of the United States. One of the acts for which he is remembered is his purchase of the Louisiana Territory. You will learn about the Louisiana Purchase later.

Thomas Jefferson made the presidency a more casual office. For example, people used to bow to President Washington and President Adams. But Thomas stopped that practice. Instead, he shook hands with his visitors, as presidents still do today. Thomas Jefferson also was known to greet important people while wearing his slippers. He said he thought more clearly when he could wiggle his toes!

### Jefferson Retires

Thomas Jefferson did not stop working just because his term as president was over. Instead, he completed one project of which he was most proud. He founded the University of Virginia. He, himself, designed the buildings. He defined the courses that would be offered. And, he hired the first teachers. At the University of Virginia, Thomas also introduced the idea of electives. An elective is a course you take because you want to, not because you have to.

After his retirement, money problems plagued Thomas Jefferson. He had spent more to run the White House than he made as president. So, he left office in debt.

Thomas spent a lot of money in his private life, too. For example, Thomas had many visitors at Monticello. In fact, one of his servants observed that "many weeks the 26 spare horse stalls were not sufficient [enough] for the visitors' mounts [horses]." Sometimes, 50 people stayed at Monticello at one time. Some visitors stayed for months!

By 1826, Thomas owed over $107,000. He needed money so badly that he even started a lottery, offering Monticello as the lottery prize. Monticello remained his home, however, when he didn't sell enough lottery tickets.

## Jefferson Dies

By the time Thomas Jefferson was in his 80s, his health was failing. By July 2, 1826, he was drifting in and out of consciousness. On the evening of July 3, he wakened and spoke his last words. "Is it the Fourth?" he asked. "It soon will be," his doctor answered. The next day, July 4th, on the fiftieth anniversary of our nation's birth, Thomas Jefferson died. Later that day, the nation's second president, John Adams, also died. John Adams did not know of Thomas' death. It is said his last words were, "Jefferson still survives."

*This photograph shows one of the buildings at the University of Virginia, which Thomas Jefferson founded.*

## Show What You Know

In 1825, Thomas Jefferson wrote a letter to his grandson. In the letter, Thomas listed ten pieces of advice. He thought that if his grandson followed this advice, he would live a better life. Here is the list Thomas Jefferson wrote:

1. Never put off till tomorrow what you can do today.
2. Never trouble another for what you can do yourself.
3. Never spend your money before you have it.
4. Never buy what you do not want, because it is cheap; it will be dear [expensive] to you.
5. Pride costs us more than hunger, thirst, and cold.
6. We never repent of having eaten too little.
7. Nothing is troublesome that we do willingly.
8. How much pain have cost us the evils which have never happened.
9. Take things always by their smooth handle.
10. When angry, count ten, before you speak; if very angry, a hundred.

Choose one of the ten points listed here. Write what you think one of the points really means and why you think it is good advice. Then, for a whole week, try to follow the advice of the point you have chosen. For example, for a week, you might count to ten every time you are angry (#10). At the end of the week, decide whether your life was better because you followed Thomas Jefferson's advice.

_____

_____

_____

_____

_____

_____

# Unit 5  1785–1860
# The U.S. From Coast to Coast

The first half of the 1800s was a time of adding on to the nation. In fact, almost all the land west of the Mississippi River was added to the United States during that time.

As each new piece was added to the country, Americans moved into it. During this time of adventure, it sometimes seemed like everyone was going west.

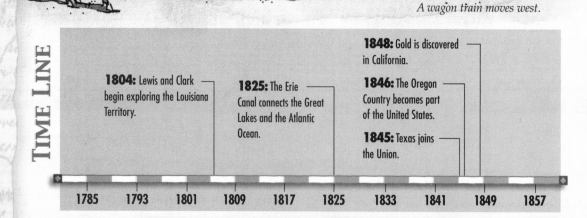

*A wagon train moves west.*

## TIME LINE

**1804:** Lewis and Clark begin exploring the Louisiana Territory.

**1825:** The Erie Canal connects the Great Lakes and the Atlantic Ocean.

**1848:** Gold is discovered in California.

**1846:** The Oregon Country becomes part of the United States.

**1845:** Texas joins the Union.

1785  1793  1801  1809  1817  1825  1833  1841  1849  1857

# SAMUEL SLATER STEALS AN IDEA

English machines made it cheaper for England than for other countries to make textiles, or cloth. England wanted to keep it that way. So, laws were passed that neither machines nor the men who ran them could leave the country. In that way, England hoped to protect the money its citizens were making from the textile industry.

## Samuel Slater Comes to America

Samuel Slater was an Englishman. When he was young, his family apprenticed him to one of the biggest textile manufacturers in the country. An apprentice is someone who learns a trade. During his apprenticeship, Samuel learned more than how to make cloth. He also memorized how the English spinning machines were built and how they worked.

Samuel heard that American companies were offering prizes to people who brought English technology to the United States. He decided he wanted to go to America.

Samuel knew that he was forbidden by law to leave England. So, he disguised himself by dressing in farmer's clothes. That way no one would suspect he worked in the mills. Then, with the machine plans safely stored in his head, Samuel boarded a ship bound for the United States. Just before the ship left, he wrote his family and told them he was going to America.

*Born in England, Samuel Slater came to the United States and built a cotton-spinning mill.*

*This illustration shows a mechanical cotton mill by a river.*

## Samuel Builds a Mill

In 1789, a Rhode Island businessman agreed to pay for Samuel to build his spinning machine. By late 1790, Samuel's cotton-spinning mill opened for business. The mill used Samuel's machines to spin cotton into yarn. Then, the yarn was given to home weavers to be woven into cloth.

Samuel built his mill on the Blackstone River in Pawtuxet, Rhode Island. At first, the mill's water wheel didn't work. It froze in place almost every night. Samuel often had to work for two or three hours in the morning to free the wheel from the ice's nightly grip.

## Samuel and the Blacksmith's Daughter

Samuel's mill almost didn't get built at all. That is because Samuel fell in love. The girl's name was Hannah, and she was a blacksmith's daughter. She also belonged to a religious group called the Quakers. Her parents wanted Hannah to marry a Quaker, and Samuel wasn't one. So, to break up the romance between Hannah and Samuel, Hannah's parents decided to send her away to school. Samuel threatened to go after her. "You may send her where you please, but I will follow her to the ends of the earth!" he said. Hannah's

*Samuel Slater used child labor in his mill. This picture, taken at a later date, shows a young girl working at a cotton mill.*

In America, it wasn't unusual for young children to work. After all, this was a farming nation. On the farms, children often began to work soon after they began to walk. In addition, Samuel treated his child workers well. Later factory owners also used child labor. However, many were not as kind as Samuel to the children who worked for them.

This poem was written about children at work in a mill:

*The golf course is so near the mill*
*That almost every day*
*The little children can look out*
*And see the men at play.*

*— by Sarah Cleghorn*

parents gave in. They allowed Samuel and Hannah to marry. Then, Samuel went back to work on his mill.

## Children Work in Samuel's Mills

Samuel brought another idea from Great Britain, too. Like the British, he used child labor. The eight boys and girls he hired for his first mill were between 7 and 12 years old. These children were not apprentices. They were workers. And, they worked for very little money—much less money than grownups made. In fact, the wages were so low that only the poorest families sent their children to work in the mills.

### Show What You Know

You have already seen a picture of the kind of machine whose workings Samuel Slater memorized. Choose one of the machines in your own home. For example, you might choose a vacuum cleaner, a VCR, a television, or a toaster. Study the machine for a few minutes. Then, turn away from the machine, and try to draw it from memory. When you have finished, turn back, and compare your drawing to the actual machine. How did you do?

# ELI WHITNEY'S COTTON GIN

## The Importance of Cotton

*About three-fourths of all the cotton the South produced was exported, or sent to other countries. Britain received most of the exported cotton. For many years, the money made from exporting cotton was greater than the money made from all other goods exported by the United States!*

E li Whitney had always understood machines. When he was just 12 years old, he made his own violin. When he was a teenager, he began to sell nails that he made with a machine he had invented.

### A Problem With Cotton

In 1792, when he was about 27 years old, Eli Whitney went South to teach. Instead, he ended up inventing. He was living on a Georgia plantation owned by Mrs. Catherine Greene, the widow of the Patriot General Nathaniel Greene. While living there, Eli spoke with Mrs. Greene. He also spoke with other farmers in the region. He found that they grew little cotton. This was because the kind of cotton that grew well in

*Eli Whitney had been a blacksmith at one point in his life. He always liked fixing and making machines.*

*Eli Whitney's cotton gin separated cotton from its seeds.*

southern soil was difficult to clean. It had small, tough seeds that were very hard to separate from the cotton itself. In fact, it took a slave a whole day to separate one pound of cotton from its seeds. For southern farmers, the cost of growing cotton was just too high.

## Eli Solves the Cotton Problem

All the people with whom Eli spoke wished there were a machine that could do the tedious, time-consuming task of separating cotton and seeds. Eli wrote to his father about what he had heard. "There were a number of very respectable Gentlemen at Mrs. Greene's," he wrote, "who all agreed that if a machine could be invented . . .

it would be a great thing both to the Country and the inventor."

Eli knew he could invent such a machine. So he set to work. First, he studied how slaves moved their hands as they cleaned the cotton. Then, he began to build a machine that made the same motions as the slaves' hands.

It took Eli only ten days to create his cotton gin. Eli's first cotton gin was cranked by hand. Even so, it separated cotton and seeds 50 times faster than could the hands of a slave!

Now, Eli Whitney's gins could supply Samuel Slater with all the cleaned cotton Samuel's mills could spin. Soon, cotton was no longer a luxury. Instead, with machines doing most of the work, its price dropped, and it became a common cloth.

When Eli first showed Mrs. Greene his cotton gin, they invited many people to come and see the new invention. They realized their mistake when the gin was easily copied, and some people went away and made their own. Someone even broke in and stole Eli's gin one night. As a result, Eli made very little money on his invention.

## Eli's Gin Encourages Slavery

With Eli's gin, the demand for cotton exploded. To meet the demand, many southern farmers began to devote their whole plantations to cotton growing. Land that was thought useless was planted with this easy-to-grow, easy-to-harvest, and—now—easy-to-clean cotton.

Until the 1790s, slavery was slowly fading away in the South. That is because southern farmers had no crops that made enough money to pay to keep slaves. Then, Eli invented his gin. Southern farmers realized they had found their cash crop. It was cotton. Soon, great plantations filled up with fields of cotton. These fields depended on slave labor. More and more slaves were bought. Within ten years, the price of a slave doubled! Slavery became entrenched in the South.

## Eli Builds 10,000 Guns

Eli Whitney could have stayed angry when others stole his gin invention. Instead, he decided to invent something else. He heard that the government needed guns made. Eli had never made a gun. Still, he wrote a letter to the government. In the letter, Eli said, "I have a number of workmen & apprentices. . . . I should like to undertake to Manufacture Ten or Fifteen Thousand Stand of Arms."

The government asked 27 companies to make guns. Most got a contract for about 1,000 weapons. But Eli's contract was different. The government knew about Eli's mechanical skills. So, his contract called for him to make 10,000 guns.

Other gunmakers made their guns by hand. Eli had a different idea. For each part of a gun, he made a metal mold. He also made the machines to make the molds. The metal molds then turned out exactly the same parts—trigger, barrel, and so on—for gun after gun after gun. This meant that the parts were interchangeable—that is, each part of one gun was exactly the same as each

*Slaves work in a cotton field.*

part of any other Whitney-made gun. Regular workers—not skilled gunsmiths—made many parts, then assembled them into many guns. This method was much faster than making guns by hand. It also was much less expensive.

Eli Whitney was not the first to think of using interchangeable parts. However, he is the one who made using them famous. Later, Eli used these same skills to make clocks from interchangeable parts. After that, more people could afford to have a clock in the house.

## Show What You Know

This is a pictograph about cotton-growing in the United States. A pictograph is a graph that uses a picture of something to represent something else. In this pictograph, each purple rectangle represents 25,000 bales of cotton.

### COTTON GROWN IN THE UNITED STATES

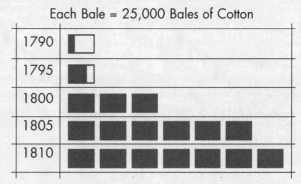

Each Bale = 25,000 Bales of Cotton

|  | |
|------|---|
| 1790 | |
| 1795 | |
| 1800 | |
| 1805 | |
| 1810 | |

Study the pictograph. Then, use it to answer these questions. Circle the correct answer for the first two questions. Write your answer on the lines for number 3.

1. In what year did the United States first produce over 25,000 bales of cotton?
   a. 1790
   b. 1795
   c. 1800

2. What do you think happened to cotton-growing by the year 1815?
   a. More cotton was grown.
   b. Less cotton was grown.
   c. The same amount of cotton was grown.

3. What effect did Eli Whitney have on cotton-growing in the United States?

   _____

   _____

   _____

# LEWIS AND CLARK EXPLORE THE LOUISIANA PURCHASE

New Orleans is, and has always been, a very important port. That is because it sits at the mouth of the Mississippi River. In the early days, farmers from all over the Midwest used the Mississippi and the rivers that connect to the Mississippi to ship their goods to New Orleans. At that great port, everything from flour and bacon to beeswax and bearskins was loaded onto ocean-going ships and sailed to markets in faraway places.

Farmers couldn't take their goods over land. The time it took could cause their produce to spoil. For many, their success or failure as farmers depended on the Mississippi River and the city of New Orleans.

The problem was, the United States did not own New Orleans. France owned it. In fact, France owned much of the rest of the country, from the Mississippi River just about to the Rocky Mountains. This entire region was

*These steamboats are docked at the Port of New Orleans.*

known as the Louisiana Territory. If France wanted, it could stop American ships from using the port in New Orleans. This had happened before, when Spain controlled the region. America couldn't let that happen. So, President Thomas Jefferson decided to try to buy the land from France.

## Jefferson Buys Louisiana

Thomas Jefferson did not think that the French would sell all of New Orleans. So, his instructions to the officials he sent to France were to try to get at least part of it. He said, "If the entire port cannot be acquired [bought], try for a good riverbank site for a dock plus warehouses—along with some land at the very mouth of the river."

President Jefferson was in for a surprise. France needed money. France also wanted to keep Louisiana out of British hands. So, France offered to sell all the Louisiana Territory to the United States. The cost was $15 million. Today, $15 million sounds like a small price to pay. However, at that time, $15 million was more money than could be found in the entire United States!

Many people were angry when the Louisiana Purchase was announced.

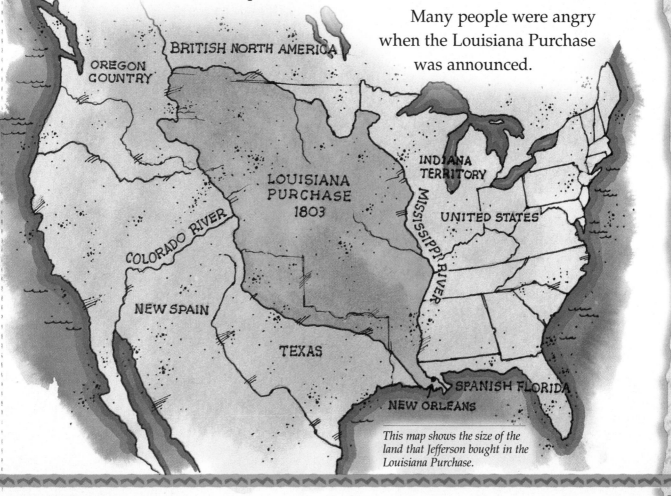

This map shows the size of the land that Jefferson bought in the Louisiana Purchase.

Some were upset about the $15 million debt. Others felt the United States would now be too big to remain one nation.

Some thought, as president, Thomas Jefferson did not have the right to make the decision by himself. That was more like what a king would do.

In the end, though, the people accepted the purchase. On December 20, 1803, in a celebration in New Orleans, the area called Louisiana officially became part of the United States of America.

## Lewis and Clark Prepare for an Adventure

No one—not the French and not the Americans—knew just how big the Louisiana Territory was. But, Thomas Jefferson wanted to know. He wanted to know everything about Louisiana. So, he asked Meriwether Lewis, his personal secretary, to explore the territory. The president told Meriwether to find out about the Indians, the animals, the soil, the stones, the birds, the bugs, the water, the weather, and anything else he saw on his trip.

Meriwether Lewis invited an old army buddy, William Clark, to join him on his journey. Both men were very interested in nature. Plus, William could draw, so Meriwether would depend on him to sketch the new animals and plants they found. Together, history will always remember them as Lewis and Clark.

It took Meriwether Lewis and William Clark months to get ready for the trip west. They had to think long and hard about what to take on the journey. After all, they knew they would be gone for a couple of years. For example, they knew there would be no place in the wilderness to get bullets for their guns. So, they stored their gunpowder in lead kegs. The waterproof kegs protected the gunpowder. And, when a keg was empty, it could be melted down into lead bullets.

*These notes and the drawing are examples of what Lewis and Clark wrote and drew during their trip.*

Lewis and Clark also assembled a great group of men for the trip. Each of the 30-or-so men chosen brought special skills to the group. For example, one was a gunsmith, one a cook, one a carpenter, and one an expert fisherman. All brought enthusiasm to the party, because they all were excited to go with Lewis and Clark. "I am so happy as to be one of them picked men," one man wrote home.

## A Two-Year Journey

On May 14, 1804, Lewis, Clark, and the rest of the men set out from St. Louis. A large flat-bottomed boat, almost 60 feet long, held most of the men and supplies. Two dugout canoes accompanied the big boat. Together the big and little boats began a long voyage of discovery. The first leg took them up the Missouri River.

By October, the men had reached the home of the Mandan and Hidatsa Indians, in present-day North Dakota. The Indians were kind and helpful. So, the explorers decided to spend the winter there. The settlement they built was called Fort Mandan.

During the winter at Fort Mandan, the Lewis and Clark party was joined by a trader and his wife. The trader's name was Toussaint Charbonneau (too SAN shar buhn OH). He was French Canadian. His wife was a Shoshone (shoh SHOH nee) Indian. Her name was Sacagewea (sak uh juh WEE uh).

Sacagewea's people lived in the Rocky Mountains. As a child, she had been kidnapped and brought to the country of the Mandan. Eventually, Toussaint Charbonneau bought her. Now, with her

*Sacagewea and her baby boy are shown on this coin.*

husband, she would help Lewis and Clark communicate with the many different Indian groups through whose lands they would travel. On her back, Sacagewea carried her baby boy, Baptiste, who was born that winter.

When spring came, it was time for the party to move on. Soon they faced the Rocky Mountains, where no large boats could sail. So, they sent their large boat back down the Missouri, home to St. Louis. The boat carried reports about what Lewis and Clark had seen and studied. It also carried samples and artifacts—such as the skins of unknown animals and specimens of unknown plants. These things were delivered to the White House, since there was no museum to house them yet.

The group moved west, always gathering information and samples and mapping the unknown land. Finally, in November 1805, a year and a half after their journey had begun, Lewis and Clark reached the Pacific Ocean.

*Sacagewea worked as a guide for Lewis and Clark.*

For the first time, the people of the United States had some idea of what they had gained when the Louisiana Territory was added to the nation.

## Lewis and Clark and Bears (Oh My!)

Grizzly bears were among the many new kinds of animals that impressed Lewis and Clark. They described the grizzly as a "furious and formidable animal" that "will frequently pursue the hunter when wounded." In fact, Lewis and Clark were so impressed with grizzly bears that two grizzly cubs

were among the hundreds of plants and animals they brought back for President Jefferson.

Meriwether wrote about one especially scary grizzly encounter. He said that six hunters had gone after one grizzly bear. They all shot at it. But the bullets only made the bear angry. It chased after the hunters, who tried to run and reload their guns at the same time. Two of the men jumped off a 20-foot cliff into a river. But, the bear jumped off after them! More shots finally killed the bear. It took eight bullets in all to bring the bear down.

## Show What You Know

Here is the route followed by Lewis and Clark on their way through the Louisiana Territory. On the map, write a 1 at the spot described in the first sentence below. Write a 2 by the place described in the second sentence. And write a 3 by the place described in the third sentence.

In the middle of May 1804, Lewis and Clark started their journey by boarding boats in St. Louis and sailing north up the Missouri River.

In the fall of 1804, they reached a place about 150 miles east of where the Missouri and the Yellowstone rivers meet. They built Fort Mandan and settled in for the winter.

In November 1805, Lewis and Clark were full of joy as they finally looked out at the Pacific Ocean.

# BOATS ON THE MISSISSIPPI RIVER

For hundreds of years before there was written history, Indians had used the Mississippi River for travel. Then the Europeans came, across the Appalachian Mountains, to settle and farm the rich soil along the Mississippi and the rivers that feed into it. They, too, used the great river for travel. When they were ready to take their goods to market, they built flatboats, which were really just rafts. They loaded the flatboats with goods and let the Mississippi River's current float them all the way down to New Orleans.

When the farmers arrived in New Orleans, they sold their goods. Then,

Flatboats were really just rafts.

## The Keelboatmen

The keelboatmen were a tough breed of workers. They thought of themselves as "half-horse and half-alligator," They worked hard, and they played hard. And, they loved to fight.

One of the best known of the keelboatmen was a man named Mike Fink. Mike used to say he could "lick five times my own weight in wildcats." But, even Mike Fink couldn't take on the steamboats He went north to try his hand at trapping. In the end, Mike died as he had lived. He was shot and killed during an argument.

they sold the wood from their flatboats. The flatboats were no longer useful to the farmers. The same strong current that helped the farmers go south made it very difficult for the flatboats to go north.

## Going North on the Mississippi

Once farmers reached New Orleans and sold their goods, they had two choices. One choice was to walk home. For many, this walk started with a 500-mile trek north on a road called the Natchez Trace—"trace" is another word for "road." The Natchez Trace was a rough road that ran from Natchez, Mississippi, to Nashville, Tennessee.

Thieves and murderers lurked along the Natchez Trace. Their targets were the returning farmers, who carried the money from the sale of their goods in New Orleans. To protect themselves, farmers traveling the Natchez Trace often traveled in groups of a dozen men or more. The farmers also sewed the coins they'd received in New Orleans into their shirts or pants for safekeeping.

*Steamboats burned coal to heat water that created steam to run their engines.*

After all, for some, the money they made in New Orleans was all the cash their families had for the year.

According to one story, that trick worked at least once. A group of farmers camping out for the night were attacked by robbers. The farmers jumped up and ran away. The robbers gathered up everything the farmers left behind. Later, as they followed the trail the robbers left, one of the farmers found his pants, which the robbers had thrown away. Still safely sewn into the pants' waistband were the farmer's four gold doubloons!

Because of the dangers of the Natchez Trace, some farmers used part of their profits to buy a ticket on a keelboat. Keelboats were long, narrow boats that were pointed on both ends. Unlike flatboats, keelboats could go north on the Mississippi. This is how they did it: On either side of a keelboat was a narrow walkway. Four or five men stood on this walkway. Each man held a long pole. At the same time, each stuck his pole through the water, into the river bottom. Then, each man leaned his shoulder against his pole and pushed as he walked toward the back of the boat. These poles pushing together moved the boat northward, against the current of the Mississippi River. When the men reached the back, they lifted their poles and hurried forward again. Then, they repeated the motions again and again, all day long.

Keelboats also could be rowed like rowboats or sailed like sailboats. Sometimes, when the water was too deep or the current too fast, the men tied a rope to the boat, got out onto the bank, and pulled the boat through the water.

It took a month to float goods from a Pennsylvania farm down the rivers to New Orleans. It took three or four months to pole a keelboat back to Pennsylvania. This meant that when a farmer left to sell his goods, he might be gone from home for four or five months—even longer if he walked back on the Natchez Trace!

## Steamboats on the Mississippi

In New York, a different kind of boat had already shortened the time it took to travel by water. In 1807, partners Robert Fulton and Robert Livingston put the nation's first steamboat into the Hudson River. It was called a steamboat because its engine ran on the steam created by boilers full of water heated with burning coal. Soon, that steamboat and others were regularly huffing and puffing up and down the Hudson River, carrying people and goods from place to place.

In the spring of 1811, work began in Pittsburgh on a new steamboat. Robert Fulton named it the *New Orleans*. Soon, the new steamboat was launched into the Ohio River. It traveled down the Ohio to the Mississippi, then down the Mississippi to New Orleans.

*Top: A keelboat could go both north and south on the Mississippi River. Bottom: Robert Fulton's steamboat, the* New Orleans, *shortened travel time on the river.*

No one doubted that the ship *New Orleans* could get to the city of New Orleans. However, many doubted that it could get back. "You have visited us in a steamboat, but we see you for the last time," one mayor cried as the *New Orleans* steamed past his town. "Your boat may go down the river, but as to coming up, the very idea is an absurd one."

The *New Orleans* faced many challenges on its maiden voyage. Perhaps the greatest challenge came one night when the boat was tied up on the Ohio River. Suddenly, the *New Orleans* trembled, and the waters of the river slammed against the river's banks. It was an earthquake. In fact, it was the worst earthquake ever to hit the central United States. It shook the earth all that night and all the next day.

The *New Orleans* continued down the Ohio and into the Mississippi, and the earth continued to shake. Whole parts of the riverbank fell into the water. Old islands disappeared. New islands popped up. The *New Orleans* passengers watched as animals ran along the shore or drowned in the river, trying to escape the unceasing quaking.

Eventually, the *New Orleans* sailed past the danger zone and went on to the city for which it was named. And, to the amazement of many, it successfully made the return trip. The *New Orleans* immediately began regular service between New Orleans and Natchez. Within ten years of the arrival of the *New Orleans*, hardly a keelboat was left on the Mississippi River. People and their goods could now travel faster by steamboat.

## Show What You Know

Reread the sentences on pages 134–135, that tell how men used long poles to move a keelboat north against the river's current. Now, imagine you work on a keelboat. You are one of the people who pole the boat. Get a broom handle or a long stick to act as your pole. Then, follow the directions given by the sentences above, and pole your imaginary keelboat forward several times. On a separate sheet of paper, write a paragraph describing what it must have been like to do that job all day long.

# THE BATTLE OF TIPPECANOE

According to legend, one March night in 1768 an Indian woman was about to give birth when she saw a meteor flash through the sky. When her baby boy was born, she named him Tecumseh— Shooting Star—in honor of that meteor that had lit up her sky.

## Tecumseh, Shawnee Leader

Tecumseh was born in the Shawnee village of Old Piqua, on the Mad River, in the southwest corner of present-day Ohio. As Tecumseh grew older, he watched as tribe after tribe sold its land to the white settlers.

### General William Henry Harrison

*General William Henry Harrison's victory at the Battle of Tippecanoe helped him become president of the United States. In 1840, the General ran for president. John Tyler ran with him, hoping to become vice president. The General won the election, in part because of his catchy slogan. The slogan he used was "Tippecanoe and Tyler too." The General had received the nickname "Tippecanoe" after his defeat of the Prophet and his followers in the Battle of Tippecanoe.*

Tecumseh felt that was wrong. He thought the land belonged to all the Indians. He thought that all the Indian groups should agree before anything was sold.

Tecumseh also wanted to keep whites from crossing the Ohio River. That way, Indians would continue to have a home on the river's west side. No one Indian group was big enough to stop the whites' western movement on its own. Tecumseh knew the different Indian groups would have to join together. Only together would they have a chance of keeping the white settlers east of the Ohio River.

Tecumseh began to travel. He traveled all the way to Wisconsin in the north and all the way to Florida in the south. On his travels, he visited many different Indian groups. Everywhere he brought his message of unity among the Indian groups.

Many agreed with Tecumseh. Some of these believers began to gather at Prophetstown, near present-day Lafayette, Indiana, where the Tippecanoe and Wabash rivers meet. Prophetstown had become a kind of capital for the Indian groups of the region.

*This picture shows Tenskwatawa, the Prophet.*

## Tenskwatawa, the Prophet

Tecumseh had several brothers and sisters. In fact, an older sister and brother helped raise Tecumseh after his father died and his mother left.

Another brother was also important in Tecumseh's life. This was a younger brother called Tenskwatawa, which means "The Open Door." This brother became better known as the Prophet. A prophet is someone who can foretell the future. The Prophet would help Tecumseh in his work to unite the tribes.

The Prophet was big and strong and mystical. He had many followers. Once, he was challenged to prove his powers by blocking out the sun. In response, the Prophet told many Indians to gather together on the morning of June 16, 1806. That morning, the Prophet appeared before them. At about 11:30, he began to point toward the sun. As the Indians watched, an eclipse occurred! During a daytime eclipse, the moon moves between the sun and Earth and, for a while, blocks out the sun's light.

To some it may have looked like the eclipse was the work of the Prophet. But scientists can predict eclipses, and historians think the Prophet had secretly learned of the eclipse that would happen that day.

## The Battle of Tippecanoe

General William Henry Harrison was U.S. governor of the Indiana territory. He worried about Tecumseh. "He [Tecumseh] is one of those uncommon geniuses," wrote the general, "which spring up occasionally to produce revolutions and overturn the established order of things. . . ." For William Henry Harrison, the "established order of things" was to write treaties that gave Indian land to white settlers. He would not let Tecumseh upset that.

General Harrison knew that Tecumseh was away. He decided it was a good time to take troops to drive out the Indians who had gathered at Prophetstown.

*General William Henry Harrison had a military career before becoming president in 1841.*

However, before Tecumseh left, he gave strict instructions not to start a fight. It was the Prophet who told the Indians to attack government troops before they reached Prophetstown. The Prophet dipped the warriors' weapons in a special brew to make sure the warriors won the battle. He promised that the white soldiers' gunpowder would turn into "ashes and sand" and the bullets would not harm them. He said if the warriors killed the white leader on his white horse, victory would be assured.

Things did not go according to the Prophet's plan. First, a keen-eyed guard spotted and shot an Indian before the rest were in place to attack. Also, the American soldiers had been ordered to sleep on their weapons. Even though the Indians attacked before dawn, the soldiers were ready for battle in an instant.

The Indians did kill the soldier on the white horse. But that day, General Harrison had mounted a different, darker horse. The Indians had killed the wrong man. One Indian later said that, when he discovered Harrison was still alive, "I knew then that the great white chief was not to be killed, and I knew that the red men were doomed."

Many soldiers and many warriors died that day at Tippecanoe. In the end, the Indians were forced to retreat. The American soldiers claimed victory. "Huzzah!" the soldiers cried as they watched the Indians carry their wounded away. "Huzzah! Huzzah!" they said. Then, General Harrison and his men marched to Prophetstown and burned it to the ground.

**Tecumseh and the Prophet**

When Tecumseh returned, he was shocked to find Prophetstown destroyed. News of the battle had not reached him in his travels. The battle ruined the union he had been trying to build. Soon, Tecumseh went to Canada to join the British in their fight against the Americans. On October 13, 1813, Tecumseh was killed in battle there.

After the battle at Tippecanoe, the Prophet lost most of his followers. In 1836, he died, bitter and ignored, in present-day Kansas.

## Show What You Know

An epitaph (EH puh taf) is a statement that is written in memory of a dead person. The statement usually describes something important about the person's life. Many times epitaphs are put on burial monuments.

Think about the life of Tecumseh and what he tried to accomplish. Then, write what you think would be a good epitaph for him.

_____

_____

_____

_____

_____

_____

_____

_____

_____

# FRANCIS SCOTT KEY WRITES THE NATIONAL ANTHEM

*Washington, D.C., was burned by the British during the War of 1812.*

THE TAKING of the CITY of WASHINGTON in America

## Battle of New Orleans

The last battle of the War of 1812 was the Battle of New Orleans. It took place on January 8, 1815. However, the Battle of New Orleans did not need to happen at all. That is because a peace treaty had been signed between the United States and Great Britain more than two weeks earlier. At that time, though, communication was poor. There were no phones or faxes or telegrams or e-mail. The American and British soldiers who fought at New Orleans did not know the war was already over.

By 1812, Great Britain and the United States were again at war with each other. In 1814, the British captured Washington, D.C. They burned much of our capital, including the White House.

Then, the British sailed north, up the Chesapeake Bay. They planned to take the city of Baltimore, Maryland. They started with Fort McHenry, which had been built to protect Baltimore.

### Francis Scott Key, Captive of the British

American Francis Scott Key, a lawyer and poet, and John S. Skinner, a government agent, went to see the British officers near Baltimore.

*Francis Scott Key wrote the words to the "Star Spangled Banner."*

behind after a battle near Washington. The letters said the Americans were taking good care of the wounded British. Because of those letters, the British decided to let Dr. Beanes go.

There was a catch, though. The British would not allow the Americans to leave until after British ships had attacked the city of Baltimore. Francis and John were to be held on the ship *Surprise*. From where the *Surprise* was anchored, they could clearly see Fort McHenry, with a giant, 50-foot-long American flag flying above its walls. They watched that flag as long as daylight lasted. And when night fell, they waited to see if the flag still flew the following day.

## The Bombing of Fort McHenry

The British bombing of Fort McHenry began at 6:00 A.M., on the morning of September 13, 1814. All day long, the British cannons fired at the fort. The British guns were more powerful than the American guns, so the British ships could stay out of Fort McHenry's range. It wasn't until evening that the British ships moved closer, and Fort McHenry's cannons finally could do some damage to the enemy. Soon, the British pulled away again.

They hoped to get the release of Francis's friend, Dr. William Beanes. The British had arrested Dr. Beanes because he had arrested three British sailors.

The British wanted to punish Dr. Beanes. But, John Skinner gave them letters from their own wounded men, who had been left

For hours and hours of that long night, the British fired their rockets and bombs at the fort. Then, the firing finally stopped. Francis and John could see nothing in the dark. They paced the deck, waiting breathlessly for day to break. Did the flag still fly over Fort McHenry? Or, had the fort surrendered to the British?

On the morning of September 14, dawn began to light the skies. Then, Francis and John could see that, yes, the flag still flew over Fort McHenry! The British had failed. Their ships were leaving. The American prisoners would soon be free to go.

### Francis Writes a Patriotic Poem

Francis was deeply moved by the sight of the American flag that morning. As he stood on the *Surprise's* deck, he took a letter out of his pocket. On the back of the letter, he began to scribble lines to a poem about that night. He finished the poem later, in a Baltimore hotel room.

The poem made its way to a printer, and the printer printed it onto a handbill. The handbill was given out to Baltimore residents and to the soldiers of Fort McHenry. The poem was also published in two Baltimore newspapers. Within a couple of months, it had been printed in newspapers all over the United States—in Washington, D.C.; Boston, Massachusetts; Richmond, Virginia; Savannah, Georgia; and Concord, New Hampshire. Soon, people began to sing the words of the poem, using the tune of an old English song for music. The old song was called "Anacreon [a poet] in Heaven." Political campaigns in the country began to use the song. The army began to sing the song as it raised and lowered the flag every day. On July 4th, celebrators in cities and towns sang the song, too.

At first, the song was called "Defense of Fort McHenry." It later became known as the "Star-Spangled Banner." This is the story of how the people of the United States made the "Star-Spangled Banner" our unofficial national anthem. It wasn't until 1931 that Congress officially named it the national anthem.

*Above right: This is the flag that flew over Fort McHenry when Francis Scott Key wrote our national anthem.*
*Above left: This is a copy of Key's original poem in his own handwriting.*

## Show What You Know

In the "Star-Spangled Banner," Francis Scott Key told the story of the attack on Fort McHenry. Read the words to the first verse below. Compare the words to the story you have just read. Then, on another sheet of paper, write a poem or a song about an event or sight you have witnessed that greatly impressed you.

> O say, can you see, by the dawn's early light,
> What so proudly we hail'd at the twilight's last gleaming?
> Whose broad stripes and bright stars, thro' the perilous fight,
> O'er the ramparts we watch'd were so gallantly streaming?
> And the rocket's red glare, the bombs bursting in air,
> Gave proof thro' the night that our flag was still there.
> O say, does that Star-Spangled Banner yet wave
> O'er the land of the free and the home of the brave?

# THE ERIE CANAL

For years, people talked about building a canal to connect Lake Erie to the Hudson River. New York's governor, De Witt Clinton, wanted the canal. In fact, he ran for office on the promise of building a canal if he were elected. The people wanted a canal. That is why they elected De Witt Clinton governor by a landslide—43,310 to 1,479. Plus, the state government agreed to pay for the building of the canal.

There was, however, one more hurdle to jump before work on the canal could begin. The money had to be approved by a special five-person government committee. Of the five, two were against building the Erie Canal and two were in favor of building it. Another one—Judge James Kent—was undecided. Here is how James Kent made up his mind and how the Erie Canal was built.

## A Threat Backfires

In 1817, Daniel Tompkins was vice president of the United States. Before he became vice president, Daniel had been New York's governor. He was opposed to the Erie Canal, and he went to speak to the committee of five before they voted.

Daniel wanted to talk the group into voting against the Erie Canal. To make sure that happened, he tried to frighten them. He told them that soon, the United

### "Low Bridge! Everybody Down!"

*About 300 bridges were built over the Erie Canal. Some of these bridges connected roads broken in two by the canal's crossing. Other bridges were built so that farmers could reach their fields.*

*To save money, these bridges usually were built low, close to the canal. As canalboats approached, the pilot would yell, "Low bridge!" so that all the passengers would duck their heads. Some bridges were so low that people had to lie on the deck to fit under them!*

*These men are working on part of the Erie Canal.*

**146**

States would again go to war against England. He said New Yorkers should spend their money on getting ready for war, rather than on a canal.

But Daniel's plan backfired. Judge Kent became very angry at the way the vice president tried to influence the group. The judge stood up and gave his vote. His became the third "yes" to the Erie Canal! "If we must have war or have a canal, I am in favor of the canal," he said. So, with a vote of three to two, the decision was made to build the Erie Canal.

## Work on the Canal

On July 4, 1817, the first piece of earth was turned for the Erie Canal. Construction started in the middle of the state, near the little settlement of Rome. This may seem a strange place to start, for Rome still was in the wilderness. However, the land there would be easier to dig than the land in the west or the east. That is because there were few rocks in this area, and the land was fairly flat. Flat land meant there would be no need for locks. A lock is a place in the canal where, in a series of steps, a ship goes from higher water to lower water, or from lower water to higher water, so that the ship can continue its journey through the canal. In all, the Erie Canal would have 83 locks along its length.

Along its length, different contractors were each charged with digging part of the canal. Each contractor then hired the men he needed to do the job. He built the workers a place to live and supplied the workers with the digging tools they needed.

*This painting shows a scene along part of the Erie Canal.*

Many came to work on the canal. They were lured by the promise of good food and good wages—"roast beef guaranteed twice a day, . . . and wages eighty cents." Many of those who came were U.S. citizens. Many others were from foreign countries. In fact, about one-fourth of all the men who worked on the canal were from Ireland.

For the next eight years, thousands of men dug a 363-mile-long, 4-foot-deep ditch across New York State. Beside it for its whole length, the men also shaped a 10-foot-wide tow path. It was along this path that horses and mules walked,

LAKE ONTARIO

LAKE ERIE

ERIE CANAL

NEW YORK

*The Erie Canal stretched from the Hudson River to Lake Erie.*

towing the sail-less, engine-less canalboats through the water by the ropes that connected horse to boat.

## Completion of the Canal

On October 26, 1825, it was time to celebrate. In Buffalo, Governor Clinton and others boarded several canalboats and began their journey down the finished Erie Canal. Almost every town they passed greeted the boats with cheers and good wishes.

When the boats reached the end of the Erie Canal, they turned south into the Hudson River. Then, they followed the Hudson all the way to New York City and the Atlantic Ocean.

When they reached the ocean, Governor Clinton poured a keg of water from Lake Erie into the Atlantic. With this "Wedding of the Waters," the entire length of the Erie Canal was open for business.

## The Importance of the Erie Canal

The Erie Canal went over budget. Originally it was to cost under $6 million. However, it ended

*Governor Clinton pours a keg of water from Lake Erie into the Atlantic Ocean to celebrate the opening of the Erie Canal.*

up costing almost $8.5 million to finish the canal. Even at that tremendous cost, the Erie Canal turned out to be a bargain. Immediately, boats filled the canal. The canalboats moved eastern goods, such as guns and needles and cloth, to western markets and moved western goods, such as potatoes and flour, to the East. The canal also moved people, as many Easterners used the boats to travel to the west to new land.

HUDSON RIVER

For every pound of product and for every human on board, a toll was charged to use the Erie Canal. This is how the canal made money. Everyone was shocked when, before a decade had passed, the Erie Canal had collected more in tolls than it cost to build the canal in the first place!

For decades, people relied on the Erie Canal. It was not until the railroads came that they turned their backs on the slow, smooth travel of the canalboats for the faster, dirty, bumpy rides of the country's new fangled trains.

## Show What You Know

These four pictures show the steps a ship must take to sail through a canal lock. Write the letter of the sentence under each picture that illustrates it.

A. The lock gates close behind the ship.

B. The gates open, and the ship leaves the lock.

C. The ship enters the gates of the lock.

D. Water is let out of the lock, and the ship is lowered to a new level of water.

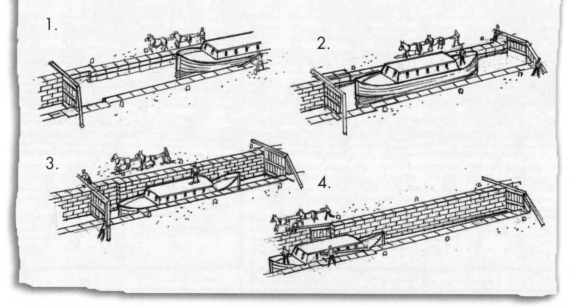

1.

2.

3.

4.

# TRAVEL ON THE OREGON TRAIL

By the 1840s, America was on the move again. Reports from Lewis and Clark and others of the land's western wonders filled the minds of Easterners. Many decided to go west. They sold their farms and their stores and almost everything else. Then, they set out for the city of Independence, Missouri. Independence was the starting point of the Oregon Trail.

The Oregon Trail was a 2,000-mile path that began in Independence, Missouri, and ended in Astoria, Oregon. For thousands and thousands of pioneers, the Oregon Trail was more than just a way west. It was a 2,000-mile test of courage and strength.

### The Price of Traveling the Oregon Trail

*Some have called the Oregon Trail "the world's longest graveyard." Thousands who traveled the Trail died due to accidents and diseases. Malaria, caused by the bites of infected mosquitoes, and cholera, caused by drinking dirty water, were especially feared and especially deadly. In fact, one of every 17 grownups and one of every 5 children who started the trip did not finish it.*

*Pioneers start their trip west on the Oregon Trail.*

## A Wagon for the Trail

Before the trip began, many pioneers bought a book called *The Prairie Traveler*. It was a kind of self-help book for people who wanted to go west. The book explained things like what to pack for the trip, how to find water, how to get a wagon down a mountain, how to cross a river, and what to do if you ran into quicksand.

According to *The Prairie Traveler*, one of the most important things the pioneers would purchase was a wagon. Most chose a kind of wagon called a Conestoga wagon. The Conestoga wagon got its name from Pennsylvania's Conestoga Valley, where it was first built.

This picture shows a Pennsylvania Conestoga wagon.

The Conestoga wagon also was called a prairie schooner—a schooner is a kind of sleek boat. That is because the long grass of the prairies hid the wheels so that, as the wagons moved, they looked like boats sailing on the ocean of grass that covered our nation's center.

A Conestoga wagon was built with its ends higher than its sides. This kept the precious cargo inside from spilling out when the wagon went up and down mountains. This wagon also had wide wheels, to help it move through the many miles of mud and sand it would have to cross. The wheels also could come off, and the wagon would float like a raft—another reason for it to be called a prairie schooner.

The wagon bed itself was usually 10 or 11 feet long by 4 feet wide by 2 feet deep. Into this space, the pioneers crammed everything they would need, both for the six-month trip and for their new life at the journey's end.

What few wagons carried, though, was human cargo. Most pioneers walked the 2,000 miles of the

Oregon Trail. This left more room in the wagon. It also spared the animals that pulled the wagon from pulling extra weight.

Mules or oxen pulled the wagons. Mules were faster, but oxen were cheaper. A team of mules could cost three times the price of a team of oxen! And, oxen were less likely to stampede. In addition, if the trip was remarkably rough, and food ran low, the oxen could supply fresh meat.

## The Larkins Travel the Oregon Trail

In 1853, the Larkin family's wagon joined other wagons at Independence, Missouri. The "wagon train" they formed set out in the spring. In spring, the grasses along the Oregon Trail are long enough to feed the animals that travel with the wagons.

Six Larkins headed to Oregon: Hiram and Hetty and their children Rachel, 14; Abraham, 10; Rebecca, 7; and Margaret, 3. Margaret is too little to know what is happening, but the other children are excited about the trip.

Hiram and Hetty Larkin decided to take their family to Oregon because they could get free land there. The government passed a law that said every new settler would get 160 Oregon acres, and every new settler's wife would get 160 Oregon acres, too. In return, the settlers had to promise to farm the land for four years.

*The Oregon Trail began in Independence, Missouri, and ended in Astoria, Oregon.*

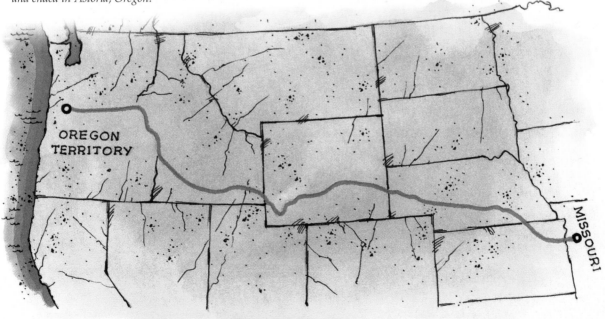

## A Good Day on the Oregon Trail

A good day for the Larkins and the 59 other families that are in their wagon train begins at 4:00 A.M., when everyone gets up. Hetty makes a fire. Then, she starts to cook breakfast. She pours pancake batter into a skillet and lets it cook. At the same time, she is baking bread or biscuits or muffins. Beans, meat, and gravy also will be added to the breakfast menu. The pioneers are going to walk all day. They need a big breakfast to give them energy.

While Hetty is cooking, Hiram rounds up the horses and cattle the family has brought on the trip. He also yokes up his six oxen, getting them ready for their day of wagon-pulling.

By 7:00 A.M., breakfast is over. Everything is packed up again. The wagon train moves out. All the Larkins walk alongside the wagon. They don't really mind walking, because the wagon ride is too bumpy anyway.

Together, they walk for five hours. They get perhaps five miles, maybe even ten miles, if they have no wagon problems. Then, they stop for a lunch of breakfast leftovers. It's time for the people and the animals to eat and rest.

All afternoon, they walk. Around 6:00 P.M., they finally stop for the night. They pull their wagons into a tight circle for protection. Hiram cares for the

*Pioneer families head west on the Oregon Trail.*

animals. Hetty cooks supper. They eat. They clean up. They do any other chores the day requires. Sometimes, they visit with their wagon-train friends. Then, the men take turns standing guard as everyone turns in for the night.

What made this a good day for the wagon train? There were no rivers to ford, or cross. There were no mountains to cross. The land still offered water to drink, for the wagons had not yet reached the desert. No one was hurt, and no one became sick. No animals were lost. Yes, it was a good day for the Larkins on the Oregon Trail.

The Larkins' wagon train made good time. In only four months, on September 10, 1853, they came to the end of the trail. Soon, they had claimed their new land, built a log cabin, and settled in for their first western winter. Together, the Larkins and their children would build a good life in Oregon.

## Show What You Know

For each person traveling on the Oregon Trail, a wagon might hold the following:

150 pounds of flour
60 pounds of bacon
50 pounds of lard
(used like butter or margarine)
15 pounds of coffee
25 pounds of sugar
10 pounds of salt

Count up the number of people who live at your house. Imagine they are all going to travel the Oregon Trail with you. Fill in the chart to tell how much you would need of each of the foods above, based on the number of people taking the trip.

A Conestoga wagon usually carried a 2,000-pound load. How many pounds of other items could you take, after you've packed all the food your family will need?

| Pounds of Food per Person | People | | | | |
|---|---|---|---|---|---|
| | 2 | 3 | 4 | 5 | 6 |
| 150 lbs. flour | | | | | |
| 60 lbs. bacon | | | | | |
| 50 lbs. lard | | | | | |
| 25 lbs. sugar | | | | | |
| 15 lbs. coffee | | | | | |
| 10 lbs. salt | | | | | |
| pounds of other items you could take | | | | | |

# REMEMBER THE ALAMO!

### Davy Crockett

*Davy Crockett was among the men for whom death at the Alamo helped create a legend. Even before he joined Texas's fight for independence, Davy already was known around the nation, both as a frontiersman and as a politician—he represented Tennessee in Congress. It is said that when the Mexicans came over the wall, Davy had no gunpowder left to fire. So, he used his rifle as a club against the attackers.*

The land that is now Texas was not always part of the United States. It actually belonged to Mexico, after Mexico became its own nation in 1821.

Not many people lived in the Texas region at that time. So, Mexico welcomed Americans who wanted to come live in Texas. The Mexican government even gave some Americans land for free. For the next 15 years, Americans poured into the region. By 1836, about 30,000 Americans had come.

Then, Mexico tried to stop the flood of Americans. The country passed a law that said no more could settle in Texas. The Mexicans resented the Americans living in Texas because they brought their own culture with them. They did not want to embrace the Spanish language or the Catholic religion.

There were ways in which Americans did not feel part of Mexico, as well. For example, in Mexico, slavery was against the law. Some Americans who came to live in Texas wanted slaves to work their land.

In 1834, Mexico's government was overthrown by Antonio López de Santa Ana. He was a general who made himself a dictator. A dictator is a leader who makes all the decisions, with no one else to say whether those decisions are fair and just. The Americans did not want to live in a dictatorship. For all these reasons, Texas decided to separate itself from Mexico.

## The Battle of the Alamo

General Santa Ana heard of the trouble in the Texas territory. He took the Mexican Army north to stop the American rebels. On February 23, 1836, the Mexican Army—about 4 or 5 thousand strong—attacked San Antonio, which was being held by about 150 Americans.

The Americans retreated to the Alamo. The Alamo was a mission. It had been built by the Spanish over 100 years before. It was empty now. The roof of its church had caved in, but it still made a fairly good fort.

Lieutenant Colonel William Barret Travis was in charge of the Americans at the Alamo. He knew that 150 volunteer fighters could never hold off an entire army. The day after fighting began, he wrote for help. Here is part of his letter:

*This is an illustration of an early American homestead in Texas, when it was still part of Mexico.*

157

"*I am besieged [under attack] with a thousand or more of the Mexicans under Santa Ana. I have sustained a continued Bombardment and cannonade for 24 hours and have not lost a man. The enemy has demanded surrender . . . otherwise, the garrison [soldiers] is to be put to the sword, if the fort is taken. I have answered the demand with a cannon shot, and our flag still waves proudly from the walls. I shall never surrender or retreat. . . .*" The letter ended with a plea to send more American fighters to the Alamo.

Only 32 Americans answered William's plea. The new volunteers slipped through enemy lines and joined the Americans already in the Alamo. Now, the soldiers in the mission numbered about 188. For 12 days, outnumbered 20 or 30 to 1, those Americans held off an entire army.

In the end, the Mexicans won. On March 6, they finally scaled the Alamo's walls. The battle was over.

THE U.S. FROM COAST TO COAST • 1785–1860

Some of the Americans may have survived the battle. If they did, General Santa Ana made sure they did not survive the surrender. All the American soldiers were killed. The Mexicans spared only a woman, her child, and a slave. The woman and the slave lived to tell other Americans of the fate of those who tried to stand up against Mexico's army.

Mexico won the battle at the Alamo. However, the cost to the Mexican Army was high. The Americans had killed hundreds and hundreds of Mexican soldiers. Historians think that maybe as many as one in four Mexican soldiers died at the Alamo. General Santa Ana called the Alamo a "glorious victory" for Mexico. But, one of his officers said, "One more such 'glorious victory,' and we are finished."

## After the Alamo

On April 21 of the same year, Texan Sam Houston led a new Texas Army against General Santa Ana and his army. He decided to attack the Mexicans outside San Jacinto. To inspire his soldiers, Sam mounted a white horse and rode among his men, crying "Remember the Alamo! Remember the Alamo!"

The battle that followed was over quickly. In just 18 minutes, the Texans had killed over 600 Mexican soldiers. They captured over 700 more. The rest of the Mexican Army fled back across the Rio Grande—the river that would become the border between Texas and Mexico.

The victory at San Jacinto ended the war. Texas was free. For almost ten years, it was an independent nation. It had its own president and its own constitution. Then, on December 29, 1845, Texas became the 28th state of the United States.

### Show What You Know

You read about how Sam Houston inspired his soldiers by crying, "Remember the Alamo!" Now imagine that you have been chosen to help Sam Houston gather together an army. Make a poster that you think would inspire Americans to join Texas's war for independence. Make sure you use the words "Remember the Alamo!" on your poster.

# THE GOLD RUSH BUILDS SAN FRANCISCO

This is what a block of gold looks like.

### As Good as Gold

Gold has been valued by humans for thousands of years. One reason is because of its beautiful color. Also, it doesn't rust or tarnish. A gold bracelet taken from a 5,000-year-old Egyptian tomb shines as if it were made yesterday.

Gold can be drawn out thinner than any other metal. A piece of gold the size of a pea can be drawn out into a wire two miles long! Gold can conduct both heat and electricity. So, it is used in computers and televisions and other machines that run on electricity.

On January 24, 1848, James Marshall went to the house of his employer, John Sutter. He told John Sutter he had something important to tell him. He hurried John Sutter up the stairs and into a room, and he insisted the door be locked behind them. Then, James Marshall reached into a pants pocket and pulled out a crumpled-up white cotton rag. He opened the rag and lifted out a yellow, shiny stone about the size of a dime. He held the stone out toward John Sutter. "I think this is gold," James said.

James was right. The nugget was gold. He found it at Sutter's Mill, in California's Sacramento Valley.

Reports of gold began to come out of California. The stories easterners heard seemed too wild to be true. Yet, many of the stories were true. Thousands and thousands of dollars worth of gold were being dug and panned out of the California's fields and streams. Some people were finding $1,000 worth of gold almost every day they mined. Remember, this was a time when a farmer might make $400 a year! Nuggets weighing 20 pounds or more were found. And, there was still much more gold to be mined. As one Californian wrote an eastern friend: "You regard our statements as the dreams of an excited imagination; but what seems to you mere fiction, is stern reality. It is not gold in the clouds, or in the sea, or in the center of a rock-ribbed mountain, but in the soil of California—sparkling in the sun, and glittering in its streams."

*These two prospectors are looking for gold during the California Gold Rush.*

Soon, President Polk himself told Congress that there was gold in California. After that, the rush for riches was on.

"Gold fever," they called it. And, it was like a fever. It swept through the East, and then through the world. Whole towns emptied as people started west, called by the promise of gold in California. One person who stayed behind watched the others leave: "All were off for the mines, some on horses, some on carts, and some on crutches, and one went in a litter [stretcher]."

## San Francisco Explodes

In 1848, before Sutter found his gold, San Francisco was just a little settlement. A few dozen houses and perhaps 800 people were all that could be found there, clustered around the San Francisco Bay.

Then came the Gold Rush. San Francisco was the nearest port to California's gold fields. So, hundreds of ships from all over the world headed for the bay. In 1849 alone, 800 ships arrived at San Francisco's port. They carried, all together, 40,000 people. These people had come to search for gold. They all poured through San Francisco on their way to the gold fields.

San Francisco immediately became an important supply center for all the gold seekers. Its population exploded. In that first full-blown year of the Gold Rush, the number of people living in San Francisco swelled from 800 to 25,000. By September, there were 500 houses, with up to 30 new ones being built every day!

By the end of the year, San Francisco was on its way to becoming a city. Here are some of the changes one visitor noticed as 1849 came to an end: "Stages run regularly to the mines, steamboats run on the river; a theatre, church and several large handsome hotels

with billiards saloons and bowling alleys and all the fixings, have been put up . . . Civilization is making rapid strides . . ."

## The Problems of Growth

This unbelievably fast growth caused problems for San Francisco, however. The problems started at the harbor. When the ships came in, their passengers hurried off, heading for the gold fields. In many cases, the ships' crews followed the passengers to the fields.

Soon, hundreds of ships lay anchored in the bay, abandoned, rotting, slowly sinking. Sometimes a ship's cargo sank with the ship, because the ship owners couldn't find anyone to unload the goods. One group of visitors observed that ". . . some three or four thousand seamen deserted from the many hundred ships lying in the bay. . . . At the time of which we write there were between three and four hundred large square-rigged vessels [in port], unable to leave on account of want of hands. Many of these vessels never got away, but in a few years, afterwards, rotted and tumbled to pieces where they were moored."

*Left: San Francisco was a small settlement before the Gold Rush.*
*Right: As a result of the Gold Rush, the population of San Francisco grew. Ships that brought people to the city were abandoned in the bay.*

Another problem caused by the Gold Rush was that there weren't enough hotels and houses in San Francisco to shelter everybody. Building couldn't possibly keep up with demand. Many people crowded into poorly built shanties. Many others lived in tents. Some even waited until high tide and hauled abandoned boats out onto land. Then, they lived in the boats. Actually, these often were better built than many of the hastily constructed houses!

There was another problem, too. The thieves and murderers who always follow honest workers caused crime to increase in the city. Some even think these criminals

*Notice that one of the buildings was made from an abandoned ship.*

set some of the many fires that roared through San Francisco during this time. Then, the crooks could loot houses from which people fled during the blazes.

## The Gold Rush Ends

Eventually, most of California's gold was dug up. The Gold Rush came to an end. Still, many who came for gold decided to stay after the gold was gone. Thanks to the Gold Rush, enough people lived in San Francisco for it to become a city. And, enough people lived in California for it to become a state.

### Show What You Know

Most miners who headed to California carried a special kind of pan. It was a shallow pan, with low sides. Its purpose was to separate gold from the sand of a creek or stream bottom. Here is how a miner used his pan. First, he scooped up sand and water from a creek bed. Then, he carefully swirled the water around and around, slightly tipping the pan so that a little water and sand sloshed out with each swirl. In the end, if the miner did it right, only gold was left in the bottom of the pan, because gold is heavier than sand or water.

Imagine you have gone to California to pan for gold. Find a shallow pan, such as a pie pan. Put some small metal screws in the pan, and pretend the screws are gold nuggets. Now, add water and sand to the pan and try to swirl away everything but the "gold."

# THE PONY EXPRESS

In 1860, this advertisement began to appear in the United States.

Who in the world would answer an ad like that? The answer is, anyone who wanted to ride for the Pony Express.

> ## RIDERS WANTED
> Young, skinny, wiry fellows. Anxious for adventure and chance to see our great WEST. Must be expert riders, willing to risk death daily.
> ***Orphans preferred.***

### The Pony Express Delivers the Mail

Hundreds of thousands of Americans now lived in the West. They felt isolated from their eastern friends and families. They also were slow to get news from the East. The fastest way mail could reach westerners was by stagecoach. And, that took three weeks or more!

Then, some businessmen thought up a new way to deliver the mail. They would use fast riders and fast horses to gallop the mail across the country. They promised that, using this "pony express," they could deliver mail from St. Joseph, Missouri to California in just ten days! St. Joseph was the starting point because the trains ended there.

To get ready for the start of the Pony Express, the businessmen bought 400 horses and hired 80 riders. They built about 190 way stations along the trail that the riders would use. At these way stations, fresh horses and fresh riders would await their turn to carry the mail.

### President Lincoln and the Pony Express

*The inaugural address given by new President Lincoln was delivered to California by the Pony Express. The address was considered so important that for that ride, the horses were changed every 10 miles along the route. Because of this, a copy of President Lincoln's speech took only 7 days, 17 hours to arrive in California.*

The Pony Express was similar to a relay race. However, in a relay race, a baton is passed from one runner to the next. Instead of passing a baton, Pony Express riders passed on saddlebags holding about 20 pounds of mail bound for California.

The race began when one man jumped onto a horse and rode as fast as he could to the next way station. There were way stations every 10 to 15 miles or so. There, he would leap off his horse and jump onto a fresh horse that was waiting for him. Then, he would ride again for all he was worth to the next way station, and then to the next.

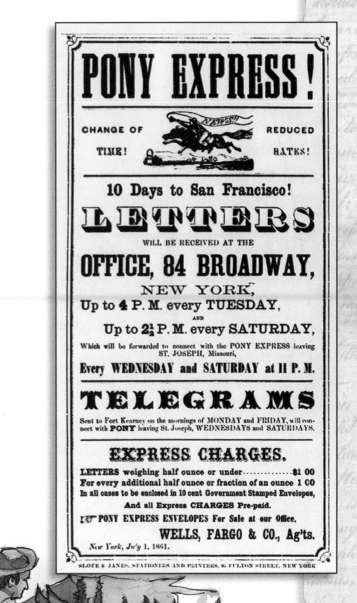

PONY EXPRESS !

CHANGE OF TIME!    REDUCED RATES!

10 Days to San Francisco!

LETTERS

WILL BE RECEIVED AT THE

OFFICE, 84 BROADWAY,

NEW YORK,

Up to 4 P. M. every TUESDAY,

AND

Up to 2½ P. M. every SATURDAY,

Which will be forwarded to connect with the PONY EXPRESS leaving ST. JOSEPH, Missouri,

Every WEDNESDAY and SATURDAY at 11 P. M.

TELEGRAMS

Sent to Fort Kearney on the mornings of MONDAY and FRIDAY, will connect with PONY leaving St. Joseph, WEDNESDAYS and SATURDAYS.

EXPRESS CHARGES.

LETTERS weighing half ounce or under..............$1 00
For every additional half ounce or fraction of an ounce 1 00
In all cases to be enclosed in 10 cent Government Stamped Envelopes,
And all Express CHARGES Pre-paid.

☞ PONY EXPRESS ENVELOPES For Sale at our Office.

WELLS, FARGO & CO., Ag'ts.

New York, Ju'y 1, 1861.

SLOTE & JANES, STATIONERS AND PRINTERS, 86 FULTON STREET, NEW YORK

When he had traveled between 50 and 100 miles, he found another, rested rider waiting for the mail he carried. He gave his mail bag to the new rider, who galloped off to cover his portion of the trip as fast as his horses would take him.

American writer, Mark Twain, described the job done by a Pony Express rider as follows: "No matter what time of the day, or night his watch came on, and no matter whether it was winter or summer, raining, snowing, hailing, sleeting, or whether his 'beat' was a level straight road or a crazy trail over mountain crags and precipices (PRE suh puh suhz) [steep cliffs] . . . he must always be ready to leap into the saddle and be off with the wind!"

## The Last Ride of the Pony Express

Even as the Pony Express riders galloped west, telegraph wires were being strung between the big cities of the East. Here is how a telegraph works: Telegraph wires carry electricity. People at one end can interrupt the flow of electricity in the wire. People at the other end of the wire can hear the interruptions as clicking sounds on a telegraph key.

A code called Morse code was used to send messages over telegraph wires. Morse code is made up of dots and dashes—short and long interruptions in the electricity flow. Each dot-and-dash combination stands for a letter. So, people can use Morse code to spell out

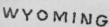

messages to each other over telegraph wires.

Few people thought a telegraph wire would ever span the country. In fact, President Abraham Lincoln called the idea "next to impossible." After all, telegraph poles would have to be raised over plains, deserts, and mountains. Three thousand miles of telegraph wire would have to be connected to the poles.

Despite these challenges, on October 24, 1861, telegraph wires and poles reached from New York City to San Francisco. Now, messages could be sent across the continent in a matter of moments, instead of in the ten days it took the Pony Express riders. One Kansas newspaper described the impact of the telegraph on the Pony Express:

". . . now the Pony had become a thing of the past—his last race is run. Without sound of trumpets, celebrations, or other noise demonstrations, the slender wire has been stretched from ocean to ocean. . . ."

Two days after the first message was telegraphed across the country, the Pony Express business closed down forever. It had lived less than 19 months. But, in that short time, its riders rode 650,000 miles to help connect one end of our big, sprawling nation with the other.

## Show What You Know

Here is a secret word, written in Morse code:

**····  ———  ·—·  ···  ·**

Use the chart on this page to figure out what the word is. (Hint: The word appears in this reading!) Then, use Morse code to write your own name, or to write a secret message about the Pony Express. Ask a friend or a family member to figure out what you have written.

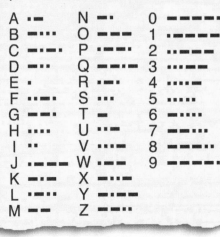

| | | |
|---|---|---|
| A ·— | N —· | 0 ————— |
| B —··· | O ——— | 1 ·———— |
| C —·—· | P ·——· | 2 ··——— |
| D —·· | Q ——·— | 3 ···—— |
| E · | R ·—· | 4 ····— |
| F ··—· | S ··· | 5 ····· |
| G ——· | T — | 6 —···· |
| H ···· | U ··— | 7 ——··· |
| I ·· | V ···— | 8 ———·· |
| J ·——— | W ·—— | 9 ————· |
| K —·— | X —··— | |
| L ·—·· | Y —·—— | |
| M —— | Z ——·· | |

*The Pony Express carried mail across land with few roads or towns.*

# UNIT 6

1840–1870

# AMERICA AGAINST AMERICA

In the United States, in the 1800s, the North and the South were different from each other in many ways. The North was a place of growing cities and new factories and few slaves. The South was a place of small towns and miles of farms and slaves by the millions. These differences—especially differences about slavery—tore the nation apart.

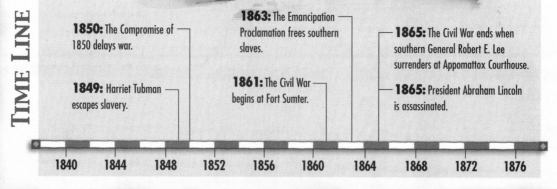

The first shots of the Civil War were fired at Fort Sumter, South Carolina.

## TIME LINE

**1850:** The Compromise of 1850 delays war.

**1849:** Harriet Tubman escapes slavery.

**1863:** The Emancipation Proclamation frees southern slaves.

**1861:** The Civil War begins at Fort Sumter.

**1865:** The Civil War ends when southern General Robert E. Lee surrenders at Appomattox Courthouse.

**1865:** President Abraham Lincoln is assassinated.

| 1840 | 1844 | 1848 | 1852 | 1856 | 1860 | 1864 | 1868 | 1872 | 1876 |

# SLAVERY IN AMERICA

For a long time in this country, slavery was accepted. George Washington, this nation's first president, owned over 200 slaves. Thomas Jefferson, who in the Declaration of Independence wrote "All men are created equal . . ." had over 180 slaves. In fact, eight of the first twelve presidents were slave owners.

*This poster shows the abolitionists' ideas about the meaning of the Declaration of Independence.*

From the beginning, some Americans thought that slavery was wrong. Slowly, others began to change their minds about slavery, too. Most of the people who were opposed to slavery lived in the northern half of the nation. Many people in the South supported slavery. That was because in the South, a plantation's success or failure might depend on the slaves who worked there.

## Slavery North and South

The rocky soil of New England did not encourage great big farms. So, New England farmers could, with the help of their families, farm their own fields. They had little use for slaves. In addition, many mills and factories were being built in the North. That meant fewer northerners were making their living by farming.

It was different in the South. There, giant farms called plantations grew up. One reason was the fertile soil. Another reason was the presence of many rivers.

These rivers made it easy to ship southern goods to market. Plus, the South had a longer growing season than the North, since it has a short winter.

Some of the crops grown on southern plantations needed a great deal of care. Tobacco especially took a lot of work. The plants are tender and had to be planted one by one. They needed to be kept clean of bugs and cut back and weeded.

Even when the tobacco was harvested, the work was not finished. The plants had to be hung and dried. Then, the workers stripped off the leaves and packed them up for sale.

The southern farmer needed help farming his many acres of tender crops. The least expensive year-round help he could get was a slave.

## What It Meant to Be a Slave

Southern slave owners did everything they could to control their slaves. For example, slaves could not marry without their owners' permission. Slaves couldn't learn to read or write. Slaves couldn't own property. Sometimes, they couldn't even name their own children—an owner would choose the baby's name instead.

Of all the terrible things about slavery, perhaps the most terrible was that a slave was considered property. That meant a slave could be sold. Children could be sold away from their mothers and fathers. Husbands could be sold away from their wives and families. Many slaves were allowed to live with their families. However, knowing that at any time this could change was one of slavery's tortures.

Despite their treatment, slaves tried to make lives of value for themselves. One man wrote about the happiness his family created during their days of slavery. Of course, he remembered the "miry cabins, frosted feet, weary toil under the blazing sun, curses and blows." But he also remembered "jolly Christmas times," "extra meat at holiday times," and "midnight-visits to apple-orchards."

Some owners did not do the day-to-day work of the plantation. They left that up to overseers. It was the overseer's job to watch over the slaves and make sure they did their work. Here, a visitor describes an overseer's role on a plantation:

*"The whole management of the plantation is left to the overseer, who as an encouragement to make the most of the crops, has a certain portion as his wages. . . . He drives and whips them [the slaves] about, and works them beyond their strength, and sometimes till they expire [die]; he feels no loss in their death, he knows the plantation must be supplied. . . ."*

*This illustration shows a woman being sold into slavery.*

## Frederick Douglass Questions Slavery

Frederick Douglass was a slave. When he was about 21 years old, though, he disguised himself as a sailor and escaped to the North.

Frederick became a writer and published the story of his life. He also started a newspaper in Rochester, New York. He called his newspaper the *North Star*, because runaway slaves followed the North Star on their way north to freedom.

Here is how Frederick Douglass felt about slavery:

*Frederick Douglass talks to people about slavery.*

### Why Am I a Slave?

*By some means I learned . . . that "God, up in the sky," made everybody; and that he made white people to be masters and mistresses, and black people to be slaves.*

*I found that there were puzzling exceptions to this theory of slavery on both sides, and in the middle. I knew of blacks who were not slaves; I knew of whites who were not slaveholders; and I knew of persons who were nearly white, who were slaves. Color, therefore, was a very unsatisfactory basis for slavery.*

*Once, however, engaged in the inquiry [question], I was not very long in finding out the true solution of the matter. It was not color, but crime, not God, but man, that afforded the true explanation of the existence of slavery; nor was I long in finding out another important truth, viz [namely]: what man can make, man can unmake.*

## Show What You Know

Line graphs are helpful for showing how something has changed over time. The line graph here shows how the number of slaves living in the United States changed between 1800 and 1860.

Study this line graph. Then, circle the correct answer for each of the questions below.

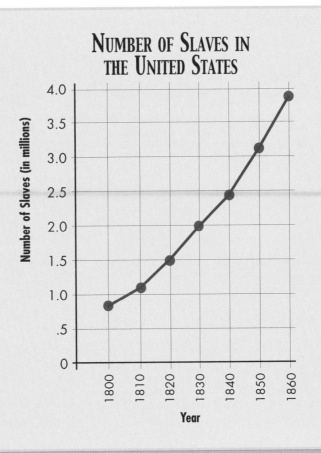

**NUMBER OF SLAVES IN THE UNITED STATES**

1. About how many slaves were in the United States when the 1800s began?

   a. about 1800
   b. a little less than 1 million
   c. a little more than 1 million

2. In what year did the number of slaves reach 2 million?

   a. in 1820
   b. in 1830
   c. in 1840

3. Did the number of slaves owned in the U.S. ever drop between 1800 and 1860?

   a. yes
   b. no

4. About how many more slaves were there in 1860 than in 1800?

   a. about 3 million more
   b. about 4 million more
   c. about 2 million more

# TRYING TO SAVE THE UNION: THE COMPROMISE OF 1850

For many years, people tried to keep the question of slavery out of politics. After a time, though, that proved impossible. Slavery was dividing the nation in two—a northern part, where there was no slavery, and a southern part, where slavery still existed. Eventually, almost every bill that came before Congress was judged on whether it was good for the North or good for

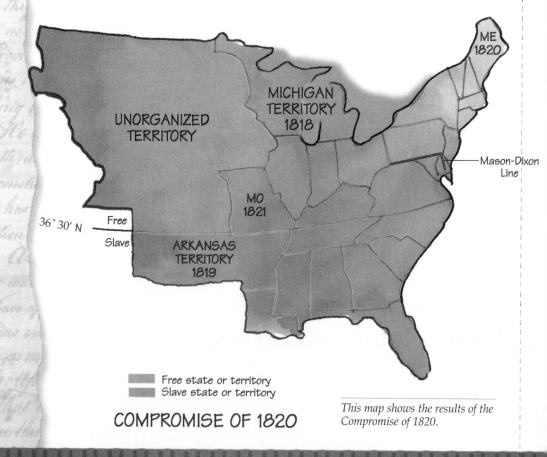

Free state or territory
Slave state or territory

COMPROMISE OF 1820

*This map shows the results of the Compromise of 1820.*

the South. The problem of slavery made people lose track of what was good for the nation as a whole. In fact, the southern states began talking about leaving the Union and becoming a separate country.

In the early 1800s, lots and lots of land was being added to the United States. The question was, would slavery be allowed in these new territories? Or, would the new lands be slave-free?

## The Missouri Compromise

In 1819, the number of free states—states that did not allow slavery—equaled the number of slave states—states that allowed slavery. Then, Missouri, which had been part of the Louisiana Purchase, wanted to become a state. It was going to be a free state. If that happened, the North would control the government.

Before Missouri was admitted to the Union, Congress had to reach a compromise. A compromise is a way to settle differences between sides by each side giving up something that it wanted. In the case of the Missouri Compromise of 1820, the North allowed more slave states to enter the Union, and the South allowed more free states to enter the Union. According to the Missouri Compromise, Missouri would become a slave state. However, first Maine—then part of Massachusetts—would enter the Union as a free state. That way, slave and free states would stay equal in number.

The Missouri Compromise of 1820 also set a line across the nation. Above that line, no slavery would be allowed. Look at the map to see where the line was drawn.

## Trying to Keep the Union Together

Congress was desperate to keep the United States together. In September of 1850, after months of arguing, the representatives, both northern and southern, passed five bills. These bills became laws after President Millard Fillmore signed them. Together, these new laws are known as the Compromise of 1850. These laws were called a compromise because in them, the North gave up some things it wanted and the South gave up some things it wanted.

For example, with the Compromise of 1850, California was admitted to the Union as a free state, which was something the South didn't want to happen. Another of the Compromise laws said that Texas, New Mexico, and Utah could each decide whether it wanted to have slavery. The North didn't like that part.

*Left: Members of Congress debate slavery issues in 1850.*
*Right: The map shows the results of the Compromise of 1850.*

## The Fugitive Slave Act

There was another law in the Compromise of 1850 that particularly upset the North. It was called the Fugitive Slave Act. According to this act, or law, blacks in the North could be taken back to the South to slavery, just on the word of a southern slave owner. It didn't matter whether the person was a runaway slave or a free black. In addition, captured blacks could not have a jury hear their case or speak for themselves at their own trials.

Free State by admission to Union

Free State by gradual abolition

Free Territory by Act of Congress

Slavr State by admission to Union

Territory open to slavery by Act of Congress

The Fugitive Slave Act also tried to make people stop helping slaves escape. Many free blacks and many northerners were abolitionists (a buh LIH shuhn ihsts). That is, they believed that slavery was wrong. They wanted to abolish, or get rid of, slavery in the entire country. Some of these abolitionists hid or fed or guided runaway slaves who were headed toward the free northern states. The Fugitive Slave Act said that from now on, anyone who helped a runaway slave could be fined $1,000. The helper also could be put in jail for six months.

These compromises worked for a while. But as time passed, more and more northerners were coming out against slavery. At the same time, in the South, support for slavery grew. The nation was becoming more and more divided.

## Two Views on Slavery

Here are examples of two views on slavery that were held by the people of the United States.

John C. Calhoun was a senator from South Carolina. He took part in the debate about the Compromise of 1850. According to John, the South should not compromise.

Instead, the North should give up every point about slavery. He did not even want to discuss slavery with northerners. If the North did not give in, John warned that the South would leave the Union. He said, "let the States . . . agree to separate and depart in peace. If you are unwilling we should depart in peace, tell us so, and we shall know what to do. . . ."

Three days after John C. Calhoun spoke, northern Senator Daniel Webster appeared before Congress. He argued in favor of the compromise. He began with these words: "I wish to speak today not as a Massachusetts man, nor as a northern man, but as an American. . . . I speak today for the preservation of the Union. Hear me for my cause."

## Show What You Know

Most of us make compromises every day. For example, Jamie asks his mother if he can stay up an extra hour. She says he can stay up an extra half-hour instead. Both have compromised.

Think of a compromise you recently made. With that compromise in mind, fill out the table below. Then, on another sheet of paper, tell whether or not you think a compromise is a good way to settle a difference and why.

### A COMPROMISE I MADE

What was the compromise? _____

_____

What I gave up_____

_____

What I got _____

_____

What the other person gave up _____

_____

What the other person got _____

_____

# HARRIET TUBMAN TAKES THE UNDERGROUND RAILROAD

Harriet Tubman was a person who was born into slavery. She was owned by Edward Brodess, a Bucktown, Maryland, farmer who also owned Harriet's mother.

Years before her birth, Harriet's grandparents had been kidnapped and taken away from their African homeland, the area now called Ghana. When Harriet's grandparents were brought to this country, they were sold into slavery. That meant their children and their grandchildren would be slaves, too.

Even as a child, Harriet thought slavery was wrong. She was often beaten and whipped by her overseers, the people in charge of the slaves. Once, she tried to stop an overseer from beating another slave. The overseer hit her in the head with a two-pound weight. Harriet lived, but for the rest of her life, she had blackouts and dizzy spells.

*Harriet Tubman risked her life to help slaves to freedom.*

## The Language of the Underground Railroad

The Underground Railroad had certain code words. This helped keep abolitionists safe when they talked about the secret escape routes that runaways used.

For example, the abolitionists who helped runaway slaves were called "agents." The safe houses where "agents" lived were known as "stations" on the Underground Railroad. And the people like Harriet Tubman, who helped guide the runaways farther and farther north, were the Underground Railroad's "conductors."

## Harriet Runs to Freedom

In 1849, when she was about 28 years old, Harriet heard she was to be sold to an owner in the deep South. She decided she would run away instead. She thought to herself, "There's two things I've a right to—Death or Liberty. One or t'other I mean to have."

Legend has it that Harriet told her parents she would let them know when she was leaving by walking past where they were

*Slaves head north to freedom on the Underground Railroad.*

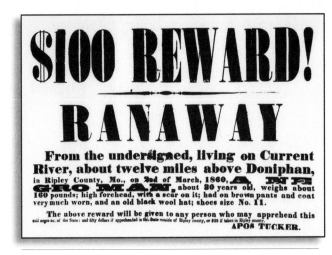

*This poster announces a reward for the return of runaway slaves.*

working while she sang this song: "When that old chariot comes, I'm going to leave you, I'm boun' for the Promised Land. . . ." The words to the song secretly told the listeners that Harriet was leaving. She was going north.

That night, Harriet ran away. Eventually, she found freedom in the free state of Pennsylvania. Years later, Harriet said that when she finally crossed the border into Pennsylvania, "I looked at my hands to see if I were the same person. Now I was free."

## Harriet Tubman Helps Others

Harriet Tubman arrived in Philadelphia in 1849. By the end of 1850, though, she was headed back to the South. She was not going back to stay. Instead, she was going to lead other runaway slaves along the paths that she had followed to freedom. She was going to become a conductor on the Underground Railroad

"Underground Railroad" was the name given to the secret series of routes and safe houses that helped runaway slaves get from the South to the North, where freedom awaited. It is said that the Underground Railroad got its name when a slave owner exclaimed that a runaway had disappeared so suddenly, it was as if he had "gone off on some underground road."

Slaves escaping on the Underground Railroad followed the North Star. That way, they were sure they continued to travel north. In some houses along the way, abolitionists lived. These abolitionists—both white people and black people—offered runaway slaves food and a safe place to rest and perhaps some money and clothes. Sometimes, the slaves could even get a boat or wagon ride to the next safe house on the route.

Every time an abolitionist helped a runaway, that abolitionist was breaking the law. That is because in 1850, Congress passed the Fugitive [runaway] Slave Act. That act made it illegal to give aid to runaway slaves.

Every time Harriet Tubman made the perilous journey on the Underground Railroad, she broke that law, too. She also risked being caught and returned to slavery. In fact, slave owners offered a huge reward for her capture!

For the next ten years, Harriet continued to risk her life and her freedom to help runaway slaves. In 19 trips on the Underground Railroad, Harriet Tubman guided some 300 slaves to freedom in the North.

## Show What You Know

Look at the picture below on this page. It is based on a true story. The white children playing in the snow are only pretending to play. They are the children of abolitionists, and they know that the men going by on horseback are slave catchers. The slave catchers are looking for the family of runaways who are hiding in the snow fort.

What happens next? Does the family escape? Do the abolitionists get in trouble? Use a sheet of paper, and draw a picture of what you think will happen next to the family of runaways. Or, if you wish, you can write a paragraph describing the next thing that happens in the runaways' journey.

# DRED SCOTT REMAINS A SLAVE

The Supreme Court is the part of our government that decides whether laws that are passed agree with the Constitution. It is made up of men and women justices, or judges. All the justices are well-educated. They also have a lot of experience in the legal system. However, like all human beings, sometimes justices are influenced by what others think. And, this means that sometimes, they make mistakes.

## Dred Scott Sues for His Freedom

Dred Scott was a slave. He belonged to a doctor named John Emerson. Dred and the doctor lived in the slave state of Missouri.

The doctor took Dred with him when he moved. First, they went to the state of Illinois. Then, they lived in what would become the state of Minnesota in the Wisconsin Territory. Both the state and the territory banned slavery. So, for several years, Dred lived as a slave where slavery was not allowed. Dr. Emerson's last move was back to Missouri. He died there in 1843.

*Dred Scott went to court to try to gain his freedom.*

Several years later, Dred Scott, with the help of several white friends, including the doctor's widow and the relative of an old owner, sued for his freedom. He said that because he had lived in the free state of Illinois and free territory of Wisconsin, he should be a free man. The case climbed the ladder of courts until in 1857, it reached the country's top court—the Supreme Court.

## The Supreme Court Decides

In 1857, there were nine justices sitting on the Supreme Court. Seven of them voted against Dred Scott. Roger B. Taney was Chief Justice, or head judge of the Supreme Court, at the time. He wrote about why the Supreme Court made the decision it did. He said that no African American—free or slave—could ever be a citizen of the United States.

Justice Taney also ruled that all slaves were property. Their owners could take them wherever they wanted. The Dred Scott decision meant that it did not matter whether a state had decided to be a free state or a slave state. Slave owners could take their slaves anywhere.

## After the Dred Scott Decision

Justice Taney and others hoped that a Supreme Court decision would stop the problem of slavery

*Fighting broke out between pro-slavery and anti-slavery forces in Kansas before it became a state.*

in the Union. Instead, it made things worse.

There were many who agreed with the Court's decision. But many others were furious. They felt the decision had set the nation on a course toward more slavery. In the end, the decision helped to further divide the nation into slavery and anti-slavery forces.

As for Dred Scott himself, what happened to him? In 1857, after the Supreme Court announced its decision, Dred Scott was freed by his owner. He lived as a free man for only 16 months before a lung disease called tuberculosis took his life.

## "Bleeding Kansas"

What happened in Kansas in the 1850s is another sign of how the question of slavery was hurting the nation. When Kansas was getting ready to become a state, it had only about 200 slaves. Yet, it became the center of a bitter battle about slavery.

People for and against slavery poured into Kansas. They wanted to influence whether Kansas would be a slave state or a free state. Then, when elections came, slavery supporters from Missouri crossed the border into Kansas and voted there illegally. These extra slave votes helped elect a pro-slavery government. That government then wrote a pro-slavery constitution for Kansas. It also passed many laws supporting slavery.

*Roger B. Taney was Chief Justice of the Supreme Court when the court voted against Dred Scott's case.*

Then, the arguments between pro- and anti-slavery groups became violent. Lawrence, Kansas—a town against slavery—was burned by supporters of slavery. white abolitionist John Brown and his supporters killed several slavery supporters. These and other violent acts gave Kansas a new nickname in the nation: "Bleeding Kansas."

Eventually, free-state groups took over the Kansas government. The constitution was changed. The pro-slavery laws were dropped. However, Kansas did not become a state until 1861. By then, the country was divided by war.

## Show What You Know

There have been other times when what Americans thought was true at that time is not considered true today. Here are three examples.

1. In 1644, the governor of Massachusetts, John Winthrop, said that democracy was the "worst of all forms of government."

2. In 1787, patriot Alexander Hamilton said that ordinary American citizens should not be allowed to vote—"they seldom judge or determine right."

3. In the 1890s, President Grover Cleveland said women should not be allowed to vote. In fact, he said, "Sensible and responsible women do not want to vote."

Choose one of these examples. Then, write a sentence or two explaining why it is not the way people feel today.

# THE BATTLE OF GETTYSBURG

The Civil War—the war between the North and the South—broke out in 1861. By the summer of 1863, it looked like the South might win. Southern General Robert E. Lee and his troops had just won two important battles in the South. One was at Fredericksburg, Maryland, and one was at Chancellorsville, Virginia.

Compare the uniforms between the Confederate soldier and the Union soldier.

### President Lincoln Speaks at Gettysburg

On November 19, 1863, people gathered to dedicate part of Cemetery Hill to those who died at Gettysburg. One of those who came was President Abraham Lincoln. He spoke only ten sentences. In those sentences, he forever honored the thousands who had died at the Battle of Gettysburg. The speech he gave became known as the Gettysburg Address. In it, he did not separate the Union dead from the Rebel dead. Instead, he honored all who fought. He hoped, he said, that "these dead shall not have died in vain—that this nation, under God, shall have a new birth of freedom—and that government of the people, by the people, for the people, shall not perish from the earth."

The general decided to move his army north. He hoped that a victory on northern soil would convince the North it could not win the war.

As his army of 75,000 soldiers crossed into Pennsylvania and headed for Harrisburg, Pennsylvania's capital, General Lee was not certain where northern troops were. He found out when some of his soldiers went to Gettysburg for supplies. Instead of the shoes for which they were searching, the southern soldiers spied Union troops. They hurried back to General Lee to report what they had seen.

## Three Days of Battle

At Gettysburg, northern and southern soldiers met for the first time on July 1, 1863. One gunner at Gettysburg later remembered that first terrible encounter. He spoke of "bullets hissing, humming and whistling everywhere; cannon

*Pickett and his soldiers charge Cemetery Ridge during the Battle of Gettysburg.*

roaring; all crash on crash and peal on peal, smoke, dust, splinters, blood, wreck and carnage [slaughter] indescribable." By the end of the fighting that first day, the southern troops had pushed the northern soldiers out of Gettysburg and into the places of higher ground to the south of town.

On the second day, General Lee ordered his troops to try to break through the line of defense northern soldiers had created. Again and again, the Confederate soldiers tried to break through. They tried at Culp's Hill. They tried at Cemetery Ridge. They tried at Peach Orchard, and they tried at Wheatfield, Devil's Den, and Little Round Top. From dawn to dusk, they fought. At all these places, all day long, the northern forces held their ground.

On the third terrible day at Gettysburg, southern General George Pickett was ordered to take the northern-held high ground called Cemetery Ridge. He knew he would have to send his forces across an open field. Of this command, he wrote to his fiancée: "My brave [soldiers] are to attack in front. God in mercy help us. . . ."

There was no help for Pickett and his men that day. It was a hopeless cause. Still, the Confederate soldiers battled bravely on, while the Union soldiers battled bravely to keep the Rebels back. One observer said that the noise of the battle for Cemetery Ridge was "strange and terrible, a sound that came from thousands of human throats . . . like a vast mournful roar."

When Pickett's charge ended, and the smoke of the battle cleared, Union troops had been victorious. The field in front of Cemetery Ridge was littered with the corpses of Confederate dead. In fact, of the Confederate soldiers who made that desperate charge, only one in four lived to retreat.

The defeat of Pickett's charge spelled the defeat of the Confederate Army at Gettysburg. After three blood-drenched days, the Union had won. The battle was over. Never again would General Lee be able to plan a major attack in the North. He had lost too much of his army at Gettysburg.

## The Cost of Gettysburg

The North won the Battle of Gettysburg. However, the cost in human life for both sides was almost unbelievable. In those three days in Pennsylvania, about 50,000 people were killed, wounded, or captured. When General Lee turned his army south again, it took a wagon train 17 miles long to haul the wounded southerners back home.

Other wounded men, both Yankees and Rebels, flooded into Gettysburg. Homes turned into hospitals, and civilians became nurses. In one Gettysburg family, five daughters all left their teaching positions to help care for the wounded and dying of both sides. One horrified nurse said of one day of work with the

GETTYSBURG

CEMETERY RIDGE

CEMETE

CODORI HOUSE

TROSTL
HOUSE

WARFIED
HOUSE

ROSE
HOUSE

wounded, "There are no words in the English language to express the suffering I have witnessed today." Only one Gettysburg civilian was killed during the battle. That was 20-year-old Jenny Wade. Jenny was baking bread at her sister's house when a bullet from a Confederate sharpshooter's gun accidentally tore through the walls of the house and killed her.

## Show What You Know

Here is a map showing some of the places where fighting took place during the Battle of Gettysburg. Read "The Battle of Gettysburg" again. Every time you find a name of a site where northerners and southerners fought, find the corresponding place on the map. Then mark the place with a "C" if it was the site of a Confederate win and "U" if it was the site of a Union win.

CEMETERY RIDGE
POWDER HILL
MEAD'S HQ
TANEYTOWN ROAD
WEIKERT HOUSE
LITTLE ROUND TOP
WHEAT FIELD
DEVILS DEN
RIDGE

# ABRAHAM LINCOLN, THE MAN

You probably know a lot about Abraham Lincoln already. You may know that he was called "Abe." You may know that he was president of the United States. And, you probably can name the penny as the coin on which he appears.

It is important to know the facts about Abraham Lincoln, the president. After all, the decisions he made and the actions he took as president during the Civil War helped bring the South back into the United States. Perhaps it also is important to know something about Abraham Lincoln, the human being.

### Young Abe Learns to Read

When Abe was just ten years old, his mother, Nancy, died of "milk sickness." This was a sickness people caught when they drank milk from a cow that had eaten a plant called snakeroot. The next year, his father remarried.

Abe's mother had loved him very much. His stepmother loved him, too. Abe's

## Abe Lincoln Leaves for Washington

*In 1860, Abraham Lincoln won the election for president of the United States. He boarded the train that would take him from his home in Springfield, Illinois, to Washington, D.C. He told those gathered to see him off what it meant to leave the city where he had lived for 25 years: "No one not in my situation can appreciate my feelings of sadness at this parting. To this place, and the kindness of these people, I owe everything. Here I have lived a quarter of a century, and have passed from a young to an old man. Here my children have been born, and one is buried. I now leave, not knowing when, or whether ever, I may return. . . ."*

*The president never again saw his beloved Illinois home. The next time he came to Springfield was to be buried there.*

stepmother, Sarah, saw that Abe was very smart. Although she herself could not read, Sarah encouraged Abe to read and write and learn.

Abe learned to love words. In fact, he wrote words anywhere he could—in snow, in mud, in dust—and just studied them. Once he wrote his name down and told a friend he couldn't believe those few letters stood for a whole person! Abe read all he could, and he wrote a lot, too. He even wrote letters for neighbors who couldn't write themselves. This was a time when schools could be far from home and children were needed to work on the farm. Many people didn't have a chance to learn to read and write.

### Abraham, the Man

Abraham Lincoln was a tall, thin, gangly man. He stood 6 feet 4 inches and weighed only 180 pounds. His arms and legs seemed too long for his body. His face had deep-set eyes and sunken cheeks, and he had a wart near the right corner of his mouth.

He was, as he said himself, "not much to look at."

What Abe Lincoln lacked in looks, he made up for in personality. For example, Abe was very funny. When he was a teenager, he told neighborhood children to walk in the mud. Then, he lifted them up, turned them upside down, and had them "walk" with their muddy feet on the ceiling of his family's cabin!

Abe Lincoln also was a modest man, and becoming president of the United States didn't change that. When he found out he would be the next president, he didn't go to a big party. Instead, he walked home by himself, said to his wife, "Mary, we're elected," and sat down on the couch to spend the evening with his family.

Abe was known for his kindness. When the Civil War ended, he was asked how the defeated southerners should be treated. The president felt these beaten people should be treated with mercy. Abe, who still sounded like an old frontiersman, said he wanted to "let 'em up easy, let 'em up easy."

Abe was also kind to animals. It was said that any trip with Abe Lincoln took a while longer than it should. That was because every time he saw a baby bird that had fallen from its nest, he stopped, got off his horse, and rescued it. Also, when the new president took his family to Washington, he took along a photograph of Fido, the family dog. He wanted his children to remember Fido, who would stay behind in Springfield.

*John Wilkes Booth sneaks up on President Lincoln while he watches a play at Ford's Theatre.*

## The End of Abe's Life

On April 14, 1865, President Lincoln took his wife and two friends to Ford's Theatre to see the play *Our American Cousin*. As the audience watched the play, at about 10:15 in the evening, a man named John Wilkes Booth sneaked up behind the president and shot him in the head. John Wilkes Booth later was caught and killed.

The president's heart still beat, but the wound was too serious for him to live. He was carried across the street and into a room in William Peterson's boarding house. They had to lay Abe in the bed diagonally, because he was too tall to fit the regular way. There he lay, unconscious, through the night. At 7:22 the next morning, on April 15, 1865, President Lincoln died.

Secretary of War Edwin Stanton was one of the people with the president at his death. After Abe drew his last breath, Stanton said of him, "Now he belongs to the ages." Those words also appear on President Lincoln's tomb in Springfield, Illinois.

## Show What You Know

One of the ways we honor our presidents is to put their likenesses on our money. For example, President Abraham Lincoln's face appears on the penny. A portrait of President Thomas Jefferson is on the nickel. President Franklin D. Roosevelt's likeness is on the dime. The quarter's president is George Washington.

Find a penny, a nickel, a dime, and a quarter. Lay the coins on a table. Put a blank sheet of paper over the coins, one at a time. Then, using only half the paper, rub a pencil point back and forth over the paper and the coin until you have made an impression of the president's face on your paper. Now, turn the coins over, and rub your pencil point over the backs of the coins on the other half of the paper.

When you have finished, cut out the eight circles you have made (four of coin fronts, four of coin backs). Match up each front with its correct back. Then, use a drop of glue to glue the two circles together. When you have finished, ask a friend or relative to identify each of the coins you created. Ask whether the friend or relative knows the names of the presidents shown on the coins.

# UNIT 7  1865–1900
# THE UNITED STATES GROWS

If you wanted to choose one word to describe the last half of the 1800s, you might choose the word "change." Between the time the Civil War ended and the next century began, the West had been settled. Indians had been forced onto reservations. The days of the cowboy had come and gone. Millions had crowded into growing cities. And, candles and gas lights gave way to electric lights.

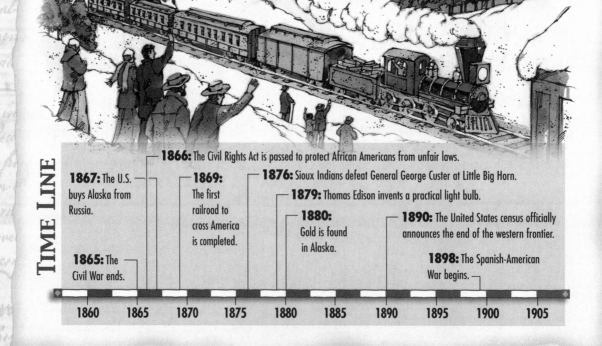

**TIME LINE**

**1866:** The Civil Rights Act is passed to protect African Americans from unfair laws.

**1867:** The U.S. buys Alaska from Russia.

**1869:** The first railroad to cross America is completed.

**1876:** Sioux Indians defeat General George Custer at Little Big Horn.

**1879:** Thomas Edison invents a practical light bulb.

**1880:** Gold is found in Alaska.

**1890:** The United States census officially announces the end of the western frontier.

**1865:** The Civil War ends.

**1898:** The Spanish-American War begins.

1860    1865    1870    1875    1880    1885    1890    1895    1900    1905

# A RAILROAD ACROSS AMERICA

The first railroads in the United States started to run in the early 1800s. By the 1860s, railroads crisscrossed much of the eastern half of the nation.

Government officials had thought about a transcontinental railroad for a long time. ("Trans" means "across." So, "transcontinental" means "across the continent.") For years, northern and southern representatives fought about the details. One reason was because each group wanted the railroad to start in its region.

It was not until after the South left the Union that northern representatives could pass a bill to build the transcontinental railroad.

| **HOW LONG IT TOOK TO SHIP PRODUCTS FROM CINCINNATI, OHIO, TO NEW YORK CITY, NEW YORK** | | |
|---|---|---|
| DATE | HOW SHIPPED | AVERAGE TIME |
| 1817 | Ohio River keelboat to Pittsburgh, wagon to Philadelphia, wagon to New York City | 52 days |
| 1843 | Ohio River steamboat to Pittsburgh, canal to Philadelphia, railroad to New York City | 18–20 days |
| 1852 | Railroad lines all the way from Cincinnati to New York City | 6–8 days |

## Work Starts

President Abraham Lincoln signed the bill into law on July 1, 1862. The law was called the Pacific Railroad Act. It gave the responsibility of building the railroad to two companies. One company was the Central Pacific Railroad. It was to lay track from Sacramento, California, toward Omaha, Nebraska. The other company was the Union Pacific Railroad. It was to start near Omaha and lay track toward Sacramento.

For each mile of track, the companies would receive money from the government. If the mile of land was flat, the company received $16,000. If the track covered a mile of mountains, the company could receive up to $48,000.

The government also gave each company land. All along the route, the land on either side of the tracks was divided up like a checkerboard. The company received every other square of land along every mile of track it completed. The companies then could sell these millions of acres to farmers. The farmers would, in turn, pay the nearby railroad to take their products to market.

*Thousands of Chinese workers helped build the Central Pacific part of the railroad.*

## Problems Building the Tracks

Both companies faced problems as they began building the transcontinental railroad. For example, during the Civil War, there weren't enough men to do the building. So, both companies looked for workers outside the country. Soon, thousands of Irish men were working on the Union Pacific's stretch of track. Thousands of Chinese workers were building the Central Pacific's part of the railroad.

Geography also caused problems for the railroad-building companies. In the West, for example, the Central Pacific workers soon faced the Sierra Nevada mountains. There was no easy pass through the mountain range. The builders had to blast tunnels through some mountains and raise bridges over others. In the mountains terrible blizzards blew snow into drifts 30 or 40 feet deep. No snowplow could clear tracks buried under mountains of snowdrifts. So, to keep the trains moving, Central Pacific workers had to enclose dozens of miles of track with dozens of miles of wooden snow sheds.

These snow sheds helped to keep the great snows off the rails.

Meanwhile, the Union Pacific was building its way across the nation's vast, treeless plains. The tons of wood it needed for ties—and most of its other supplies, too—had to be hauled all the way to Omaha. From there, goods were loaded onto train cars that followed the finished track—perhaps hundreds of miles—to where the men were working.

## How the Train Tracks Were Laid

Here is how one writer of the time described what he saw as he watched Union Pacific workers lay track:

*A light [railroad] car, drawn by a single horse, gallops up to the front with its load of rails. Two men seize the end of a rail and start forward, the rest of the gang taking hold by twos until it is clear of the car. They come forward at a run. At the word of command, the rail is dropped in its place, right side up, with care. . . . Less than 30 seconds to a rail for each gang, and four rails go down to the minute. Quick work, you say, but the fellows on the Union Pacific are tremendously in earnest.*

*The moment the car is emptied, it is tipped over on its side of the track to let the next loaded car pass it, and then it is tipped back again; and it is a sight to see it go flying back for another load, propelled by a horse at full gallop at the end of sixty or eighty feet of rope. . . .*

*Close behind the first gang come the gaugers, spikers, and bolters, and a lively time they make of it. It is a grand Anvil Chorus that these sturdy sledges are playing across the Plains; it is in triple time, three strokes to a spike. There are ten spikes to a rail, four hundred rails to a mile, eighteen hundred miles to San Francisco— twenty-one million times are they to come down with their sharp punctuation before the great work of modern America is complete.*

## A Golden Spike Finishes the Railroad

After years of work, the two rail

lines met each other in Utah, at a place called Promontory Point. There, on May 10, 1869, officials gathered to watch the last tie be laid and the last spike be driven to connect the western rail line with its eastern half. The last tie was made of laurel wood. The last spike was made of gold.

Actually, two of the officials were supposed to take turns using a sledgehammer to pound in the last, golden spike. However, each of them missed his mark, and the man who finished the rails was one who had helped build them. As he finished, telegraphs all over the country tapped out the message: "Done." Then, the engines from the Central Pacific and the Union Pacific inched forward over the newly completed track until their noses touched. The nation's first transcontinental railroad was completed!

## Beginnings and Ends

A nationwide celebration followed the completion of the transcontinental railroad. Guns were fired. Cannons boomed. Church bells rang. And, fireworks lit up the night in cities all over the country. In fact, the railroad united the country as nothing had before. The New York Times announced that now, "The inhabitants of the Atlantic seaboard and the dwellers on the Pacific slope are henceforth emphatically one people. . . ." The railroad also encouraged an explosion of settlement across the Great Plains.

The transcontinental railroad meant the end of some things, too. The Pony Express and wagon trains died away quickly. People began traveling by the fast-moving trains, instead of slower steamboats or stagecoaches. Perhaps the saddest end was the end of the wandering way of life of the Plains Indians, who watched and fought as their prairies were cut up by the rails and parceled out to white farmers.

Left: This photo shows the completion of the nation's first transcontinental railroad, which took place at Promontory Point, Utah.
Right: A golden spike like this one was the last spike used to finish the transcontinental railroad.

**1865–1900**

# RAILROADS AND TIME ZONES

Before the railroads spanned the continent, the people of America set their clocks by the sun. When the sun was directly above a place, it was 12:00 noon in that place. This meant that from place to place, time could be different, even if the places were not so far apart.

Then, the trains came. And with the trains, came train schedules. With different times from place to place, it was difficult to make and keep to a train schedule. So, in 1870, a teacher named Charles F. Dowd came up with the idea of time zones. According to his plan, every place in a time zone has its clocks set for the same time.

Look at the map of time zones. Notice how, as you travel west, each time zone is one hour behind the one to its east. That is because the earth rotates, or turns, in an eastward way. This means that, if it is 4:00 in the afternoon in New York City (in the Eastern Time Zone), it is only 3:00 in the afternoon in St. Louis, Missouri (in the Central Time Zone—one time zone west of the Eastern Time Zone).

Circle the correct answer for each of these questions.

1. If it is 7:00 A.M. in New York City, what time is it in St. Louis?
   a. 6:00 A.M.
   b. 7:00 A.M.
   c. 8:00 A.M.

2. It is 1:30 P.M. in Philadelphia. In which of these cities is it also 1:30 P.M.?
   a. Bismarck
   b. Salt Lake City
   c. Atlanta

3. According to the name of its time zone, what kind of land would you expect to find around Denver, Colorado?
   a. mountainous land
   b. flat land
   c. land near the Pacific Ocean

4. In which time zone do you live?
   a. Eastern Time Zone
   b. Central Time Zone
   c. Mountain Time Zone
   d. Pacific Time Zone
   e. Alaska Time Zone
   f. Hawaii Time Zone

# PIONEER LIFE ON THE GREAT PLAINS

This poster advertises rich farming lands along the Union Pacific Railroad.

**RICH FARMING LANDS!**
ON THE LINE OF THE
**Union Pacific Railroad!**
Located in the GREAT CENTRAL BELT of POPU-
LATION, COMMERCE and WEALTH, and
adjoining the WORLD'S HIGHWAY
from OCEAN TO OCEAN.
**12,000,000 ACRES!**
*3,000,000 Acres in Central and
Eastern Nebraska, in the Platte Valley, now for sale!*
We invite the attention of all parties seeking
a HOME, to the LANDS offered for sale by this Company.

O. F. DAVIS,
Land Commissioner, U. P. R. R.
OMAHA, NEB.

The United States government generously offered land to encourage railroad companies to build railroads through the American West. To sell some of the land, the railroad companies ran advertisements about the wonderful opportunities of the Great Plains. The ads spoke of the prairie's pure water and calm climates. They told how, on the Great Plains, a farmer could plow for miles in a straight line. Some of what the ads said was true, but some was not.

## The Problem of Water

There was pure water on the Great Plains. However, most of it was underground. The plains do not receive much rainfall. That was one reason the region was, for a long time, known as the Great American Desert.

Prairie farmers couldn't rely on the rain to provide enough water for their crops. So, many farmers practiced "dry farming." That is, they found ways to keep moisture in the ground, instead of letting it evaporate into the air. For example, some farmers learned to plow across a slope, instead of up and down the slope. Then, when there was rain, it didn't just flow down the slope. Instead, the furrows caught the rain,

## The Homestead Act

*Many of the pioneers who came to the Great Plains gained their land because of a government law passed in 1862 called the Homestead Act.*

*The Homestead Act said that any head of household who was over 21 years old could claim 160 acres of land. The land was free, except for a small fee. To keep the land, the settlers had to agree to spend five years living there and improving the land.*

and it sank into the soil. Also, in winter, the cross-wise cuts helped snow stay on the slopes. In the spring when the snow melted, the water would run into the ground. This and other dry-farming techniques helped farmers depend less on rainfall for the success of their crops.

## The Problem of Wood

One of the first problems prairie pioneers faced was building a house. They couldn't build wooden houses, because trees were scarce on the Great Plains. Instead, many built their first houses of sod. Sod is created when the top layer of soil becomes matted with the roots of thousands of years of plants. There was plenty of sod on the Great Plains.

To make a sod house, or soddy, farmers first cut long strips of sod from the earth. Then, they cut the sod strips into big rectangular bricks. They piled these big bricks up on top of each other. Sometimes, the roof was made of sod. It took about an acre of sod to make a one-room, 16-by-20-foot soddy.

Sod made a pretty comfortable house. The thick, earthen walls made the house like a cool cave in the summer heat. Those same thick walls held in heat when winter winds howled outside. Plus, sod houses didn't burn, and fire was always a danger on the prairie.

Sod houses did have problems, though. They were dark and smoky, and bugs lived in the walls. Sometimes they smelled like dirt. Plus, when it rained, mud from a sod roof could drip down onto everybody and everything!

### The Problem of Grasshoppers

In the summer of 1873, James Kyner was driving his wagon back to the family farm. He was thinking happy thoughts about how tall and strong the corn was growing when he noticed the sky growing dark. Suddenly, thousands and thousands of grasshoppers flew out of the sky and swarmed around him. They flew into the horses' faces and crunched under their hooves. The wagon filled with grasshoppers. James heard their bodies pop like popcorn under the wagon wheels as he struggled to keep the horses moving toward home.

When James finally reached the farm, he saw that the cornfields, of which he had been so proud and on which his family had depended, now were wrapped in a moving, eating, 4-inch-thick blanket of grasshoppers. It took the hungry bugs only two hours to eat up all the corn. Even most of the corn stalks were eaten. James said that, "where many a stalk had stood, a hole in the ground

*Left: The Great Plains stretch across many states.*
*Right: Pioneers built sod houses where there were few trees.*

was all that remained—a hole where the grasshoppers had eaten the stalk off an inch or more below the ground." That year, the Kyner corn crop was completely ruined. So were the crops of many of their neighbors.

The grasshoppers did not eat people, but they did eat just about everything else. Clothes and curtains and the handles on plows and pitchforks—all were dinner for the swarms of grasshoppers.

The grasshoppers even ruined things they didn't eat. Farmers lost livestock when hogs and other animals ate themselves to death on the flying feast. The meat of chickens and turkeys that had gorged on grasshoppers tasted like grasshopper and couldn't be eaten!

## Other Problems of the Plains

Weather was always a challenge to farmers on the Great Plains. In the summer, there could be tornadoes and horribly hot temperatures. Winter brought frozen weather and blizzards.

Perhaps the greatest challenge faced by the people of the Great Plains was the challenge of loneliness. Many were lonely for the families and land and lives they left behind. Many others were lonely for human company. One man who grew up on the plains described the loneliness this way:

*This photo shows a typical sod house on the Great Plains.*

*You look on, on, on, out into space, out almost beyond time itself. You see nothing but the rise and swell of land and grass and then more grass—the monotonous, endless prairie! A stranger traveling on the prairie would get his hopes up, expecting to see something different on making the next rise. To him the disappointment and monotony were terrible. "He's got loneliness," we would say of such a man.*

## Why the Pioneers Stayed

Faced with all these problems and challenges, many left the Great Plains. Still, many stayed, and others came to take the place of those who went back home.

The settlers of the Great Plains grew to love the endless sameness of the prairie. One woman, looking back on the good and the bad of her pioneer life on the flat lands of Kansas, explained why her family stayed. She said, "It might seem a cheerless life, but there were many compensations: the thrill of conquering a new country; the wonderful atmosphere; the attraction of the prairie, which simply gets into your blood and makes you dissatisfied away from it; the low-lying hills and the unobstructed [unblocked] view of the horizon; and the fleecy clouds driven by the never failing winds. The pioneer spirit was continuous in our family."

## Show What You Know

Pictured below is part of a chart that was meant to help pioneer children learn arithmetic, or mathematics. The chart used things from a farmer's life at that time to show sample arithmetic problems.

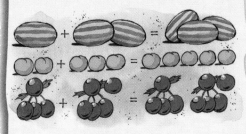

Imagine you are a teacher today. Make up three math problems like the three problems shown here. Make your math problems by using objects from your everyday life today. For example, you might draw:

$$1 \text{ TV} + 2 \text{ TVs} = 3 \text{ TVs}$$

When you have finished, give your math problems to a younger friend or relative. Ask that person to solve the problems you have created.

# JOHN WESLEY POWELL EXPLORES THE COLORADO RIVER

*This photo is a portrait of John Wesley Powell.*

### The Grand Canyon

In 1903, a year after John Wesley died, President Theodore Roosevelt came to see the Grand Canyon. He couldn't get over what he saw there. "It is beautiful and terrible and unearthly!" he exclaimed. He knew it should be kept the way it was. He declared that he wanted the Grand Canyon to be preserved without a "building of any kind, not a summer cottage, a hotel, or anything else, to mar the wonderful grandeur, the sublimity, the great loveliness and beauty of the Canyon. Leave it as it is," the president said. "You cannot improve on it." In 1919, the Grand Canyon became a national park.

When John Wesley Powell was young, he thought he would be a minister, like his father. Then, he fell in love with nature. He decided to become a scientist instead.

### War Delays Powell's Plans

John Wesley's plans to be a scientist were delayed for a while by the Civil War. As soon as the war began, John Wesley signed up. He served from the beginning of the war until the war's end. During that time, he became a major. In fact, some of the men who later worked for him called him "The Major" as a kind of nickname.

At the Civil War's Battle of Shiloh, John Wesley was wounded. Because of that wound, doctors had to amputate, or remove, his right arm at the elbow.

After the war, John Wesley taught science at colleges in Illinois. Sometimes, he took his students on field trips. Some

*These drawings show John Wesley Powell on his boat during his first exploration down the Colorado River in 1869.*

of John Wesley's field trips took him and his students all the way to the Rocky Mountains.

## John Wesley Goes Exploring

In 1869, John Wesley was hired by the U.S. government to take a trip west. His assignment was to explore the Colorado River. John Wesley was glad to go exploring for his country. He said he hoped that what he learned would "add a mite [little] to the great sum of human knowledge."

John Wesley chose nine men to go with him on his journey down the Colorado River. On May 24, 1869, at Green River City, Wyoming, their voyage began.

## Trouble on the Trip

John Wesley, his nine men, and his three boats—there were four but one crashed—had been roaring down the Colorado River for almost three months. They had traveled hundreds of miles. Now, they were running low on supplies. Also, they were entering a place where the river ran through a canyon—a canyon whose great, mile-high walls now towered above them.

John Wesley was very worried. In his diary, he wrote, "We have an unknown distance yet to run; an unknown river yet to explore. What falls there are, we know not; what rocks beset the channel, we know not; what walls rise over the river, we know not. Ah well! We may conjecture [guess] many things. The men talk as cheerfully as ever; jests [jokes] are bandied about freely this morning; but to me the cheer is somber and the jests are ghastly."

John Wesley was right to be worried. He didn't know it, but his little boats were about to enter the deep, dark, 277-mile-long Grand Canyon.

## The Challenge of the Grand Canyon

The Colorado River formed the Grand Canyon. It took millions and millions of years. For all those years, day after day, the waters of the river slowly carved out a course through the rock of the region.

Deeper and deeper the waters dug, through layer after layer of rock, until, in places, the canyon walls they created reached more than a mile up from the river.

Into this canyon, John Wesley's boats plunged. For days, they battled the "mad waters" of 160 sets of rapids. One week passed, then two weeks. Still the men fought on.

Finally, on August 28, three of the now starving men in John Wesley's party decided to climb out of the canyon. Shivwit Indians lived on the canyon's rim. The men climbed right into their midst and were killed.

If those three men had sailed with John Wesley for just one more day, they would have lived. That is because, on August 29, the survivors rowed their way out of the canyon, as the Colorado River flowed into the sunlight beyond the canyon's walls.

The Spanish explorer Coronado was the first white man to see the region. However, John Wesley and the others on his expedition were the first white men to explore the great Grand Canyon.

## Show What You Know

Pictured below is a map that shows the route John Wesley Powell took down the Colorado River during his 1869 expedition. The map also shows places where interesting or frightening things happened to John Wesley and his men.

Study the map. Then, use the information on the map and below the map to write "before" or "after" in each of the blanks below.

1. The *No Name* was wrecked _____ John Wesley Powell reached the Grand Canyon.

2. John Wesley Powell found Indian ruins _____ he started his journey into the Grand Canyon.

3. John Wesley Powell got to the Grand Canyon _____ he started down the Colorado River.

① **May 24, 1869:** John Wesley Powell and nine other men start the journey on which they will explore the Colorado River.

② **June 7:** One of John Wesley's four boats—the *No Name*—is lost when it is swept away by rapids and smashes into a boulder. Its captain missed John Wesley's warning signal that rapids lay ahead. The four men on the boat all are rescued.

③ **August 13:** John Wesley and his men sail the Colorado River into the Grand Canyon.

④ **August 17:** John Wesley and his party come upon Native American ruins in the canyon.

⑤ **August 28:** The men are running dangerously low on food. Three of the men climb up the canyon walls and right onto the land of the Shivwit Indians. All three men are killed.

⑥ **August 29:** The men who have survived the journey come out the other end of the Grand Canyon.

# CHIEF JOSEPH AND THE NEZ PERCE

The railroad trains brought merchants, miners, ranchers, and farmers by the thousands into the Great Plains and the American West. Many different Native American groups had lived in the regions west of the Mississippi River. They were all squeezed out so white people could take over their land.

Some Native American groups decided to fight. In the 1850s and 1860s, some Cheyenne, Arapaho, Sioux, and several other groups all waged war against white people.

## What Happened to Shirt On?

Suhm-Keen, or Shirt On, and his parents were among the lucky Nez Perce. They, along with 30 or 40 others, actually made it to Canada. Once there, Chief Sitting Bull and his group of Sioux took them in for a while.

In 1878, Shirt On's family moved back across the border. They worked on white people's farms for a while. Then, they returned to Lapwai and its reservation.

Shirt On went to college. He became a police officer on the Flathead Indian Reservation in Montana. He worked there for 20 years. Then, he retired and moved back to Idaho.

In 1903, Shirt On went with Chief Joseph to Washington, D.C. Chief Joseph had been to Washington before to plead for the return of Wallowa Valley to the Nez Perce. This was the chief's last trip. The next year, he died—some say of a broken heart.

In 1878, American General Philip Sheridan explained why some Native American groups chose to go to war against the United States and its settlers. He wrote, "We took away their country and their means of support, broke up their mode of living, their habits of life, introduced disease and decay among them, and it was for this and against this that they made war. Could anyone expect less?"

## The Nez Perce and the White Men

The Nez Perce Indians were given their name by French fur trappers who thought they all had pierced noses—nez percés—which

they didn't. They called themselves Nimipu—the people—but adopted the name Nez Perce.

For many years, the Nez Perce had little contact with white

This is a portrait of Chief Joseph. This map shows the path that Chief Joseph of the Nez Perce followed in his fight for freedom.

people. That is because they lived in the far northwest, in the land where present-day Idaho, Washington, and Oregon meet.

Lewis and Clark were among the first to bring back information about the Nez Perce tribe. Meriweather Clark described the people as "Stout likely men, handsome women, and very dressy in their way." He said the men wore "white buffalo robe or elk skin dressed with beads." The women, he said, "dress in a shirt of ibex [mountain goat] or goat . . . skins which reach quite down to their ankles."

Meriweather also said that of the Native American groups they had met along their way, the Nez Perce were "among the most amiable [friendly] we have seen." The Nez Perce remained friendly, first with white explorers, then with white settlers. For many years, it was a point of pride for the Nez Perce that no one of their tribe had ever killed a white person.

## Trouble Begins for the Nez Perce

More white settlers began to fill up the Northwest. They wanted to farm Nez Perce land. Then, gold was found where the Indians lived.

The prospectors wanted the Nez Perce land, too.

The U.S. government began to take Nez Perce land. Eventually, almost all the Nez Perce were forced onto the Lapwai Reservation in Idaho. Only a group living in Oregon's Wallowa Valley remained on its homeland. That group was led by Chief Joseph.

By 1877, settlers wanted Chief Joseph's valley, too. The government gave the chief and his Nez Perce group 30 days to move to the Lapwai Reservation. Most of Chief Joseph's group started peacefully on their journey. However, a few of the young men rebelled. They killed a group of white people. That marked the start of the Nez Perce War, also called the Flight of the Nez Perce. That is, perhaps, a better name, because the Nez Perce did not want to fight the white soldiers. They wanted only to escape to Canada.

As Chief Joseph's group traveled north, more Nez Perce joined them. Soon, there were three or four chiefs, in addition to Chief Joseph. Together, they helped the group outsmart and outfight the United States Army for 1,500 miles. Together, they almost made it to freedom.

## The Race for the Border

Suhm-Keen (Shirt On) was ten years old when he traveled with Chief Joseph and the other Nez Perce on their flight toward freedom. On August 8, 1877, they set up camp at Big Hole, in the Montana Territory. Most were sleeping when, at 4:00 in the morning, U.S. soldiers attacked.

Shirt On remembers his wounded grandmother pushing him from the tepee. She cried to him to run and hide in the woods. "I raced up the slope as fast as I could . . . bullets kept whizzing past clipping off leaves and branches all around me. I was very afraid . . . soon some other boys joined me there and we watched trembling at the awful sight below. Our tepees were set afire and our people shot as they tried to run for cover in the timber."

The Nez Perce fought off the soldiers at Big Hole, but 63 were killed. Of that number, 31 were women and children.

Big Hole was not the only place where the Nez Perce held off the bigger, better-armed U.S. Army. Even before the Battle of the Big Hole, 24 Nez Perce warriors had held off the army at Clearwater, Idaho, while the rest of the group escaped. In fact, the Nez Perce fought off over a dozen army attacks as they fled through the mountains of this treacherous territory. They won every battle but the last.

## The Final Battle

Over three months had passed. The exhausted Nez Perce were almost at their destination. Canada's border was only 40 miles away!

On September 29, the Nez Perce stopped to rest at the Snake Creek, in Montana's Bear Paw Mountains. They thought they were "two suns," or two days, ahead of the soldiers. Suddenly, a scout up on a ridge fired his gun and waved his blanket: "Soldiers coming—soldiers coming," his signals said.

In the next few moments, two lines of soldiers rode down from the ridges, firing on the camp. Day after day, the Nez Perce warriors fought off the army. But the Nez Perce could not win this battle. On October 5, Chief Joseph raised the white flag of surrender. Here are the words he spoke to the white victors:

*I am tired of fighting. Our chiefs are killed. Looking Glass is dead. Toohulhulsote is dead. The old men are all dead. It is the young men who say yes or no. He who led the young men is dead. It is cold and we have no blankets. The little children are freezing to death. My people, some of them, have run away to the hills and have no blankets, no food. No one knows where they are—perhaps freezing to death. I want to have time to look for my children and see how many of them I can find. Maybe I shall find them among the dead.*

*Hear me, my chiefs. I am tired. My heart is sick and sad. From where the sun now stands I will fight no more forever.*

After he had spoken, Chief Joseph covered his face with his blanket so that no one could see his shame. He and his people became prisoners of the U.S. Army.

*Chief Joseph of the Nez Perce surrenders to cavalry officers.*

## Show What You Know

The animals on which the Plains Indians relied were actually bison, not buffalo. Bison have bigger heads, a large hump at their shoulders, and more ribs than true buffalo. For some reason, though, most Americans use the word "buffalo" to describe that shaggy-haired, horned, bearded beast of the Great Plains.

Before the railroads crossed the United States, perhaps 20 million bison roamed the Great Plains. Then, the trains brought "buffalo" hunters to the region. Some of the buffalo hunters were even hired by the train owners, who hated the bison. A herd of bison grazing around the tracks could delay a train for hours. A bison stampede could knock a train right off its tracks.

Some of the buffalo hunters shot the bison just for fun. Some shot them for their hides. Millions were slaughtered, and millions of bison bodies were left to rot on the Great Plains.

By 1889, only 541 bison could be found in the whole United States. Only then did some Americans begin trying to protect the bison from extinction, or disappearing from the earth.

Imagine that you are living in the 1890s. You want to save the bison. Draw a poster that shows why the bison should be saved. Or, if you prefer, draw a poster using an animal that is in danger of extinction today. This includes animals such as the American crocodile, the blue whale, the red wolf, and the tiger.

# BELL AND EDISON CHANGE THE WORLD

The second half of the 1800s was a time of invention in America. American Christopher Sholes invented the first usable typewriter in 1867. Typewriters allowed people to produce work faster and neater than they could with regular handwriting.

In 1874, American Joseph F. Glidden created barbed wire. Great Plains farmers used the thorny wire to fence in their new farms.

*This picture shows what a gramophone looked like.*

There were other important inventors of the time, too. One of them was Alexander Graham Bell. His invention helped people talk to each other over distances. Another was Thomas Edison. One of his inventions lit up the world.

## Bell Invents the Telephone

Sound was always important to the Bell family. Elisa Bell was a musician. Her husband, Alexander Melville Bell, taught deaf people to talk. It made sense that their son, Alexander Graham Bell, would study sound, too. Like his mother, he became a musician. Like his father, he became a teacher of the deaf.

### How to Use a Phonograph

When Thomas Edison invented the phonograph, no one was exactly sure what to do with it. So, Thomas thought of these ten ways to use a phonograph:

1. Letter writing
2. Records that would speak to the blind
3. The teaching of good English
4. To reproduce music
5. Have family members record their memories for future generations
6. Music boxes and musical toys
7. Clocks that tell the time aloud
8. Record different languages so we will always know exactly how the words were pronounced
9. For education
10. Connect a phonograph to a telephone and record conversations

*This picture shows one of the earliest telephones.*

voice come out of the receiver. He rushed into Alexander's room and cried, "I can hear the words!" Because of that accident, with the genius of Alexander Graham Bell, the telephone was invented.

In 1871, Alexander came to America from Scotland, where he was born. He came to teach deaf children in Boston, Massachusetts. He also taught teachers of the deaf. Then, he began to experiment with inventing a way to send voices over wires. Alexander called his invention the telephone.

For months, Alexander and his helper, Thomas A. Watson, experimented with transmitters, or senders, and receivers. Then, the remarkable day came when the first voice was heard over a telephone. That day was March 10, 1876. Alexander was in one room with a transmitter. Thomas Watson was in another room with a receiver. Alexander accidentally spilled dangerous battery acid on his pants. Quickly he said into his transmitter, "Mr. Watson, come here, I want you." In the other room, Thomas heard Alexander's

## The Wizard of Menlo Park

Thomas Edison could not serve in the Civil War, because he was deaf in one ear. During the war, he became a telegrapher. Many telegraphers had gone to work for the northern and southern armies. There was a lot of work for Thomas.

Near the end of 1869, when he was about 22 years old, Thomas left his telegraph job. One paper announced what he planned to do next: "T. A. Edison has resigned his situation and will devote his time to bringing out his inventions."

Even as a young man, Thomas was inventing things. Unfortunately, some of his first inventions were designed to fool an employer into thinking Thomas was working when he really was napping!

As a grown-up, some of Thomas's first inventions were improvements in the telegraph business. For example, he invented a new telegraph that quickly reported the buying and selling of stocks. When Thomas finished his invention, he offered to sell it to the Gold and Stock Telegraph Company. The company asked him how much he wanted for the rights to the machine. Thomas said, "Make me an offer." Secretly, he hoped he might get $3,000 for it. He must have almost fainted when he was offered $40,000! After he got the $40,000 check cashed, Thomas stayed up all night, because he was afraid someone would break in and steal his money.

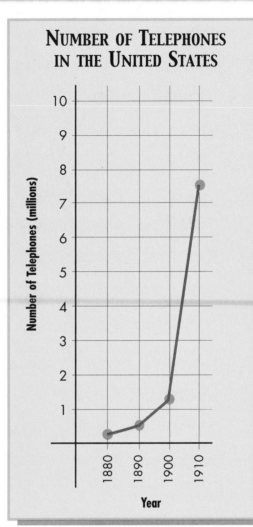

**NUMBER OF TELEPHONES IN THE UNITED STATES**

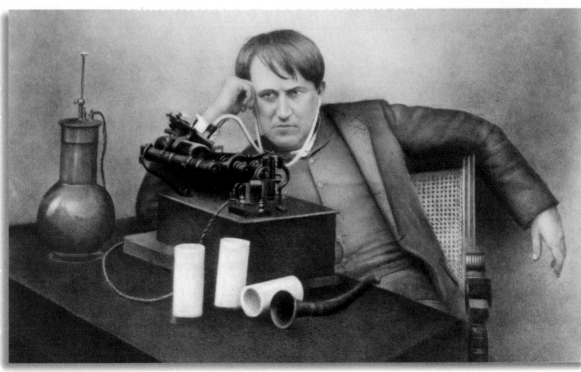

*Thomas Edison looks quite tired after having worked five days and nights to perfect the phonograph.*

In 1876, Thomas built a laboratory near Newark, New Jersey, in the town of Menlo Park. He soon became known as the "Wizard of Menlo Park" because of all the things he invented there. He once said that at Menlo Park, he and his assistants produced "a minor invention every ten days and a big thing every six months or so."

One of the "big things" Thomas invented is something you might have in your home. It was the phonograph, or record player. Another "big thing" was the world's first motion picture machine. However, the "big thing" for which he is best known today is the electric light bulb.

Thomas Edison did not actually invent electric light. But, he did invent the light bulb that makes it possible to have electric light.

Thomas ran into a problem with his electric light bulb. There had to be electricity for the light bulbs to work. To answer this need, Thomas began building electric power plants. Before the 1800s ended, there were hundreds of Edison Power Plants making and sending electricity to thousands of people. No longer were nights lit only by candles and gaslights. Electric light bulbs had turned darkness into light!

*Electrical wires were a new necessity, especially in cities.*

## Show What You Know

At his Menlo Park Laboratory, Thomas Edison and his staff worked on at least 40 projects at one time. His laboratory applied for 400 patents each year.

Under Thomas' direction, he and his staff were responsible for over 1,300 United States and foreign patents. Most if not all were applied for under Edison's name.

Use reference books, your local library, and the Internet to find the names of ten of Edison's interesting inventions and the year their patents were issued. Write your findings in the chart below.

| Name of Invention | Date of Patent |
| --- | --- |
| | |
| | |
| | |
| | |
| | |
| | |
| | |
| | |
| | |
| | |

# JANE ADDAMS FOUNDS HULL HOUSE

*The Nobel Prize bears the image of Alfred Bernhard Nobel.*

## The Nobel Prize

*The Nobel prizes are named after a Swedish chemist, Alfred Bernhard Nobel. He became rich when he invented dynamite—an explosive that was safer than other explosives being used at that time.*

*Alfred wanted to do something good with his money. He set aside $9 million. Each year, part of the interest that money earns goes to the people who have done the most good in the world that year.*

*The Nobel Peace Prize is one of the prizes that is given out. Nobel prizes are awarded in other categories, too, such as medicine and writing.*

At the end of the 1860s, newspaperman Horace Greeley observed that "We cannot all live in cities, yet nearly all seem determined to do so." That is how it seemed in the last decades of the 1800s. Cities in the East, cities in the Midwest, and cities in the West all grew rapidly during this time.

## People Crowd Into the Cities

Some of the people who came to make a new life in the cities were America's farmers. New farm machines could do the work of several people at once. That meant that many farmers found themselves out of work. Thousands decided to try their luck in the cities.

Farmers were not the only people flooding into the nation's cities. Immigrants, too, were arriving by the thousands. An immigrant is someone who leaves his or her homeland to make a new home in another country.

Some of the immigrants who came had a little money in their pockets. Many, though, had spent all their money to book ship passage to the United States. They arrived penniless. They had no money to go anywhere else. So, they crowded into the slums of the cities where they arrived.

Russian Anzia Yezierska arrived in New York in 1886. Here is how she described her first day in the city: "Between buildings that loomed like mountains, we struggled with our bundles . . . through the swarming streets of the ghetto. I looked about the narrow streets of squeezed-in stores and houses, ragged clothes, dirty bedding oozing out of the windows, ash cans and garbage cans cluttering the sidewalks. A vague sadness pressed down my heart the first doubt of America. . . . I looked out into the alley below, and saw pale-faced children scrambling in the gutter. 'Where is America?' cried my heart."

*Left: New technology allowed skyscrapers to be built.*
*Below: Booming city populations meant crowded streets.*

## New Problems for Cities

As populations exploded, cities struggled to keep up with the needs of the newcomers. For all these new people, the cities had to provide police officers and firefighters. The cities had to make room in their schools and build more transportation routes. They had to bring in more drinking water and run more electric lines and telephone wires. It is surprising that the cities could function at all!

Many times, the cities failed. Trash piling up in the streets became a common city sight. Jane Addams, who lived in Chicago, examined what she thought was an unpaved street. She found that the street was actually paved. But, its pavement was buried under almost two feet of garbage! One writer said of Chicago, "The river stinks. The air stinks. People's clothing, permeated by the foul atmosphere, stinks. No other word expresses it so well as stink."

Of the people who came to live in the cities, many remained poor. That is because there were more workers than there were jobs. That meant bosses didn't have to pay much to get someone to work. It also meant that some people didn't have jobs at all.

## Jane Addams Helps Chicago's Poor

Jane Addams decided to try to help the immigrants who settled in Chicago. She rented a big building in an immigrant-filled, rundown section of the city. She chose the place because, she said, "I gradually became convinced that it would be a good thing to rent a house in a part of the city where . . . actual needs are found." The name of the building was Hull House. In September 1889, Jane, with the help of friend Ellen Gates Starr, opened its doors to the poor.

At Hull House, immigrants could receive English lessons, medical care, and advice about jobs and life in America. There were also nurseries, schools, and playgrounds for their children.

Hull House became a model for new settlement houses around the country. A settlement house is a house that offers services to the poor, like Hull House did. Hull House itself continued to grow. By the time Jane died in 1935, Hull House had expanded to 13 buildings. It took up a whole Chicago block!

*Jane Addams founded Hull House in Chicago. Immigrants received much of the help that they needed at this settlement house.*

## Jane Addams's Other Good Works

Many Americans in need, including immigrants, the poor, children, and women, benefitted from the good works of Jane Addams. For example, Jane fought for eight-hour days for working women. She fought to get women the right to vote in America. She fought to keep young children from going to work instead of to school. She also fought for peace in the world. In fact, Jane won the Nobel Peace Prize in 1931.

One way Jane succeeded in her battles was to find other citizens who believed as she did. Then, she organized the citizens into a group. The group would write to and talk to the lawmakers about problems that were important to them. She knew that lawmakers wanted to know what Americans thought. Organizing groups of citizens was an effective way to tell them.

JANE ADDAMS

## Show What You Know

The graph at right is called a bar graph, because it uses bars to show certain information. On this graph, the bars show us about how the population of three American cities changed between 1870 and 1900.

Use the bar graph to answer these questions. Circle the correct answer.

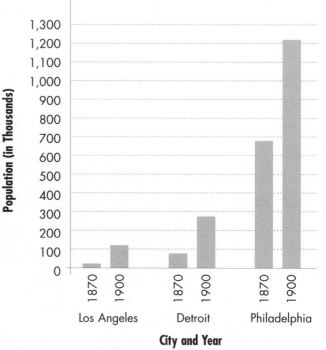

### HOW CITIES GREW

1. Which of the cities shown had the highest population in 1870?

   a. Los Angeles
   b. Detroit
   c. Philadelphia

2. Based on the bar graph, which of these statements is true about Detroit?

   a. In 1870, Detroit had fewer people than Los Angeles.
   b. Between 1870 and 1900, Detroit's population more than doubled.
   c. Between 1870 and 1900, Detroit was the biggest city east of the Mississippi River.

3. From your reading in history, you know that eastern cities were settled long before cities of the western part of the nation. Based on the graph, which city would you guess is in the East?

   a. Los Angeles
   b. Detroit
   c. Philadelphia

# BOOKER T. WASHINGTON, EDUCATOR

*This photograph is a portrait of Booker T. Washington.*

It was difficult for African Americans after the Civil War ended. Most had no money. When they were slaves, they received no money at all for their work. This meant that many could not afford to leave the plantations on which they had served as slaves. In addition, most ex-slaves had no education. In many places, it was against the law to teach slaves to read and write, although many wanted to be educated.

After the war ended, some northern teachers came south to teach ex-slaves. Some of these teachers were sent south by the U.S. government. Others were sent by northern church groups. Some of the first students eventually became teachers themselves, and they, too, took on the job of teaching ex-slaves to read and write. By 1870, one of every two teachers in the South was an African American.

## A Famous Tuskegee Teacher

*In 1896, Booker T. Washington asked George Washington Carver to teach at Tuskegee Institute. George, too, had been born into slavery. Now, he was a scientist.*

*George taught the students at Tuskegee. He also worked on finding uses for certain southern crops. He knew that the more uses he could find, the more valuable a crop would become. In his lifetime of work, George found more than 300 uses for the peanut. In fact, he found ways to create from peanuts almost anything from soap to face powder. George also created 60 new products from pecans. And, he found 100 new ways to use a sweet potato. He also studied ways to save the soil and taught African American farmers how to improve the amount of crops they could grow and harvest.*

What did ex-slaves think about having a chance to be educated? One student spoke for many when he told his teacher, "My Lord, ma'am, what a great thing learning is!"

## Booker T. Washington Becomes a Teacher

Booker Taliaferro Washington believed in education for everyone. He worked hard to educate himself. Then, he worked hard to educate others.

Booker was born into slavery in Virginia. He was 9 years old when the Civil War finally ended slavery. The Washington family, now free to leave, moved to West Virginia. There, Booker was able to go to the area's first school for African Americans. Booker helped the family by working in a salt mine from 4:00 to 9:00 every morning before he went to class. Later, he worked in a coal mine.

It was when Booker was down in the coal mine that he heard two miners talking about a new school for African Americans. Its name was the Hampton Normal and Agricultural Institute. He moved closer

to the men and listened as they described a school that would teach African Americans a trade—a skill with which they could make a living. Here is what Booker thought about what he heard:

*As they went on describing the school, it seemed to me that it must be the greatest place on earth. . . . I resolved at once to go to that school, although I had no idea where it was, or how many miles away, or how I was going to reach it; I remembered only that I was on fire constantly with one ambition, and that was to go to Hampton. This thought was with me day and night. . . .*

Booker made his dream come true. In 1872, he arrived at the Hampton Institute. He had only

*George Washington Carver is shown here teaching chemistry at Tuskegee Normal and Industrial Institute.*

50 cents in his pocket. He spent the next three years working as a janitor to pay for the cost of going to school there.

After Booker graduated from Hampton, he became a teacher. He taught children during the day, and he taught adults at night. He once said that, "Few were too young, and none too old, to make the attempt to learn."

## Booker T. Washington Starts a School

In 1879, Booker went back to the Hampton Institute, this time however, as a teacher.

After teaching at Hampton for two years, Booker started a brand-new school for African Americans.

It was called the Tuskegee (tuhs KEE gee) Normal and Industrial Institute. The name "Tuskegee" came from the Alabama town in which the school was located. Booker served as the school's principal. He also was a teacher there.

Booker knew that, in the United States at that time, black people did not have the same rights as white people. He felt that the way to get those rights was to learn a skill. With a skill, Booker believed an African American could work hard, save money, buy land, and become an economic force in the nation. To this end, Tuskegee taught African Americans how to be carpenters, printers, blacksmiths, and shoemakers.

When Booker started the Tuskegee Institute, the school was housed in a few tumbledown buildings. It had only 40 students and very little money. As the school's leader, Booker worked hard to make it a success. He tirelessly raised money for the school, from supporters in the North and the South.

All Booker's hard work paid off. By the time he died, in 1915, Tuskegee was a school of 100 buildings. It had over 1,500 students and almost 200 teachers.

The school's future was secured, because of the money Booker T. Washington had raised for it during his lifetime—almost $2 million in all!

Through his work at the Tuskegee Institute, Booker gained the respect of people all over the nation. Presidents asked for his advice. He often spoke to congressional representatives about the treatment and hopes of America's black people.

Not everyone agreed with everything Booker did and said. For example, Booker did not fight segregation. Segregation is the separation of people because of their race, their religion, or some other reason. Much of the country had segregated African Americans because of their race.

Booker said that the races could be separate sometimes. Though when it was for the good of the country, the races should work together. "In all things that are purely social," Booker said, "we can be as separate as the fingers, yet one as the hand in all things

essential to mutual progress." This angered some people, who felt that blacks and whites should work together in all things. Yet, that would not happen for many years to come.

## Booker's School Lives On

The Tuskegee Institute still exists today. It is known as Tuskegee University. Its new name reflects the fact that it now offers many courses in many subjects. For example, today's students can major in art or agriculture or engineering. Students can decide to become veterinarians or teachers or nurses. Also, Tuskegee University is no longer a school for only African Americans. Today, people of all races receive an education there.

*This photograph shows Tompkins Hall (cafeteria and student union) at Tuskegee University as it looks today.*

## Show What You Know

Study this photograph of a history class being taught at Tuskegee Institute. Then, answer the questions based on what you see there.

1.  Name three things you see in this photograph that you also could see in a modern-day classroom.

    _____

    _____

    _____

    _____

    _____

2.  Name three things you see in this photograph that you probably wouldn't see in a modern-day classroom.

    _____

    _____

    _____

3.  On the chalkboard, this history teacher has written about what happened to Captain John Smith. The chalkboard tells that the captain was a colonist at Jamestown. It says that Captain Smith was captured by Indians, and that his life was saved by an Indian woman named Pocahontas. Imagine you are a teacher. You have just told your class to read "Booker T. Washington, Educator." Write three important facts from the reading that you would choose to write on the chalkboard.

    _____

    _____

    _____

    _____

    _____

    _____

    _____

# UNIT 8
# 1890–1920
# A TIME OF CHANGE

In this unit, you're going to read about some remarkable changes for the United States. For example, you will read about how the makeup of the American people changed, as immigrants by the millions poured into America. You'll also read about how transportation changed with the invention of the automobile and the airplane.

You're going to read about another change, too. For the first time, Americans begin to look outward, beyond the shores of their own continent, for other lands to claim.

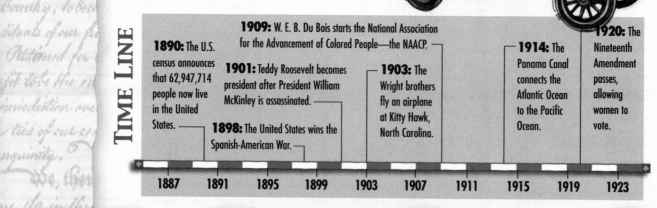

## TIME LINE

**1890:** The U.S. census announces that 62,947,714 people now live in the United States.

**1898:** The United States wins the Spanish-American War.

**1901:** Teddy Roosevelt becomes president after President William McKinley is assassinated.

**1909:** W. E. B. Du Bois starts the National Association for the Advancement of Colored People—the NAACP.

**1903:** The Wright brothers fly an airplane at Kitty Hawk, North Carolina.

**1914:** The Panama Canal connects the Atlantic Ocean to the Pacific Ocean.

**1920:** The Nineteenth Amendment passes, allowing women to vote.

1887   1891   1895   1899   1903   1907   1911   1915   1919   1923

# ELLIS ISLAND WELCOMES NEWCOMERS

Ellis Island is located in New York Harbor. It sits close to the New Jersey shore. Ellis Island got its name from the farmer, Samuel Ellis, who owned the island long ago. Before that, it was called Oyster Island, because of the beds of delicious oysters found there. And, before that, it was called by its Indian name—Kioshk, or Gull Island, because for many years, seagulls were its only residents.

## The Government Buys Ellis Island

In 1808, the United States government bought Ellis Island. For a while, soldiers were stationed at a fort built there. Later, the island was used as a place to store ammunition.

In 1890, the government decided to use Ellis Island in another way. It would become the receiving center for immigrants headed for the port at New York City.

*An immigrant family arrives in the United States.*

Immediately, the government began its work. The new main building housed receiving rooms and baggage rooms. It also had places where newcomers could exchange their money for American money or buy railroad tickets. Other buildings offered services that immigrants might need. For example, there was a laundry and a dormitory. Those came in handy for immigrants who had to stay overnight. There also was a restaurant and a kitchen. There was even a hospital for immigrants who were sick when they arrived.

The government not only built buildings on Ellis Island, it also built up the island itself. The original Ellis Island was only a little more than three acres.

However, it grew as workers added thousands of tons of soil to it. Much of this dirt came from New York when its subway system was built. Eventually, the island measured over 27 acres.

## Ellis Island Opens for Business

On January 1, 1892, 15-year-old Annie Moore of Cork, Ireland, became the first immigrant to be processed through Ellis Island. Her two brothers were second and third. For the rest of that year, and for many years to come, Ellis Island was overwhelmed with immigrants from all over the world. Every day, seven days a week, an almost unbelievable number of people passed through Ellis Island. On some days, the number of people reached over 5,000!

*For many immigrants, the huge main building on Ellis Island was their most enduring memory of the trip to America.*

There actually were over 70 other places where people could be processed into the country. San Francisco, New Orleans, Boston, and Savannah were among those ports where immigrants landed. Yet, for the next 60 years or so, three of every four newcomers to the United States came through the gates of Ellis Island.

## Processing Millions of Immigrants

To process this many people, Ellis Island set up a maze of iron-fenced pens. People moved from pen to pen as doctors poked them and prodded them and officials asked them questions.

Here is how author H. G. Wells described what he saw when he visited Ellis Island in 1905. "On they [the immigrants] go, from this pen to that, pen by pen, towards a little metal wicket [gate]—the Gate of America. Through this wicket drips the immigration stream—all day long, every two or three seconds an immigrant, with a valise [suitcase] or bundle . . . into a new world."

Some immigrants failed the tests at Ellis Island. They were not allowed to come into the United States. This happened if someone was sick with something others could catch. It also happened if the person was a criminal. Mentally ill people were not allowed into the country, either. People who failed the tests usually were sent back to their homelands.

Most immigrants—four of every five—passed all the tests they were given at Ellis Island. Officials supplied them with a landing card. That was the important paper that allowed them to settle in this country. Then, they took a ferry to the mainland.

About one-third of the immigrants who passed through Ellis Island stayed in the New York City area. The other two-thirds spread out to help populate every region and every corner of the nation.

## The Statue of Liberty

Ellis Island sits in the shadow of another famous American landmark, the Statue of Liberty. Often, the first sign that told immigrants they had reached America was the Statue of Liberty, standing watch over New York Harbor. Here is how one immigrant remembered how some people reacted when the Statue of Liberty came into view: "Many older persons among us, burdened with a thousand memories of what they were leaving behind, had been openly weeping ever since we entered the narrower waters on our final approach toward the unknown. Now somehow steadied, I suppose, by the concreteness of the symbol of America's freedom, they dried their tears."

In 1903, a plaque was added to the base on which the Statue of Liberty stands. On the plaque is a poem by an

American woman named Emma Lazarus. In the poem's last lines, Emma tells what she thinks the statue would say if it could speak to other countries:

*Give me your tired, your poor,*
*Your huddled masses yearning to breathe free,*
*The wretched refuse of your teeming shore,*
*Send these, the homeless, tempest-tost to me,*
*I lift my lamp beside the golden door.*

### Ellis Island Closes Its Doors

By 1924, the number of immigrants coming through Ellis Island's processing center had dwindled. Still, its doors didn't officially close for another 30 years, in 1954. In all, over 15 million immigrants had started their American lives by passing through the gates of Ellis Island.

## Show What You Know

You have read about the welcome that is added to the base of the Statue of Liberty. Imagine that you are helping to design the wire pens that will help Ellis Island process thousands of people a day. On each pen, you decide to put a different phrase or sentence that will help the immigrants feel welcomed to the United States. For example, you might decide to have one sign read, "Welcome, New Friends!" Another sign might read, "Have a Great Life in America!"

Think of something you might write on a welcoming sign on an Ellis Island gate. Then, write it in the space below. *(You may write it in any language you wish.)*

_____

_____

_____

_____

_____

_____

_____

_____

# Henry Ford's Fords

Henry Ford did not build the first car. Still, when people think of the earliest automobiles, they often think of Henry Ford. That is because Henry Ford was the first to build an inexpensive, reliable car.

## Henry Ford's Model T

Henry Ford started his Ford Motor Company in 1903. At first, the cars he made were like the

cars others were making. That is, his cars were expensive.

Henry knew people were very interested in automobiles. He also knew that most people couldn't afford them. So, Henry decided to build a car that almost everyone could buy. He planned to make the car "so low in price that no man making a good salary will be unable to own one."

In 1908, the Ford Motor Company introduced a new car. It was called the Model T, and it was a homely, boxy, rattly thing. It also was inexpensive—it sold for just $825. Americans fell in love with it.

The Model T had other advantages besides price. For example, it was such a simple machine that it was an easy car to fix. It was a sturdy car, too. It could handle the bumpy, rocky roads better than many expensive cars. Plus, attachments for the Model T made it able to pump water and plow fields!

Henry Ford was not satisfied with the $825 price tag for his Model T. He kept thinking up new ways to save money in the making of the car. When he did, he passed those savings on to his customers. By 1916, the price of a Model T had dropped to $345. By 1924, a brand-new Model T Ford cost only $290!

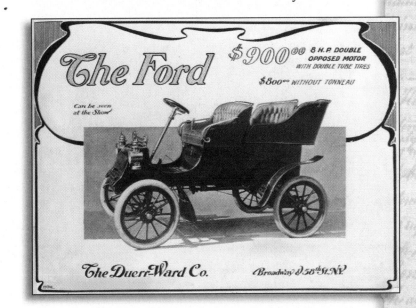

*This picture shows an early advertisement for the Model T Ford.*

Some couldn't understand why Henry Ford kept dropping the price of his Model T. But, Henry had a reason behind his decision. Here's what Henry believed: "Every time I lower the price a dollar, we gain a thousand new buyers."

## Henry's Assembly Lines

Early cars were all crafted by hand. That meant that each car was slightly different from the next. It also meant that each car took a long time to make.

Henry had a different idea. Here is how he planned to make his cars: "The way to make automobiles is to make one automobile like another automobile . . . to make them come through the factory just alike." No longer would Henry's cars be handmade. Instead, they would be put together—each in exactly the same way—with the help of an assembly line.

In an assembly line, workers stay in one place. All day long, a moving belt, called a conveyor belt, brings their work to them. Each worker has one assignment. It might be to screw two pieces together, or it might be to tighten a connection. Then, the work goes on to the next worker, and the next, and the next. Each worker does his or her small, exact part of the job, until all the workers together have created a finished product.

An Assembly Line
of the
Ford Motor Company

*Henry Ford's plan for lines of assembly changed manufacturing all over the world.*

Using an assembly line, Henry could turn out cars much faster than he could when each car was made individually. In just a few years, his factory was churning out a car every 1 1/2 hours. By 1911, his company was making more than $10 million every year.

## What Cars Meant to Americans

It is hard to think of any one thing that has changed life in the United States as much as the car. What had been faraway in the days before the automobile was faraway no more. In pre-car days, most people depended on horses, boats, trolleys, and their own feet to get them where they needed to go. That meant they'd better live near where they worked. And, they'd better shop near where they lived.

Now, with inexpensive cars like Henry's Model T, people could drive a longer distance to work. Cars also let people shop far from home. They could take a weekend vacation miles away and still be back at their jobs on Monday morning. Almost overnight, the United States became a nation on wheels, thanks to Henry Ford and the others who created the car industry.

*This illustration shows a family going for a Sunday drive in 1920.*

245

## Jokes Help Sell Fords

Henry Ford's cars became the subject of jokes for many years. Comedians could be counted on to make fun of Fords. There were even little books of Ford jokes that you could buy on trains—"two hundred good jokes for only fifteen cents"!

Henry didn't mind. In fact, he once said, "The jokes about my car sure helped to popularize it. I hope they never end."

Here are some of the jokes people told about Henry's Fords.

*I hear they're going to magnetize the rear bumper of the Ford.*

*Why would they do that?*

*So it can pick up the parts that fall off.*

---

*Ford is the perfect car for people with children. It even has a rattle for the baby!*

---

*I don't need a speedometer. When my Ford is going five miles per hour, the hood rattles. When it goes 10 miles an hour, my teeth rattle. And when it goes 15 miles per hour, the engine falls out.*

## Show What You Know

Use newspapers, magazines, and flyers that you may cut apart. Then, look through the materials you have collected to find pictures of automobiles. Cut out any pictures you see. Choose five or six pictures you like best. Glue them together onto a white sheet of paper to create a car collage.

Then, look at your car collage, and make a list of reasons why people use cars today. Your list might include reasons such as going to the grocery store or taking children to school.

_____

_____

_____

_____

_____

_____

# THE WRIGHT BROTHERS FLY

Orville and Wilbur Wright were brothers. They grew up in Dayton, Ohio. Wilbur was the older brother. He was born in 1867. Orville was born in 1871.

## Orville and Wilbur Yearn to Fly

Orville and Wilbur Wright both loved to think about and talk about flying. They read everything they could find about the subject. They also built all kinds of gliders, which they tested in a wind tunnel they made themselves.

Orville and Wilbur made and sold bicycles in their own Dayton bicycle shop. Perhaps you thought that people who loved flying so much would become pilots. The Wright brothers did not become pilots, because, at that time, there was no such job.

### The Flyer

*The Flyer was 21 feet, 1 inch long. The frame was made mainly of wood. Cotton cloth was stretched over its wings—one above the other, and each was 40 feet, 4 inches wide. A Wright-made, 12-horsepower engine ran two wooden propellers that sat in front of the wings. There was no real seat for the pilot. Instead, he had to lie in the middle of the bottom wing. You can still see the Flyer today. It is on display at the National Air and Space Museum in Washington, D.C.*

**247**

No one had even been able to keep a machine in the air that weighed more than the air itself. In other words, no one had yet invented an airplane.

## A Historic Day at Kitty Hawk

On December 8, 1903, the *New York Times* announced that no human would fly for another 1,000 years. Nine days later, Wilbur and Orville Wright proved the newspaper wrong.

December 17, 1903, was a windy day near Kitty Hawk, North Carolina. It was often windy on this Atlantic Ocean beach. That is one reason the Wright brothers chose it for their experiment. Up on a little sand knoll called Kill Devil Hill, Orville waited in the Flyer—that was the name of the airplane he and his brother had built at their bicycle shop. Then, he started the Flyer's homemade

*Above: The Wright brothers ran a bicycle shop in Dayton, Ohio.*
*Right: Wilbur and Orville built a successful airplane; many other people had tried but failed to do so.*

*The Wright Brothers made their first flight on December 17, 1903, at Kitty Hawk, North Carolina.*

engine. Here is how Orville described what happened next: "After running the motor a few minutes to heat it up, I released the wire that held the machine to the track, and the machine started forward into the wind."

Wilbur ran alongside, holding onto the wing to make sure it stayed steady. Then, he let go, and up went the Flyer! The plane stayed in the air for 12 seconds. It covered a distance of 120 feet. The Wrights and their plane made three more flights that day. The longest lasted almost one whole minute!

**After Kitty Hawk**

Just before that first historic day of flying, Orville sent a telegram to his father. "Success assured," it said. "Keep quiet." But Orville didn't actually have to tell his father to be quiet about the first flight.

For some reason, no one seemed to notice the event. Only two newspapers in the whole nation even reported what happened at Kitty Hawk.

The Wright brothers didn't mind, though. They wanted to keep working in quiet.

It wasn't until 1908, five years later, that people began to take notice of the Wright brothers and their airplanes. By then, they had improved on their original plane. The new model could stay in the air for over an hour! They began to show the public what their planes could do. They even gave some flying lessons.

Wilbur died of typhoid fever in 1912. Orville lived for another 36 years. During that time, he saw planes become weapons of war. He saw planes reach speeds of over 650 miles per hour and heights of over 30,000 feet. He saw planes cross the oceans. He even saw planes circle the world.

## Show What You Know

Using a separate sheet of paper, follow the order of the folds in the picture to create your own airplane. Follow the directions on this page to create your own paper airplane. Then, fly your airplane three times. Each time you fly your plane, measure the distance it goes. Figure out the average distance the plane traveled. Add up the three measurements. Divide that total by 3. That will tell you how far the plane traveled, on average.

The Wright brothers found that if they changed the wings a bit and changed the tail a little, their plane flew better. Use another sheet of paper to see if you can design a better airplane than the one you just made. You can test your design by flying your plane three times and figuring the average distance. Then, compare this average distance with the average distance your first plane traveled.

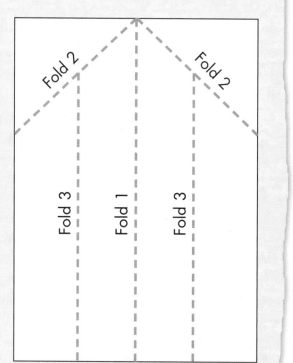

# AMERICA BUILDS THE PANAMA CANAL

Panama is one of Central America's smaller countries. Yet, in the eyes of the world, Panama is big in importance. That is because of a human-dug waterway that crosses the country. That waterway is called the Panama Canal. It connects the Atlantic Ocean to the Pacific Ocean.

Even as early as 1534, Spaniards thought about how useful a canal connecting the two oceans could be. They even explored the possibility of cutting a canal across Panama. In the end, though, the Spanish king said no to the idea, because his religious advisors believed it went against the plans of God.

## Traveling the Panama Canal

*Shipping companies pay a toll to use the Panama Canal. The toll charged is based on the weight of the ship. The toll can run thousands of dollars. However, the time and distance the Panama Canal cuts off can save a shipping company $50,000 or more! So, the cost of the toll is worth it.*

*A boat travels through the Panama Canal.*

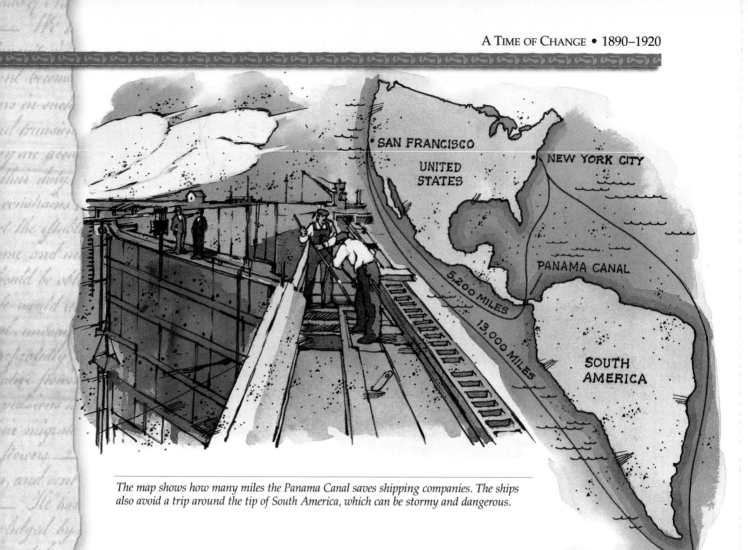

*The map shows how many miles the Panama Canal saves shipping companies. The ships also avoid a trip around the tip of South America, which can be stormy and dangerous.*

## The French Begin a Canal

In 1879, the French decided to build a canal in Panama. French builder Ferdinand de Lesseps had already built the Suez Canal through Egypt. That canal connects the Mediterranean Sea to the Red Sea and cuts the distance between England and India by 6,000 miles. Ferdinand was sure he could make the almost impossible happen in Panama as well.

By 1885, Ferdinand and his canal builders were in trouble. They were behind schedule, and they were over budget. One reason for the problems was that mudslides often erased a month of work in a moment. Plus, no one could figure out how to control the Chagres River. The Chagres wandered back and forth across the path of the proposed canal. It frequently flooded when tropical rains swelled its waters, increasing the chance of mudslides.

Death was another reason the French were failing. Historians think that over 20,000 workers died during France's attempt to build the canal. In fact, the death rate was so high that many workers wrote their wills before they left for Panama. Some even brought their own coffins with them, just in case. Most who died, died of yellow fever or malaria. Both of these diseases are common in tropical lands. At the time, no one knew what caused them, and no one knew a cure. By 1889, the French admitted that the jungle had defeated them. They stopped building the canal.

## The U.S. Decides to Build a Canal

After the Spanish-American War ended, the United States had territories in both the Atlantic and the Pacific oceans. However, traveling from ocean to ocean could take over two months. Even ships sailing from New York to San Francisco had to travel a distance of 13,000 miles. The ships had to sail all the way south around the tip of South America. These great distances meant that, to protect its territories, the United States would have to keep two navies, one in each ocean. Or, it would need to shorten the distance between the Atlantic and the Pacific oceans. The government decided to try to shorten the distance. It would take over building a canal in Panama.

## The U.S. Conquers Two Diseases

Two things helped the United States succeed where France had failed. One was its victory over yellow fever and malaria. The other was learning how to use the Chagres River.

Scientists discovered that both yellow fever and malaria are carried by certain kinds of mosquitoes. That meant that, for example, when a mosquito infected with yellow fever bites a new victim, it can leave behind in the wound yellow fever germs. Then, the new victim comes down with yellow fever, too.

Panama was paradise for mosquitoes. In fact, one visitor to the building site said he saw "mosquitoes so thick I have seen them put out a lighted candle with their burnt bodies."

Armed with this new knowledge about the connection between sickness and mosquitoes, Colonel William Gorgas, who was a doctor, proceeded to wipe out the places along the canal route where mosquitoes bred, or laid their eggs. This included marshes and swamps and any place where water collected—all common in tropical countries like Panama.

Together, the colonel and his men built new sewer systems and water systems. They drained one million square yards of swamp. They cut back 16 million square yards of brush a year and cut down 30 million square yards of grass. Also, they regularly emptied one million garbage cans. In addition, Colonel Gorgas made the men sleep under mosquito netting and boil drinking water to kill anything living in it.

All this work caused the death rate to drop dramatically. Still, 5,600 men died in the ten years it took for the United States to finish the Panama Canal.

## The U.S. Uses the Chagres River

Another reason the United States succeeded in finishing the Panama Canal was because the engineers decided not to fight the Chagres River, as the French had done. Instead, they used the raging waters of the Chagres to help run the canal.

The Panama Canal has three sets of locks. A lock is a chamber that has waterproof gates that can be opened or closed. A ship heading down the Panama Canal is guided into a lock. The gates shut behind the ship. Then, thousands of gallons of water pour into the lock. The water level rises and, with it, the ship rises. Then, the next set of

*This boat sits in a lock chamber of the Panama Canal.*

gates opens, and the ship sails out at this higher water level. The lock is kind of a stairstep to help ships cross from higher to lower areas or from lower to higher areas.

You might wonder where the thousands of gallons of water come from to fill the locks of the Panama Canal. They come from the Chagres River. In fact, engineers dammed the river and created a lake that stores water to use in case the river runs low. So,

without the Chagres River, there would be no water to feed the locks of the Panama Canal.

The United States completed the Panama Canal in 1914, at a cost of over $300 million. The canal shortened the distance by ship between New York and San Francisco to about 5,200 miles— a reduction of almost 8,000 miles. Even today, the Panama Canal is still considered one of the greatest engineering feats of all time.

## Show What You Know

Imagine you are charged with helping the government decide where to build a canal between the Atlantic and the Pacific oceans. Also imagine that Panama has said no to a canal across its land.

Study this map of Central America. Then, draw on the map the canal route you would suggest to the government. Make a list of the reasons for your suggestion of where to locate a canal.

# WOMEN GET THE RIGHT TO VOTE

When the 1900s began, women in the United States had few legal rights. A woman couldn't sue anyone. She couldn't write a will. Her children, her property, and any money she made belonged to her husband. And, she couldn't vote. That meant she couldn't change the laws that limited her rights. The only other Americans who couldn't vote at that time were criminals, the mentally ill, and the mentally challenged.

## The Seneca Falls Convention

In 1848, a convention was held in Seneca Falls, New York. This was the first time there had ever been a convention to talk about women's rights. One of the things that came out of that convention was a new document. It was called the Declaration of Sentiments. It started very much like the Declaration of Independence. The difference was that this version included women. It said, "We hold these truths to be self-evident: that all men and women are created equal. . . ."

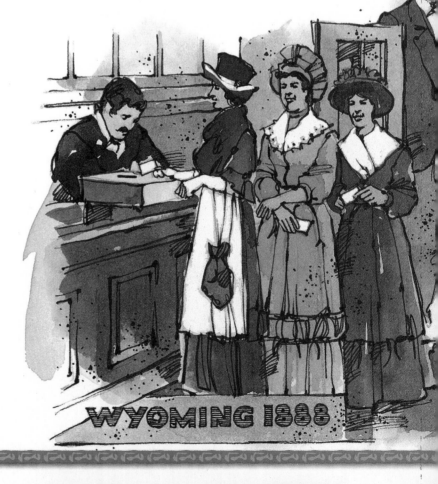

WYOMING 1888

## Western Women Get to Vote

The western states gave women suffrage, or the right to vote, earlier than the eastern states. Perhaps that was because it was still fresh in voters' minds how pioneer women had worked beside the men to help settle the western half of the country.

It also was fresh in the minds of western women. Men and women had been equal partners as they settled the Great Plains and the West. It took the work of both husband and wife to keep a family fed and clothed.

One woman explained that she expected nothing less than equality when she became a pioneer bride. "I was a woman now," she said, "and capable of being the other half of the head of the family. His [her husband's] word and my word would have equal strength."

Women got to vote in Wyoming in 1869. Wyoming was still a territory then. Twenty years later, Wyoming was ready to become a state. However, some did not want to let Wyoming's women vote once Wyoming was part of the United States. Here is what Wyoming's government had to say about that: "We will remain out of the Union 100 years rather than come in without the women."

The next year, Wyoming—including its women voters—became the Union's 44th state.

## The Nineteenth Amendment

Many in the nation did not feel the same way about women voting as the people in Wyoming did. For example, one magazine of the time said that if women could vote, the voting process would take two weeks instead of one day. This is because each woman would have "to stop and powder her nose, and fix her hair, and adjust her belt, and look through her handbag, and wonder who the occupant of the next booth is voting for. . . ."

Even before the United States was founded, there had been supporters for the rights of American women, including the right to vote. In 1776, Abigail Adams wrote a letter to her husband, John. At the time, John was in Philadelphia helping to form the new country. He later became our second president. In her letter, Abigail warned that if the Founding Fathers ignored women's rights, "we are determined to foment [stir up] a rebellion, and will not hold ourselves bound to obey the laws in which we have no voice or representation."

Women knew that the only way to assure their right to vote was to have an amendment added to the Constitution. An amendment is a way to change the Constitution. In fact, the Fifteenth Amendment had changed the Constitution to give the right to vote to African Americans, but only to the men.

Starting in 1848, Congress turned down a women's suffrage amendment every year for 40 years. Then, when it was introduced for the 41st time, it passed. The amendment was sent to the states for their approval. Three-fourths of all states must approve an amendment before it can become part of the Constitution.

The people who supported women's suffrage did everything a democracy allows them to do to influence the thoughts of other American citizens. They marched. They gave speeches. They picketed the White House. They protested at state capitals all over the country. And, they talked to their government representatives.

All their work paid off. The Nineteenth Amendment passed just in time to let women vote in the 1920 presidential election.

Here is what the Nineteenth Amendment promises: "The right of citizens of the United States to vote shall not be denied or abridged by the United States or by any State on account of sex."

## Show What You Know

The map below shows the year in which each state gave women the right to vote. The states in green did not have women's suffrage until 1920 when it became law in the United State.

Use crayons or colored pencils to color each box in the key a different color. Next, color in the corresponding states the same color, according to their dates.

Now, study your completed map. Tell how the map either supports or does not support this statement: "The western states gave women the right to vote earlier than the eastern states."

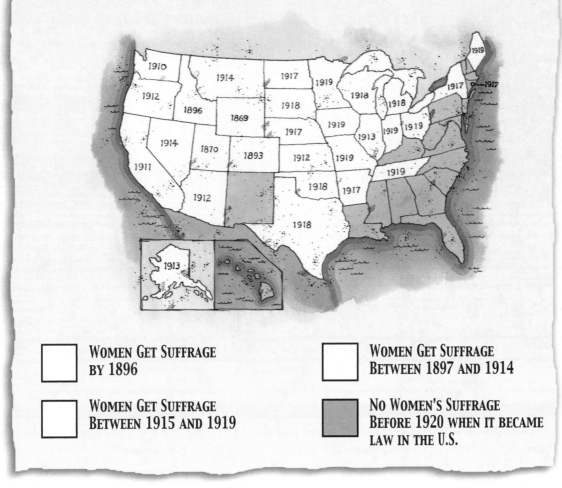

☐ WOMEN GET SUFFRAGE BY 1896

☐ WOMEN GET SUFFRAGE BETWEEN 1915 AND 1919

☐ WOMEN GET SUFFRAGE BETWEEN 1897 AND 1914

■ NO WOMEN'S SUFFRAGE BEFORE 1920 WHEN IT BECAME LAW IN THE U.S.

UNIT 9 1914–1945

# A TIME OF TROUBLES

Troubles visited the United States and its people during the first half of the 1900s. In those 50 years, two wars claimed the lives of Americans and others around the world. Between the wars, the United States and other nations were plunged into a terrible economic depression. Through these difficulties, though, Americans faced the challenges and made this country a leading world power.

TIME LINE

**1917:** The United States enters World War I.

**1918:** World War I ends.

**1927:** Charles Lindbergh flies across the Atlantic Ocean.

**1929:** The stock market crashes.

**1939:** World War II begins in Europe.

**1941:** The United States enters World War II.

**1945:** World War II ends.

**1914:** World War I begins in Europe.

| 1910 | 1915 | 1920 | 1925 | 1930 | 1935 | 1940 | 1945 | 1950 | 1955 |

# WORLD WAR I: A WAR OF AIRPLANES AND U-BOATS

World War I was a war like no other war that had come before. It was so different because of technology. New weapons such as machine guns, tanks, and poison gas made this war far more deadly. In fact, almost 10 million people died before the "Great War" finally ended.

## Airplanes Become Weapons

World War I was the first war fought on the land, in the sea, and in the air. The Wright brothers had flown their first airplane only eleven years before the war began. So, airplanes were still a very new invention.

### The Nation Drafts an Army

When the United States entered World War I, it had only about 208,000 soldiers. It needed millions more. So, it decided to have a draft to determine who would go to war.

There were 4,500 local draft centers. Every man between the ages of 21 and 30 was told to go to his local draft center and was given a number.

The highest the numbers went at any of the draft centers was 10,500. So, 10,500 tiny capsules, each with one number in it, were all put into a bowl. Every man with that number had to report for service. By the end of the war 3 million men had been drafted.

The first wartime airplanes were used to watch what the enemy was doing. If a pilot came upon an enemy plane, he leaned out of his seat and used his handgun to try to shoot his enemy out of the sky.

Then, in 1915, the Germans figured out how to attach a machine gun to a plane. This was harder than it sounds, because the machine gun's firing had to be timed so the bullets didn't hit the plane's propellers as they spun around. Now, planes had become deadly weapons. Then, someone figured out how to tie bombs under a plane's wings, and airplanes became deadlier still.

## U-Boats Terrorize the Seas

A submarine is a ship that can travel under water. You can tell its meaning from the word itself—*sub* means "under," and *marine* means "water."

The submarine was not a new invention for World War I. During the Civil War, a submarine first sank an enemy ship; the Confederate submarine *Hunley* sank the Union ship *Housatonic*. However, it was during World War I that the Germans showed how deadly a submarine could be. In fact, their use of submarines, or U-boats as they called them, helped draw the United States into the war.

Great Britain is an island nation off the northwestern coast of mainland Europe. Much of what it needs is shipped across the oceans from other countries. During World War I, Germany tried to starve Great Britain into surrender. Germany sent its U-boats to the waters off England, the largest part of Great Britain. Then, Germany announced it would sink any ship that tried to bring supplies to the British.

The U-boats did not target only supply ships. They attacked all kinds of ships. One of these was a passenger ship called the *Lusitania*. The date was May 7, 1915. The *Lusitania* had almost completed its voyage from New York to Liverpool, England, when a torpedo from a German U-boat tore through its hull. The ship sank in 18 minutes. Altogether, 1,198 men, women, and children died when the Lusitania went down. Included in that terrible total were 128 Americans.

The people of the United States were enraged at the Lusitania's sinking. The United States might have entered the war then, but Germany agreed to stop torpedoing innocent ships.

Two years later, in 1917, Germany changed its mind. It declared that, once again, its U-boats would sink anything they saw. Germany proved it meant what it said when it blasted several U.S. cargo ships out of the water.

Germany's attempt to control the seas with its U-boats was one important reason the United States decided to enter World War I. The U-boats proved, as ex-President Teddy Roosevelt said, that "There is no question about going to war. Germany is already at war with us." In fact, President Woodrow Wilson specifically mentioned U-boats when he asked Congress to declare war on Germany. "The present German submarine warfare is a warfare against mankind," he said. "It is a war against all nations." On April 6, 1917, Congress agreed with President Wilson. The United States officially entered World War I.

## Show What You Know

This poster was printed by the U.S. government to encourage men to join the Army. The poster was so popular that it was used even after the war ended.

Use a blank sheet of paper or piece of poster board to create a poster that you think will encourage men and women to enlist in the Army today.

*This Uncle Sam poster was used to recruit young men for the U.S. Army during World War II.*

# CHARLES LINDBERGH CROSSES THE ATLANTIC

Charles Lindbergh, American aviation pioneer, once predicted the future of airplanes in this country. "Undoubtedly in a few years," he said, "the United States will be covered with a network of passenger, mail, and express lines." Not only was Charles Lindbergh correct, he also helped make it happen.

## Lindbergh Flies to France

On May 20, 1927, at 7:52 A.M., Charles Lindbergh and his one-winged, one-engine *Spirit of St. Louis* took off from Roosevelt Field, in New York. His destination was Paris, France. If he made it, he would become the first person to fly across the Atlantic Ocean alone. He also would win a $25,000 prize. If he failed, however, he knew he could die.

All that day, all that night, and all the next day, people the world over waited to hear news of Charles's historic flight. They heard how his plane, heavy with fuel, barely cleared a telephone wire as it took off.

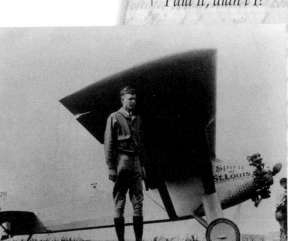

*Charles Lindbergh stands beside his plane, the Spirit of St. Louis.*

### Coast to Coast

In 1911, newspaper owner William Randolph Hearst offered $50,000 to the first person who could fly across the United States in 30 days or less. Cal Rodgers, a flight student of Orville Wright, entered the contest.

Cal crashed many times, had mechanical failures, and was even attacked by eagles. Since the flight took him 49 days, Cal lost the contest. But he didn't care about losing the money. He had shown that transcontinental flight—flight across the country—was possible. He knew that was the important thing. He said, "What matters is, I did it, didn't I?"

They heard that he'd been spotted flying low over the tree tops at Cape Cod. They knew he and the *Spirit of St. Louis* had left the safety of the continent behind for the skies above the Atlantic Ocean.

For 10 hours, Charles flew. Then, for another 10 hours. Then, for another 10. Finally, at 10:21 P.M., he brought the *Spirit of St. Louis* in for a landing at Le Bourget airfield, near Paris. Charles had been flying for 33 hours and 30 minutes.

## Lindbergh Becomes a Hero

Charles Lindbergh did not know that the world had been following his adventure. His first clue probably came when he looked down on the landing field and saw it was alive with perhaps 100,000 French citizens. They had come to celebrate his victory with him. As he climbed out of his plane, they surged toward him. Then, shouting and cheering, they picked Charles up above their heads and carried him across the field. The shy, handsome Charles Lindbergh had become an instant hero.

Charles was a hero at home, too. When he came back to the United States, President Calvin Coolidge gave him a medal. New Yorkers showered him with 1,800 tons of confetti during a parade

through that city's streets. He received 55,000 telegrams of congratulations. A new dance was named after him—the Lindy Hop. A new song, called "Lucky Lindy," told of his flying feat. "Just like a child he simply smiled/While we were wild with fear," went two of the lines.

## Lindbergh Makes the Headlines Again

There were two more times in his life when Charles Lindbergh made the front-page news. The first time, it was personal. The second time was for political reasons.

*Lindbergh reached Paris after a 33 1/2-hour flight.*

After Charles's historic flight, he met and married Anne Morrow. Anne was the daughter of the United States' ambassador to Mexico. Charles and Anne had a son and named him Charles Augustus Lindbergh, Jr.

On March 1, 1932, someone broke into the Lindbergh's New Jersey home and kidnapped baby Charles. About ten weeks later, the baby's body was found just a few miles from the Lindbergh house. A carpenter named Bruno Hauptmann eventually was found guilty of the crime.

The story of the Lindbergh kidnapping caught the attention of America. Reporters and photographers hounded the family while people searched for the baby, while police searched for the kidnapper, and while Bruno Hauptmann was on trial. Finally, after three years of hounding, the Lindberghs were forced to move to Europe to escape all the attention.

*Lindbergh was honored with a parade in New York City.*

Charles and his family came back to the United States in 1939. It was two years after that that Charles was in the news again.

By then, World War II had begun. European nations were at war with each other. Charles felt the United States should stay out of the war. He joined an organization called the America First Committee. Everyone in the Committee believed as Charles did.

Many others in the country, though, thought Charles was wrong. They felt the United States needed to enter the war. To some of them, Charles's speeches and activities seemed un-American.

Later, after the United States had entered the war, Charles changed his mind. He tried to enlist, but the government wouldn't let him. Instead, he served as a civilian advisor for both the Army and the Navy.

## Show What You Know

Charles Lindbergh's historic flight started at an airfield in Long Island, New York. He continued north to Newfoundland, where he turned east over the Atlantic Ocean. He flew to Ireland, then across England and the English Channel, and on to Paris, France.

Reread the description above of the route Charles Lindbergh followed across the Atlantic Ocean. As you read, plot the route on this map. When you have finished, use a ruler and the map scale to figure out the distance Charles Lindbergh traveled on this trip. Round your answer to the nearest 100.

### CHARLES TRAVELED ABOUT _____ MILES.

# THE GREAT DEPRESSION

In every economy, there are good times and there are bad times. A good time is sometimes called a boom. A bad time is sometimes called a depression.

The 1920s seemed like a boom time. But, times were not booming for everyone. New inventions helped increase the amount farmers could produce. However, farmers produced so much, that the prices of some crops dropped. This meant that, although farmers produced more, they often made less money. So, many farmers did not share in the boom of the 1920s.

During the 1920s, some people made a lot of money, but most did not. Those who wanted to buy things began buying on credit. That is, they gave some money at the time they made the purchase. Then, every month, they made a payment until the item was paid for.

## Hunger in a Land of Plenty

One odd thing about the Great Depression was that, although many people were hungry, there was plenty of food in the nation. However, farmers were paid so little money for their crops that it wasn't worth the cost of transporting the crops to market. At one point, the price of corn was less than the price of coal. So, at least one county burned corn instead of coal to heat its courthouse.

People also began spending a lot of money to buy stocks. A stock is a share in the ownership of a company. People watched as stock prices doubled during the 1920s. They wanted a share of that wealth, too. For the same reason, many banks and businesses also bought stocks during this time.

### The Stock Market Crashes

In October 1929, stock prices began to drop. They dropped again and again. On October 24, 13 million shares of stock were sold. On October 29, 16 million shares changed hands. Many, many people wanted to sell their stocks, but few wanted to buy. This caused the prices of stocks to drop even

more. People were forced to sell their stocks for much less than the original prices. The people, businesses, and banks with money invested in the stock market lost a fortune that October.

In addition, businesses now found that no one had money to buy their products. To stay in business, they often had to fire workers. Other businesses had to close. By 1933, almost one of every four

American workers had no job. Many who were still employed had to take pay cuts or work fewer hours.

Banks, too, were in deep trouble. Many people who had borrowed money from the banks now couldn't pay back that money. In the next few years, thousands of banks were forced to close their doors. People who had accounts in those banks lost all their savings.

Usually, depressions last for a year or two. The depression that began in 1929 lasted for over a decade. In fact, it lasted so long and was so bad that to this day, it is known as the "Great Depression."

During the Great Depression, thousands of families lost their homes, because they couldn't make their mortgage payments. All over the country, shantytowns sprang up where people built shelters from flattened tin cans and cardboard or car bodies or anything else they could find. Many called these shack cities "Hoovervilles," because they felt that President Herbert Hoover was partly to blame for their condition.

People who didn't have jobs found there were no jobs to be had. Some became shoe shiners. Others sold apples on city streets. Still they starved. America was full of scenes such as the one a woman witnessed in a Chicago alley: "One vivid, gruesome moment of those dark days we shall never forget," she said. "We saw a crowd of some fifty men fighting over a barrel of garbage outside the back door of a restaurant. American citizens fighting for scraps of food like animals!"

*Men line up for free soup during the Great Depression.*

271

## The President Responds

Herbert Hoover was president during this time. He didn't believe the national government should help the people. He argued that in times like these, it was the responsibility of individuals to look after their neighbors. What individuals couldn't do, the local or state governments should do. The national government—at least as long as Herbert Hoover was president—would give aid only as a "last resort." According to the president, that time of "last resort" didn't come during his presidency. As a result, the national government offered little aid to the nation's overwhelmed states, cities, and citizens.

## A Shameful Story

One of the darkest days of the Great Depression happened in Washington, D.C., near the Capitol Building, where Congress meets. In the summer of 1932, 15,000 World War I veterans straggled into Washington. They were part of perhaps 2 million men who had lost almost everything since the depression began.

As veterans of the war, they were holders of bonus certificates. These certificates were to mature, or reach their full worth, in 1945. The veterans hoped to talk Congress into letting the certificates mature in 1932.

Congress voted not to advance the bonus money. So, most of the veterans went back to their home states. About 2,000, though, stayed in Washington. Many of these men had no homes they could return to. They set up places to live in a shantytown they built near the Capitol Building.

*U.S. troops force the Bonus Army to disperse and leave its shantytown near the Capitol Building in Washington, D.C.*

President Hoover worried that the 2,000 veterans in the nearby shantytown might become violent. Plus, their presence was embarrassing to him. So, he told the U.S. Army to make the veterans leave the area.

On July 28, 1932, Chief of Staff Douglas MacArthur ordered the Army to scatter the veterans. Troops armed with tear gas, tanks, guns, and bayonets forced out the desperate, hopeless men, women, and children of the "Bonus Army." Then, the Army burned the shacks of their shantytown.

Later, General MacArthur defended his actions. He said that the veterans were a bunch of "riotous elements." Regardless of what he said, many Americans were furious with his and President Hoover's treatment of people who had faithfully served their country during World War I. The *Washington News* spoke for many when it said, "What a pitiful spectacle is that of the great American Government, mightiest in the world, chasing unarmed men, women and children with Army tanks. . . . If the army must be called out to make war on unarmed citizens, this is no longer America."

Many Americans had become frustrated with President Hoover's failure to end the depression. Many, too, were horrified by his treatment of the veterans in Washington. A cry went out for new leadership for these difficult times.

## Show What You Know

Every day, newspapers list the prices of different stocks. The stock report also tells whether the price went up or down since the day before. Plus, the stock report tells the highest and lowest prices for which the stock has sold in the past year.

HIGHEST/LOWEST PRICES IN THE LAST 52 WEEKS

FINAL PRICE AND CHANGE FROM THE DAY BEFORE

52-week

| High | Low | Stock | Div | Last | Change |
|------|------|-----------|-----|-------|--------|
| 28.88 | 14.00 | Company A | .24 | 18.88 | –.25 |

ANNUAL PROFIT

Study this stock report for Company A. Then, circle the answer to each question.

1. According to the stock report, how much money would you need to buy a share of Company A's stock?

   a. $18.88
   b. $28.88
   c. $14.00

2. Did Company A's stock go up or down in value since one day ago?

   a. up
   b. down

3. How does today's price for Company A's stock compare with the highest and lowest prices of the past year?

   a. Today's price is nearer the highest price for the year.
   b. Today's price is nearer the lowest price for the year.
   c. Today's price is the same as the price of the stock a year ago.

# FRANKLIN ROOSEVELT'S NEW DEAL

This photo shows Franklin Delano Roosevelt, the 32nd president of the United States.

In 1932, it was again time for U.S. citizens to elect a president. The Republicans renominated Herbert Hoover, who had been president since the Great Depression began. The Democrats nominated Franklin Delano Roosevelt, the governor of New York.

Franklin Roosevelt felt that the national government had to start helping Americans who were hurt by the depression. He believed that "To . . . unfortunate citizens, aid must be extended by the government—not as a matter of charity but as a matter of social duty." He promised that if he were elected president, he would help end the depression with "a new deal for the American people."

The American people believed Franklin's promise of a "New Deal." They proved it by electing him president in 1932.

## The New Deal: New Agencies, New Laws

March 4, 1933, was a chilly, somber day. It also was the day that Franklin Delano Roosevelt became president of the United States. First, he took the oath of office that every president takes. Then, he made his first speech as president.

### FDR Gets Polio

In 1921, when Franklin Roosevelt was 39 years old, he contracted polio. Polio is a disease that can paralyze or even kill its victims. Today, there is a vaccine that can keep you from contracting polio. But, the vaccine didn't exist then. The disease attacked Franklin's legs. From then on, he had to use braces or a wheelchair to get around.

Some tried to urge Franklin to give up his hopes for a life in politics. But, Franklin would not give up. Eleven years after polio had left him paralyzed, Franklin Delano Roosevelt became the president of the United States.

He said, "This great Nation will endure as it has endured, will revive [come back to life] and will prosper. So, first of all, let me assert my firm belief that the only thing we have to fear is fear itself." He also told the American people "this is no unsolvable problem if we face it wisely and courageously."

President Roosevelt did not just talk about change. He acted, too. One of the first things he did was set up a series of new agencies. Each of these agencies helped to put unemployed Americans back to work.

One of the agencies President Roosevelt set up was The Works Progress Administration, the WPA. The WPA put the unemployed to work building and repairing bridges, roads, and public buildings; writing guidebooks; and creating murals. The Civilian Conservation Corps, the CCC, was another important agency. It put young, unmarried men to work planting trees, building forest trails, and doing other things that conserved the natural environment. Then, there was the National Youth Administration, the NYA. It offered part-time work for students so they would stay in school.

As you can see, many of the New Deal agencies came to be known by their initials. There were so many that President Roosevelt's government was sometimes called a "government by alphabet." Even the president himself became known as FDR.

Under President Roosevelt, the government also passed a series of laws to help the citizens especially hurt by the depression. For example, to help farmers keep their farms, the Agricultural Adjustment Act set prices on some farm products. To help homeowners keep their homes, the Home Owners Loan Act helped people pay their mortgages.

*Roosevelt's New Deal agencies put many Americans back to work so that they could support their families.*

The Social Security Act of 1935 was another very important new law. It provided the elderly with a monthly pension, or retirement income. It also gave money to the states to help them care for the homeless, the visually handicapped, and other needy Americans.

## What the New Deal Did

The New Deal did not end unemployment in the country. Neither did it bring the depression to its knees. However, the New Deal did help Americans believe in America again. It showed that the government has a responsibility to help its citizens when its citizens need help.

## Show What You Know

Artists were among the people that the Works Progress Administration employed. Some of the art they created, like the art on this page, showed scenes from everyday life in America.

Imagine you have been asked to draw a mural that shows something about everyday life in America today. Decide what you would like to draw. Then, use a big sheet of drawing paper to draw the scene you chose. On another sheet of paper, write a few sentences telling about the scene you drew.

*This mural was painted by an artist hired by the Works Progress Administration.*

# Dust Bowl Children Build a School

Grass grows plentifully on the southern Great Plains. Its long, tangled roots help hold the soil in place when the winds blow. By the 1930s, though, the grass was gone. It had been plowed under by farmers, who planted wheat instead. The wheat's roots didn't hold the soil. Allowing too many farm animals to graze was another reason that the grass was destroyed.

It had been dry in the southern Great Plains. For four years, little rain had fallen. The soil on the ground was loose and crumbly, just waiting for a strong wind to blow it away.

*This photograph shows a typical dust storm on the Great Plains during the 1930s.*

## A Song About Okie Strength

*Many Okies were proud that they had lived through the terrible times of the 1930s. One song they used to sing starts by telling how they did it:*

It takes a little courage,

And a little self-control,

And a grim determination,

If you want to reach the goal,

It takes a deal of striving,

And a firm and stern-set chin,

No matter what the battle,

If you really want to win.

The winds started in 1935. Forty times that year, windstorms blew across the southern Great Plains. Each time, the winds sucked up tons and tons of loose topsoil and just swept it away. Because of the blowing, dusty winds, the entire region became known as the Dust Bowl.

For the next three years, the dust-filled winds blew and blew. They were so terrible that some children walked backwards to school to keep the dust from stinging their faces. At night, families often slept with washcloths over their faces to make sure they didn't breathe in dust. In the mornings, children had to dig out buried chickens and clean out the dust-clogged noses of the family's cattle.

All over the Dust Bowl, crops failed. That meant farmers couldn't pay back the money banks had loaned them. So, they lost their farms. To make sure a farmer moved away from his farm, a bank sometimes sent a tractor to push over the farmer's house. The farmers called this being "tractored out."

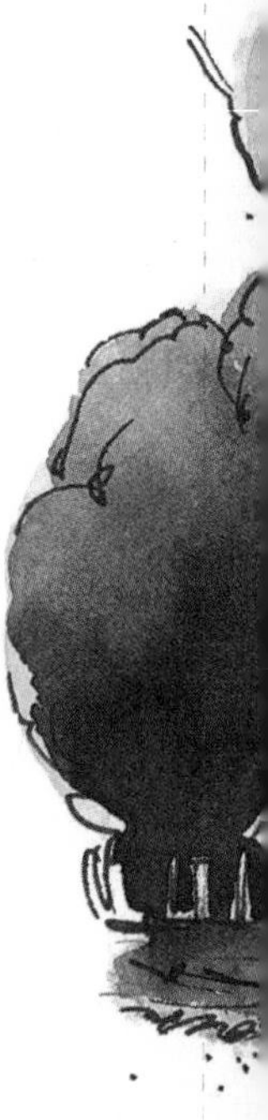

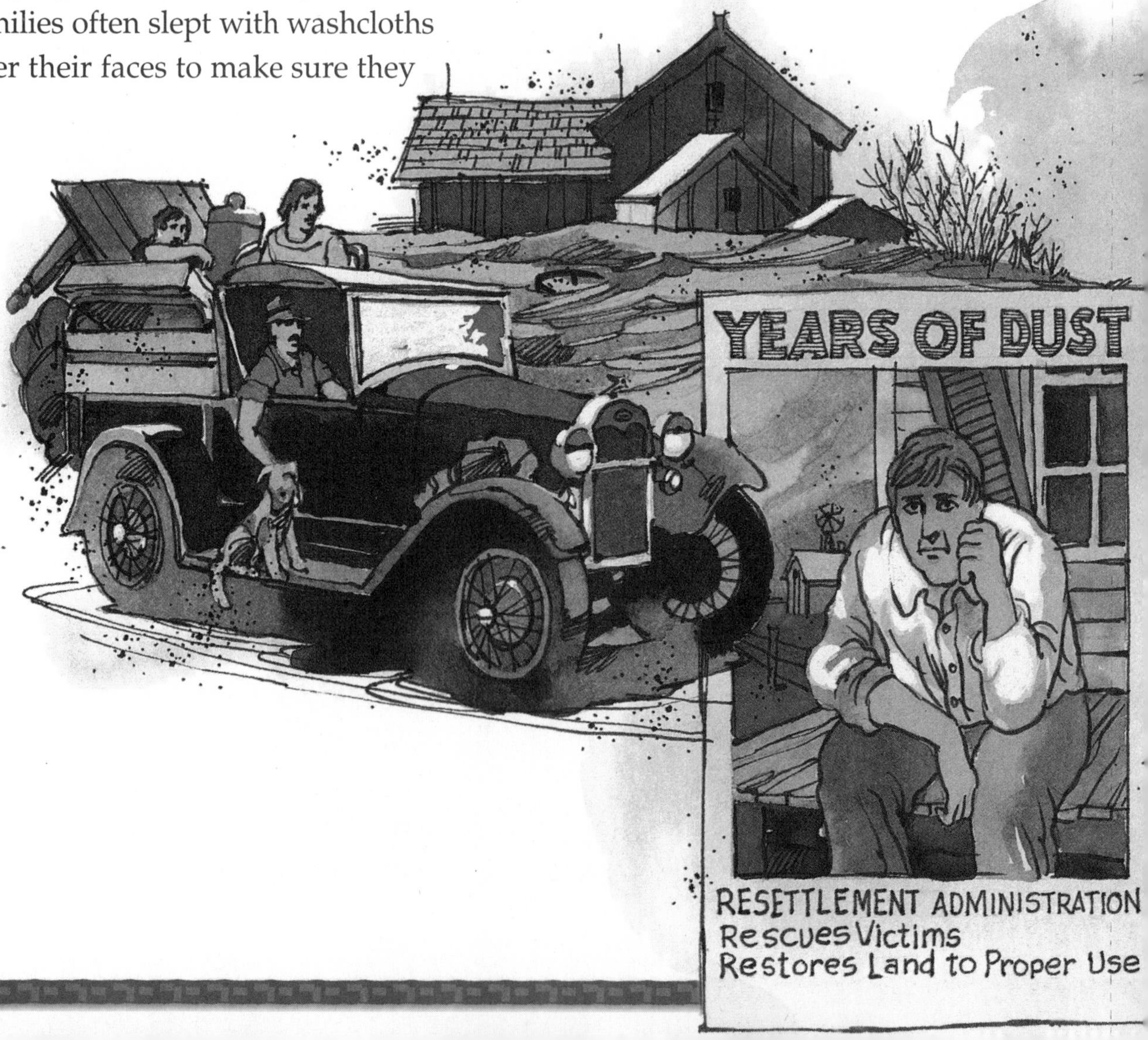

YEARS OF DUST

RESETTLEMENT ADMINISTRATION
Rescues Victims
Restores Land to Proper Use

## Okies Try for a New Life in California

Thousands of families packed up everything their cars or trucks could hold or everything they had left. So many were from dust-scoured Oklahoma that "Okies" became a kind of nickname, whether they were from Oklahoma, Colorado, Kansas, Texas, or New Mexico. These Okies went looking for new work and a new life.

Many Okies headed toward California. They heard there were still jobs there. Some California growers had actually advertised for workers to come to California. However, when the Okies got to California, they found there were no jobs. Signs announcing "NO JOBS HERE" and "10 MEN FOR EVERY JOB" were posted outside many California towns. The Okies found that the hunger, homelessness, and joblessness that had driven them from the Great Plains were waiting for them in California, too.

American author John Steinbeck wrote a book about the life of Okies in California. He called it *The Grapes of Wrath*. The book quickly became a bestseller, and it showed the rest of America the living conditions of the Okies. Before that, John Steinbeck wrote a pamphlet about a Dust Bowl refugee's first months in California. He wrote, "There is no work. First the gasoline gives out. And without gasoline, a man cannot go to a job if he could get one. Then the food goes.

*The green shading on the map shows the area of the Dust Bowl.*

And then it rains, with insufficient [not enough] food, the children develop colds because the ground in the tents is wet. I talked to a man last week who lost two children in ten days with pneumonia. His face was hard and fierce and he didn't talk much."

The Okies faced another problem in California, too. That was the problem of prejudice. Many Californians didn't like the Okies. They felt the Okies wanted to take their jobs. Also, Californians had to pay to educate Okie children in their schools and treat them in their hospitals. Some stores posted signs that said, "No Okies Allowed." Cruel "Okie jokes" became popular.

For many Okie children, school was probably the worst part of the day. Some teachers made Okie children sit on the floor in the back of the room. Plus, Okie students often were behind the others in their school work, because they had been out of school during the months it took the family to reach California.

## A School at Weedpatch Camp

To help the homeless Okies, the national government set up several camps around southern California.

In these camps, an Okie family could stay in a cabin for $1 a week, if they had it. Okie children could have a good breakfast for a penny a day.

One of the camps was called the Arvin Federal Camp. However, because it was on Weedpatch Highway and near the town of Weedpatch, it became known as Weedpatch Camp.

One day the children of Weedpatch Camp had a visitor. His name was Leo Hart. He was the new head of schools for their county. Leo knew that the schools didn't want to teach the children of Weedpatch Camp. He also knew that the children were "ordinary kids, with the same hopes and dreams the rest of us have."

Leo decided to give Weedpatch Camp its own school. He knew that Californians wouldn't want to pay for a new building. So, he and eight teachers he hired taught the children how to build their own school. The children learned plumbing and carpentry. They learned how to plaster a wall and provide a room with electric lights. While they learned, they built.

The children were proud to build something for themselves.

Even their parents helped. Two days after they started, the school had running water. Two months later, there were four brick classrooms. In the months that followed, the children built bookshelves and a chemistry lab. They built their own chairs and desks. They started a garden to help supply food for their families. They also built a cafeteria, where food from their own garden was served.

Classes started long before the school was finished. In fact, for a long time, the students were divided into two groups. In the morning, one group took classes while the other group worked on the school. After lunch, the groups switched. That way, everybody got an education, and everybody helped to build the school.

## The New School and Neighbors

Interestingly, some of Weedpatch Camp's California neighbors began to donate items for the school. Food and clothing came. So did farm equipment and cans of paint and bricks.

Another interesting thing happened. Weedpatch School became known for the excellent education it offered its students. Suddenly, Californians began asking whether their children could go to Weedpatch School, too.

According to the government, Weedpatch School was built as an emergency school. Its real name was the Arvin Federal Emergency School. The rules said that emergency schools could stay emergency schools only for five years. So, the Arvin Federal Emergency School—the school that gave students confidence and hope in addition to an education—became part of the local school district.

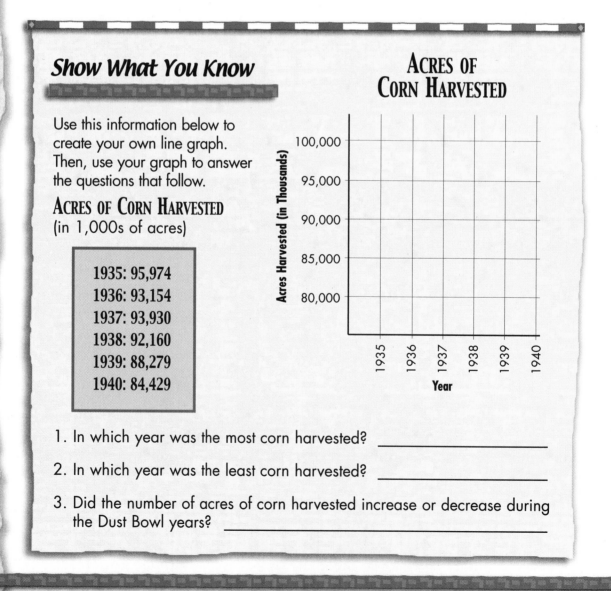

## Show What You Know

Use this information below to create your own line graph. Then, use your graph to answer the questions that follow.

### ACRES OF CORN HARVESTED
(in 1,000s of acres)

1935: 95,974
1936: 93,154
1937: 93,930
1938: 92,160
1939: 88,279
1940: 84,429

### ACRES OF CORN HARVESTED

Acres Harvested (in Thousands)

100,000
95,000
90,000
85,000
80,000

1935  1936  1937  1938  1939  1940

Year

1. In which year was the most corn harvested? _____

2. In which year was the least corn harvested? _____

3. Did the number of acres of corn harvested increase or decrease during the Dust Bowl years? _____

# JESSE OWENS PROVES HITLER WRONG

*Jesse Owens (right), runs a race during the 1936 Olympic Games in Berlin, Germany.*

The year was 1936. Adolf Hitler was the leader of Germany. He was looking forward to the Summer Olympic Games. The games would be held in Berlin, Germany, that year. The eyes of the world would be on Germany. Hitler thought it would be a perfect time to show the world his dream of a master race, which he called "Aryans." He wanted to prove that his hand-picked blond athletes were better than gypsies, Jews, blacks, and all other kinds and colors of human beings. This would happen, Hitler was sure, when Germany took all the Olympic medals at the games.

## The Other Germans

*Many Germans did not agree with Adolf Hitler's beliefs. The story that follows is an example of that.*

*Jesse Owens was having trouble with his long jump. For a couple of jumps, it even looked like he wouldn't qualify for the finals.*

*Then, a fellow athlete— German jumper Luz Long—offered Jesse advice about how to jump better. Later that day, Jesse won the long jump. First to congratulate him was Luz, who came in second.*

*Jesse and Luz never saw each other again. Luz served in the German Army and was killed during World War II. "Luz was a wonderful guy," Jesse later said. "It took a lot of courage for him to befriend me in front of Hitler."*

There was one thing Adolf Hitler hadn't planned on. That one thing was an American runner whose name was Jesse Owens.

## Jesse Owens' Young Life

James Cleveland Owens was born in Oakville, Alabama. His nickname, Jesse, came from his initials—J.C. His grandparents had been slaves. His parents were sharecroppers—farmers who farm someone else's land in return for a part of the harvest.

A sharecropper's life was a poor life. Everyone had to help if a family was to survive. Even as a young boy, Jesse, like the children of other sharecropping families, joined his parents as they labored in the cotton fields. During harvest time, Jesse spent many hours a day "blacking a strip"—that is, picking all the cotton on one strip of earth, so that there were no little white bolls left on that strip. In fact, Jesse remembered that he could go to school "only when it wasn't cotton-picking time."

When Jesse was 7 years old, his family moved to the Ohio city that also was his middle name—Cleveland. The Owens were still poor. However, that didn't matter so much now, because Jesse Owens had learned how to run. "We had nothing to do but run," he said, looking back on his childhood. "We couldn't afford any kind of equipment, so we ran and ran and ran."

By the time he graduated from high school, Jesse was such a great runner that he was given a scholarship to Ohio State University.

*Jesse Owens receives his gold medal after winning the 200-meter race in the 1936 Olympic Games.*

In the 1936 Olympics, Jesse Owens won four gold medals. He won the 100-meter race, the 200-meter race, and the long jump. And, he helped win the gold medal in the 400-meter relay race.

In the end, Germany did, indeed, win the most medals in the 1936 Summer Olympic Games. Still, Jesse Owens showed the world the lie behind Adolf Hitler's idea of an Aryan "master race."

There, he kept running faster and faster. On May 25, 1935, at one racing event, Jesse broke three world records and tied for a fourth—all within 45 minutes! He broke the world records for the 220-yard dash, the 220-yard low hurdles, and the running broad jump. He tied the world record for the 100-yard dash.

### Jesse Owens Races in Berlin

In 1936, Jesse Owens was a member of the American team that went to Berlin to take part in the Olympic Games. Jesse went to Germany to make the United States proud. He went to run the best he could. Time and time again, Jesse beat Germany's best. In fact, Jesse beat everyone else at the games!

## Show What You Know

When Jesse Owens was only 15 years old, he could run 100 yards in 9.9 seconds. Ask a friend or relative to go with you to a place where you can run. It can be in your backyard, in a nearby park, or even on the running track of the local school. Mark your starting point. Then, ask the person with you to time you for 10 seconds while you run. When ten seconds are up, stop running, and mark that place. Use a measuring tape to measure how far you ran in 10 seconds. Compare how far you ran with how far Jesse Owens could run when he was 15.

# THE WAR AT HOME

In the late 1930s, Germany and Italy began invading neighboring countries. As a result, World War II broke out in Europe in September 1939. During World War II, there were two main powers that fought against each other. On one side were the Axis powers—Germany, Italy, and Japan. On the other side were the Allies—Britain, France, and the United States. However, the United States was not involved in the war at first. The United States did not enter the war until December 1941, after Japan bombed Pearl Harbor, Hawaii. Eventually, 15 million men served in U.S. armed forces during World War II. These millions of men had to be clothed and housed and fed. They had to be trained and armed. They had to be moved from one place to another, had to have medical attention, and had to have a thousand other needs met in order to be effective fighters. All American citizens pitched in to help in the war effort.

This poster describes how donated "junk" was used in the effort to win World War II.

SAVE YOUR CANS
Help pass the Ammunition

PREPARE YOUR TIN CANS FOR WAR
1 REMOVE TOPS AND BOTTOMS
2 TAKE OFF PAPER LABELS
3 WASH THOROUGHLY
4 FLATTEN FIRMLY

## Americans Support Their Troops

Some of the needs of the armed forces were met by U.S. businesses. Many businesses stopped making their regular products and began making products needed for war. For example, one canning company shifted from canning food to making ship parts.

A pencil factory stopped making mechanical pencils and started making bombs instead. Car manufacturers went from making automobiles to making airplanes and tanks.

The U.S. government also ordered some changes in production in the country. For example, few washing machines or refrigerators were made during the war years because the government needed the metal for war materials. Even the production of safety pins was cut in half. In fact, one Pennsylvania hospital didn't have enough safety pins to pin diapers on the newborn babies. (At this time, reusable cloth diapers were used.) Nurses taped babies into their diapers until the local Lions Club came to the rescue by collecting 6,000 safety pins for the hospital. Other metal products in short

supply included hairpins, needles, zippers, and alarm clocks.

The American people pitched in, too. For example, the government needed all the metal it could get. After all, everything from rifles to hand grenades, to ships and planes, were made of metal. So, the people of the United States held gigantic metal drives. During the drives, they collected anything made of metal to give to the government. Pots, pans, padlocks, old bicycles, and empty toothpaste tubes are just a few examples of the metal goods people donated to the government.

*Factory workers found themselves making products for the war effort instead of their usual work.*

## Americans Face Rationing

Even a country as large and as rich as the United States could hardly produce everything both its citizens and its military needed. So, the government decided to ration some things. To ration something is to set a limit on the amount of that product that people can buy. Gasoline was one of the things the government decided to ration.

The military used huge quantities of gasoline. Even a light tank took 54 gallons of gas to fill up. In one night of maneuvers, a division of tanks could use almost 100,000 gallons of gasoline! That was just for practice fighting!

The government's need for gasoline meant that gasoline had to be rationed. Gasoline rationing was tough on car-loving Americans. That was especially true because most people could buy only 3 gallons of gas a week! For some, that meant starting car pools to share the ride to work. Others found they could no longer take their Sunday drives.

Some even found that their jobs were in danger. *Newsweek* magazine reported that "Service station operators . . . felt they could no longer make a living. . . . Chauffeurs by the hundreds saw their jobs sputter as tanks went dry. Parking lot operators found potential playgrounds on their hands. Businessmen in suburban shopping centers feared the worst."

## Americans Plant Victory Gardens

Americans also faced the rationing of some foods. Little ration books limited the amount of foods such as sugar, meat, coffee, cheese, and butter people could buy. Rationed foods had two "prices." One was the price in dollars and cents. The other was the price in ration points. These points told how many ration stamps an item would cost.

With so much food going to feed the soldiers, Americans decided to help feed themselves. Millions of people who had never farmed before now planted gardens to supply their families with fresh vegetables. These gardens became known as Victory Gardens. They appeared in backyards, jail yards, window boxes— anywhere there was a small plot of soil. In 1943 alone, over 20 million Victory Gardens were growing everything from tomatoes to corn to lettuce to radishes. Those gardens yielded 8 million tons of food! That was enough food to supply a third of all the fresh vegetables the country's citizens needed that year!

**Enemies in Our Midst?**

The people who lived on the Pacific Coast worried about an invasion by the Japanese. In fact, civilians had helped rescue American sailors from a ship that was sunk by the Japanese off the California coast. Many began to look with suspicion at the 112,000 Japanese and Japanese Americans living in California. They worried that these Japanese Americans might be spies sending secret messages to Japanese soldiers. Or, they worried that, if Japan attacked the United States, the Japanese living here would join the enemy.

Because of these fears, many Americans demanded that people of Japanese descent be moved away from the coast.

*Food rationing caused many people to grow their own vegetables.*

In March 1942, the U.S. government forced people of Japanese descent living in California, Oregon, Washington, and Arizona out of those states and into government-built camps far from the coast. These camps were called relocation camps. However, the camps were surrounded by barbed wire and had armed guards. This made the camps more like prisons.

The people who were moved to these camps lost their businesses, homes, and most possessions. Also, the camps were very primitive. The people often lived in army-like barracks that had no electric lights, running water, or private bathrooms. In fact, one camp had only one washroom for every 100 families!

Although they were treated harshly, most Japanese Americans remained loyal to the United States. They still helped with the war effort, as they had before they were taken from their homes. For

*Japanese Americans were taken to camps that looked and felt like prisons.*

example, some made camouflage nets. Others created posters to encourage Americans to join the Armed Forces. Many young men begged to be allowed to join the Army. "I only ask that I be given a chance to fight to preserve the principles that I have been brought up on and which I will not sacrifice at any cost," wrote Henry Ebihara to America's Secretary of War. "Please give me a chance to serve in your armed forces."

In 1943, the Army began to accept some young Japanese American men. In the end, over 1,000 served during World War II. And, they served with bravery and honor. Together they won hundreds of Purple Hearts, Oak Leaf Clusters, and Bronze and Silver Stars. In 1943, too, some of the people began to be released from the camps. It was not until the war's end, though, that all were free to leave.

*This photograph shows pages from an American cookbook sold during World War II.*

## Show What You Know

As you have read, many foods were rationed during World War II. Sugar, coffee, tea, meat, canned fruits, canned vegetables, eggs, butter, cheese, and fresh milk all were either rationed or hard to get—or both.

With the help of an adult, plan a dinner menu that does not use any of the foods listed above. You might want to include soup or salad, a main course, and a dessert in your menu. If you have permission, prepare the dinner for your family or for a friend. Then, ask the people who eat your dinner which of the foods they would have missed most if they had lived through the World War II years.

# WOMEN AT WAR

During World War II, millions of American men served their country. Millions of American women did, too. Some of these women served in the Army, the Navy, and the Marines. Other women served at home.

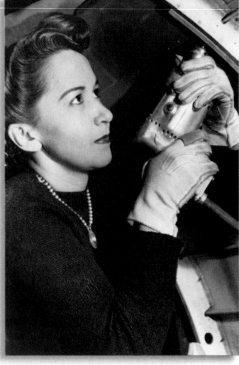

*During World War II, Lola Boyle worked at a job done mostly by men before the war.*

## Door-Key Children

*During World War II, many women moved to where the work was. Their children, who were used to mothers at home, now found themselves alone after school.*

*Some children were sent to daycare centers. At that time, though, there were few daycare centers. So, many children were responsible for taking care of themselves after school. These children often wore their house keys around their necks, so they could let themselves into their houses. Because of that, they became known as "door-key children" or "latch-key kids."*

## Civilian Women Working

Unemployment had plagued the country all during the Great Depression. Unemployment, however, almost disappeared when the United States entered World War II. In all, over 15 million American men went to fight in World War II. All their old jobs needed new workers. Plus, there were plenty of new jobs in shipyards, airplane factories, and gunpowder plants, because the United States needed ships, planes, and gunpowder to win the war.

With so many millions of men away in the service, who would fill all these job vacancies? It was America's women who went to work.

Millions of women went to work in government offices and businesses and factories. Many others went to work building war weapons. For example, before the war, only about 4,000 women worked in the aircraft industry. By the end of the war, 360,000 women were putting together the nation's planes. Two out of every five workers making ammunition were women.

As the war went on, a new picture of the American woman began to form. In that picture, the woman was wearing safety goggles and slacks—at that time, most women wore skirts. Altogether, over 6 million women entered the work force during World War II.

## Women in the Military

All over the nation, women enlisted in the armed forces. They were not allowed to go into combat, but they took over jobs that freed men to fight the war. Women became car mechanics and truck drivers.

*Many women worked during the war at jobs traditionally done by men.*

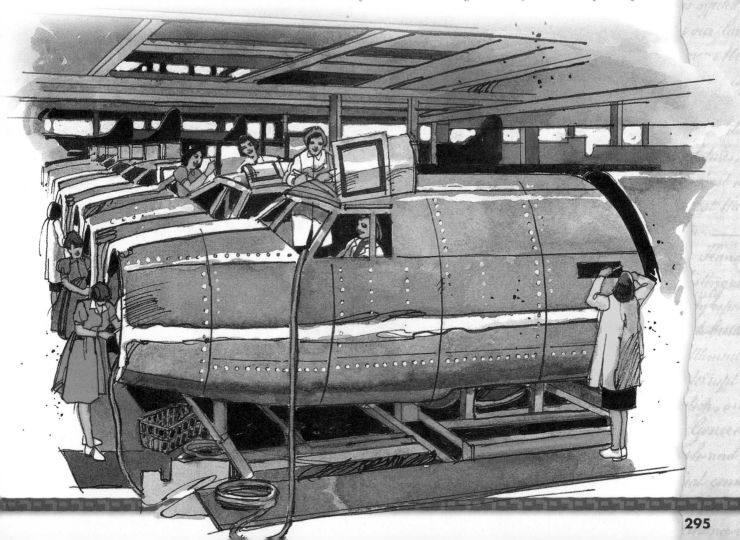

They served as typists and clerks and decoders and cooks and in hundreds of other support positions. Some, like Yvonne Pateman, even became airplane pilots.

Yvonne Pateman's mother had always admired the early women flyers. So, when Yvonne decided she wanted to fly airplanes, her mother supported her decision. Her brothers and father thought it was wrong. After all, few women worked outside the home at that time. However, her mother told them firmly, "Yvonne is going to do something with her life."

Yvonne heard that the women of the WASPs were starting to fly airplanes. WASP stands for Women's Air Force Service Pilots. The WASPs worked with the Army Air Force, but WASP women were not considered part of the Army Air Force.

The WASPs were training in Sweetwater, Texas. So, Yvonne took a train to join them there. Yvonne and the 1,000 or so other women who became pilots at Sweetwater found that WASPs lived a dangerous life. They delivered planes from factory to airfield in any kind of weather. They test-flew the newest planes that the Army

This World War II poster helped to convince women to work and to join the war effort.

Air Force had. They also flew target planes. These were planes that towed targets behind them as they flew. Fighter pilots-in-training then tried to shoot the targets the WASP pilots were towing.

By the end of the war, over 330,000 American women had served in the armed forces. This woman spoke for many of those servicewomen when she described the contribution she made when she enlisted: "I wish I could think of some way I could tell the gals back home what being in the service would do for them. Inside, you can say I am doing something.

I am helping. I shall continue doing all I can and be grateful for the chance. . . ."

## The End of World War II

On June 6, 1944, British, Canadian, and U.S. troops came by boat and landed on the beaches of Normandy, in northern France. This was called D-Day. This important event helped to end the war in Europe. These Allied soldiers advanced eastward, and the Soviets came from the west into Germany. On May 8, 1945, the Germans surrendered.

In the Pacific, in August 1945, atomic bombs were dropped on Hiroshima and on Nagasaki—two cities in Japan. This ended the war in the Pacific. Japan surrendered on September 2, 1945.

## Show What You Know

The bar graph at right shows the number of women working during the World War II years. However, the bar graph is not completed. Use the information that follows to complete the bar graph.

1940: 11,970

1941: 13,000

1942: 15,170

1943: 18,200

1944: 18,850

1945: 18,610

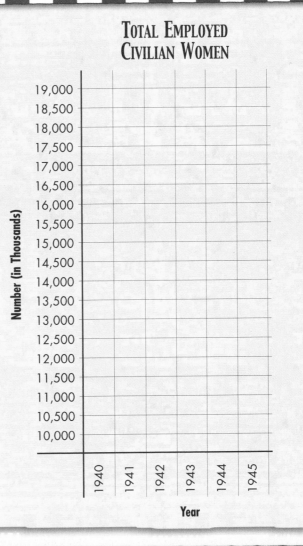

TOTAL EMPLOYED CIVILIAN WOMEN

Number (in Thousands)

19,000
18,500
18,000
17,500
17,000
16,500
16,000
15,500
15,000
14,500
14,000
13,500
13,000
12,500
12,000
11,500
11,000
10,500
10,000

1940  1941  1942  1943  1944  1945

Year

# UNIT 10
## 1950–PRESENT
# NEW FRONTIERS

The last half of the twentieth century was a time when the United States faced many new frontiers. It was a time of wars and almost-wars, of tests inside the country and with other nations. It also was a time when many Americans began to speak up for their civil rights.

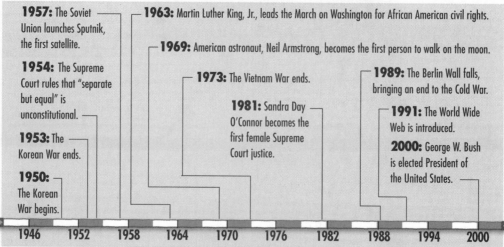

**TIME LINE**

**1957:** The Soviet Union launches Sputnik, the first satellite.

**1954:** The Supreme Court rules that "separate but equal" is unconstitutional.

**1953:** The Korean War ends.

**1950:** The Korean War begins.

**1963:** Martin Luther King, Jr., leads the March on Washington for African American civil rights.

**1969:** American astronaut, Neil Armstrong, becomes the first person to walk on the moon.

**1973:** The Vietnam War ends.

**1981:** Sandra Day O'Connor becomes the first female Supreme Court justice.

**1989:** The Berlin Wall falls, bringing an end to the Cold War.

**1991:** The World Wide Web is introduced.

**2000:** George W. Bush is elected President of the United States.

1946  1952  1958  1964  1970  1976  1982  1988  1994  2000

# LINDA BROWN GOES TO SCHOOL

*Supreme Court Justice Thurgood Marshall*

Seven-year-old Linda Brown was an African American. She lived in a segregated world in the 1950s. That meant that, in her hometown of Topeka, Kansas, Linda had to go to a school for African American children. The problem was, the African American school was far from her home. To get there, this little girl had to cross railroad tracks. Plus, she had to ride a bus for a long time every morning and afternoon.

Linda's father knew that there was an all-white school much closer to the Brown home. So, he decided to sue the Topeka Board of Education. He hoped to force the Board to let his daughter go to the school nearby.

*Linda Brown's father sued the Topeka Board of Education so that she could go to a school closer to her home.*

## Thurgood Marshall

*Thurgood Marshall was born in Baltimore, Maryland, in 1908. He became a lawyer in 1933. In 1938, he went to work for the National Association for the Advancement of Colored People (the NAACP). It was while he worked for the NAACP that he helped argue the case for school integration before the Supreme Court.*

*In 1967, President Lyndon Johnson appointed Thurgood Marshall to the United States Supreme Court. Justice Marshall became the first African American to sit on the Court. He remained a voice for equal rights until he retired from the Supreme Court in 1991.*

The Topeka Board of Education would not change its mind. After all, it was obeying the law. Over 50 years earlier, the Supreme Court had ruled that "separate but equal" schools were legal. Mr. Brown—and many, many others, both black and white—did not think that Supreme Court decision was a fair one. He took his case before the Court to ask the judges to think again about the issue of segregated schools.

### Brown v. Board of Education of Topeka

In 1952, the Supreme Court agreed to hear the case of *Brown v. Board of Education of Topeka*. First, the justices heard arguments from people who were for segregated schools, then from people who were against them. For example, Robert Figg, an attorney for the defense, told the Court that "states have the right to separate the races in public schools. . . . It is a normal and not an abnormal procedure." On the other side, lawyer Thurgood Marshall argued that "The Negro child is

**The News**

**HIGH COURT BANS SEGREGATION IN PUBLIC SCHOOLS**

made to go to an inferior school; he is branded in his own mind inferior. This sets up a road block to his mind which prevents his ever feeling he is equal." After all the lawyers had a chance to speak, the Supreme Court justices spent months and months thinking about the issue.

Finally, on Monday, May 17, 1954, just after noon, the Supreme Court announced its decision. It said, "We conclude, unanimously, that in the field of public education, the doctrine of 'separate but equal' has no place. Separate educational facilities are inherently [by their nature] unequal." In other words, Linda Brown should be allowed to attend an all-white school. In fact, according to the Supreme Court, there shouldn't be any all-white or all-black schools.

You might think that this ruling changed everything right away. Eventually, it did, but it took years for some people to follow what the Supreme Court said. In fact, it took the federal government to force some schools to let African Americans attend.

*The National Guard prevented African American students from attending an all-white school in Little Rock, Arkansas, so U.S. troops had to be sent in by the president.*

## Trouble at Central High School

The Little Rock, Arkansas, School Board decided to try to support the Supreme Court's decision. It would let nine African American children attend the all-White Central High School.

But Arkansas's governor, Orval Faubus, had different ideas. He warned that there would be trouble if the nine students tried to go to Central High. He even called out the National Guard to surround the school. The governor said the National Guard was there to keep order. However, what the National Guard did was keep the African American students from entering the school.

Now, it had come to the point that the federal government had to get involved. A governor could not defy a Supreme Court ruling. So, President Dwight Eisenhower sent 1,000 U.S. troops to Little Rock. On September 24, 1957, many of these soldiers surrounded Central High. Still other soldiers escorted those brave African American children through jeering crowds and into the school. For the rest of the year, soldiers protected the African American students as they went to their classes.

The first African American to graduate from Central High School was Ernest Green. His graduation day was May 29, 1958. Ernest later remembered that day.
He said, "When they called my name, there was nothing, just the name, and then there was eerie silence. Nobody clapped. But I figured they didn't have to . . . because after I got that diploma, that was it. I had accomplished what I had come there for."

## Show What You Know

Find all these terms in the word search puzzle on this page. Words can be found written up, down, across, diagonally, or backwards. Then, in the space below the word search, write a sentence using at least three of the terms you have found in the puzzle.

| Linda Brown | courage | Topeka | Supreme Court |
| separate but equal | brave | NAACP | |
| Thurgood Marshall | school | board of education | |

```
N T H U R G O O D M A R S H A L L D
O A S E P A R A T E B U T E Q U A L
B R A M U B R A V E Y A O Q U T D L
H I S C H O O L I N E R P B A G B E
G O N L P O A S U M T D E I L O R F
L H L I N D A B R O W N K C I O O L
T R U O C E M E R P U S A Q N D D Y
N P B O A R D O F E D U C A T I O N
C O U R A G E N M O R B W H E A D L
```

_____

_____

# JOHN F. KENNEDY'S LEGACY

John Fitzgerald Kennedy was the son of privilege. His father, Joseph, was rich. Joseph had made a lot of money in the wild stock market of the 1920s. Then, he kept his money by selling off his stock before the stock market crashed in 1929. John's mother, Rose Fitzgerald, was the child of a Boston mayor. Together, Joseph and Rose had nine children. John Fitzgerald was their second.

## JFK Joins the Navy

John was plagued by illness during his life. He suffered from everything from measles to scarlet fever to liver illness to back problems at one time or another.

*John F. Kennedy was a skipper of a PT boat during World War II.*

### How to Be a Peace Corps Volunteer

*To volunteer for the Peace Corps (kor), you have to be at least 18 years old, be an American citizen, and be willing to sign up for two years. You also have to want to help other people. Many Peace Corps volunteers have college degrees, but a college degree is not required.*

*Once you have been accepted by the Peace Corps, you face an 8- to 14-week training time. During that time, you get a course on the language and culture of the country to which you're assigned. Then, you're ready to start your work.*

In fact, his brothers used to say that John was so sickly, a mosquito that bit him might get sick itself!

When World War II began, the Army rejected John because of his bad back. However, he was determined to serve. So he spent five months doing exercises that helped strengthen his back muscles. Then, he was accepted by the Navy.

On August 2, 1943, John was in command of a PT boat in the South Pacific.

Suddenly, a Japanese destroyer appeared and sliced John's boat in two. Two men were killed. The ten survivors clung to the wreckage of the boat through the night. In the morning, John ordered the men to swim for their lives. They swam for hours before they reached land. The trip was especially hard for John. He had hurt his back again. Plus, he was swimming for two—he was towing an injured crewman along as he swam by holding onto the crewman's life-jacket strap with his teeth!

Five days later, John and his men were rescued. Because of his bravery and leadership during that time, John was rewarded with several medals.

## President Kennedy Starts the Peace Corps

On January 20, 1961, John F. Kennedy became the 35th president of the United States. He did not serve his entire 4-year term. That is because, on November 22, 1963, an assassin's bullets took his life. Yet, the short time during which John Kennedy served as president was a very exciting time for the country.

Even before he became president, John Kennedy talked about the idea of a peace corps (kor). He knew that much of the world was suffering from hunger and poverty. He also knew that money was not the answer to these problems. He envisioned an "army" of trained Americans going to other countries to teach life skills to those in need. "There is not enough money in all America to relieve the misery of the underdeveloped world," John said while he was still campaigning for president. "But there is enough know-how and knowledgeable people to help those nations help themselves."

Just six weeks after he became president, John Kennedy established the Peace Corps. Since it began, over 140,000 American volunteers have gone to 96 countries around the world. To the people of each country, volunteers have brought goodwill, American know-how, and hope for a better future.

## John Kennedy and the Space Program

By the time John Kennedy became president, the space race already had begun. This was more than just a race to get a human into space and safely back to earth again. This was a race between two great, powerful nations. The two nations were the United States and the Soviet Union. The race was to show the world which country was smarter and stronger.

In 1957, the Soviet Union stunned the world by putting its first satellite into space.

A month later it sent a dog into space. In 1959, the Soviet Union sent a probe all the way to the Moon. And in 1961, at the beginning of John Kennedy's presidency, the Soviet Union sent the first person into space. His name was Yuri A. Gagarin, and he went all the way around the Earth one time.

President Kennedy knew the United States was losing the space race. So, he decided to set a goal for the nation that, if met, would put the United States firmly in front of the Soviets. On May 21, 1961, the president announced his

*Above: Neil A. Armstrong was the first person to walk on the moon. Below, left: This photograph is a portrait of astronaut John H. Glenn, the first American to orbit Earth. Middle: The space shuttle Discovery blasts off. Below, right: President John F. Kennedy and John Glenn inspect the spaceship that took John Glenn into space.*

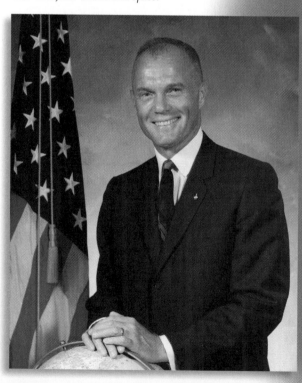

plan to Congress. He said, "I believe that this nation should commit itself to achieving the goal, before this decade is out, of landing a man on the moon and returning him safely to earth. No single space project in this period will be more impressive to mankind, or more important for the long-range exploration of space; and none will be so difficult or expensive to accomplish."

President Kennedy did not live to see whether the United States could rise to the challenge of landing a man on the Moon. He would have been proud to know that it did. On July 20, 1969, an American

spaceship touched down on the Moon's surface. All over the world, televisions broadcast pictures of astronaut Neil Armstrong taking humankind's first steps on the Moon. Millions also heard him speak the first words ever spoken on the Moon: "That's one small step for a man, one giant leap for mankind."

## Show What You Know

John F. Kennedy gave a wonderful speech on the day he was inaugurated president. One of the sentences many people remember from that speech is this: "And so, my fellow Americans: ask not what your country can do for you—ask what you can do for your country."

Use a sheet of paper to draw an example of a way in which people can help their country. If you'd rather not draw, cut out pictures from magazines and newspapers that show people doing things that are good for the country. Use the pictures to create a collage. Then, write a caption telling how the people in your picture are helping their country. Display your picture and caption for others to see and read.

# MARTIN LUTHER KING, JR.

Rosa Parks's workday was over. She got on the Montgomery bus that would take her home. She paid the fare. Then, she sat down in Row 11, just behind the "white" section of the bus.

The bus started to fill up. Pretty soon, all the "white" seats were filled. When the next white person—a man—got on, the bus driver told the African Americans, including Rosa, in Row 11 that they had to move. This was because the city of Montgomery, Alabama, in 1955 had a law that said on buses, whites would never have to sit with blacks. It said, "Every person operating a bus line shall provide equal accommodations . . . in such a manner as to separate the white people from the Negroes."

## Words of Wisdom from Martin Luther King, Jr.

*How did Martin Luther King, Jr., forgive the white people who hated African Americans? He told us we should love the people who hate us. They have been taught to hate us. Therefore, they are not fully responsible for their hate.*

*Why did Martin Luther King, Jr., decide to be nonviolent in his protests? He said we will wear down the people who hate us by showing our strength. This show of strength will cause them to give us our rightful freedom and earn their respect at the same time.*

*Rosa Parks is fingerprinted after her arrest in Montgomery, Alabama, on December 1, 1955.*

Rosa Parks would not give up her seat. The driver stopped the bus and called the police. Rosa was arrested for breaking the Montgomery law. She was found guilty and had to pay a $10 fine, plus $4 in court costs.

Something else happened in Montgomery after Rosa was arrested. The African Americans there decided to stop riding the buses. They carpooled. They hitchhiked. They took cabs. And, they walked. But, they stayed off the buses. They decided to stay off the buses until the bus companies changed the rules.

*Martin Luther King, Jr., is shown here during one of his first nonviolent confrontations with police.*

The Montgomery bus boycott lasted over a year. A boycott is a way of protesting by refusing to buy or use certain products—like the Montgomery buses. This boycott didn't end until the U.S. Supreme Court agreed that the Montgomery law went against the Constitution.

## Martin Luther King, Jr., Becomes a Leader

One of the great leaders to come out of the Montgomery bus boycott was a man named Martin Luther King, Jr. Martin was born in Atlanta, Georgia. He went north to receive training as a minister. Then, he came south again, to work in a Montgomery, Alabama, church.

Montgomery's black leaders asked Martin to run the bus boycott. Martin agreed that the African Americans should protest their treatment. He also agreed that protests, like the bus boycott, should be nonviolent.

The Montgomery bus boycott eventually ended. However, the African American movement for equal rights did not end then. Martin's role as leader in the fight for civil rights did not end either.

## Martin Goes to Washington

For the next twelve years, Martin Luther King, Jr., organized and took part in many nonviolent protests. One of the most famous of these protests took place in Washington, D.C., in 1963.

President John Kennedy sent Congress a civil rights bill to consider. Martin wanted to make sure it passed. So, he organized the March on Washington.

On August 28, 1963, over 200,000 people—both black and white—gathered in front of the Lincoln Memorial. They listened as Martin Luther King, Jr., spoke. In his speech, called "I Have a Dream," Martin said he believed that one day the people in the United States would live according to the words in the Declaration of Independence: "We hold these truths to be self-evident: that all men are created equal."

Martin told the audience that he dreamed about the day when the descendents of former slaves and the descendents of slaveowners would live together in brotherhood. It was his hope that all people of this nation would be judged by their character and not by the color of their skin. He said that freedom for all people will allow us—all races and religions—to one day join together and sing the words of the old Negro spiritual, *"Free at last! Free at last! Thank God Almighty, we are free at last."*

## Martin Dies for His Cause

Martin knew that what he was doing was very dangerous. There were many Americans who wanted him in jail. There were even some who wanted him dead.

Martin told his fellow civil-rights fighters that, if something happened to him, they should go on fighting without him. He told them that God would be with the movement.

On April 4, 1968, in Memphis, Tennessee, Martin Luther King, Jr., was killed by an assassin's bullet. He was buried in Atlanta, Georgia.

Over his grave, his tombstone uses words from the same Negro spiritual Martin quoted in his Washington speech. It says, *"Free at last, free at last, thank God Almighty, I'm free at last."*

### Show What You Know

The civil rights Martin Luther King, Jr., wanted for African Americans are the same rights the Constitution guarantees to all U.S. citizens. In fact, the Constitution guarantees many freedoms for American citizens. The First Amendment of the Constitution guarantees five rights by itself!

Below are the rights the First Amendment guarantees. Think about each right. Next, rate them, from 1 to 5, in order of how important each is to you. Then, write a paragraph telling why you think your first choice is so important.

_____ Freedom of religion—This means all Americans can worship as they choose.

_____ Freedom of speech—This means all Americans are free to express themselves in words.

_____ Freedom of the press—This means that people can express themselves in newspapers, on radio and television, and in other media.

_____ Right to assemble—This means that people can freely gather together.

_____ Right to petition—This means that people can ask the government to fix wrongs and deal with citizens' concerns.

# THE INTERSTATE HIGHWAY SYSTEM

The idea of an interstate highway system had been talked about for years. President Franklin Roosevelt was interested in the idea. He knew building highways would create many jobs. However, plans for a highway system to cross the country were put on hold when the United States entered World War II.

## Dwight D. Eisenhower Forms a Highway Plan

The war actually helped Dwight D. Eisenhower get elected president. He spent much of World War II in charge of the U.S. troops in Europe. He planned several invasions by Allied forces. He was the one who said "OK, let's go!" to the D-Day invasion of Allied troops at Normandy. By 1944, Dwight Eisenhower was a five-star general. That is the highest rank in the Army! By the time he returned home, he was an American hero.

Even before he became president, Dwight was thinking about transportation in the country. One reason for this was a trip

## Numbering the Interstate Highways

*You can tell interstate highways from other highways because interstate highways are always marked with a red, white, and blue shield. In the red of the shield appears the word "Interstate." In the blue field is the name of the state through which you're passing, as well as the number by which that interstate route is known. If the number is an odd number, it means the interstate highway goes north and south. If the number is even, the interstate highway goes east and west.*

**NORTH**

**INTERSTATE COLORADO 25**

he took across the country in 1919. He was just a young lieutenant colonel when he accompanied a group of Army vehicles as they traveled from Washington, D.C., to San Francisco. He saw firsthand the problems they faced as they struggled along the nation's narrow, poorly paved, poorly kept roads from the East Coast to the West Coast.

Dwight learned another transportation lesson during World War II. When the Allies invaded Germany, Dwight saw how much easier it was for the troops to travel once

they reached Germany's Autobahn (superhighway). Adolf Hitler had started building this four-lane highway system years before the war. Dwight later explained how both these trips helped form his vision of a highway system for the United States. He said that the 1919 trip "had started me thinking about good, two-lane highways, but Germany had made me see the wisdom of broader ribbons across the land."

## Highways for Defense

Dwight realized that a good system of roads would help make sure the country could be defended. World War II had ended. But, the Cold War had begun. The Cold War got its name because there was no actual fighting during this time. Instead, the Cold War describes a time of mistrust and fear and suspicion between democracies like the United States and communist countries, led by the U.S.S.R. (Union of Soviet Socialist Republics).

During the Cold War, many countries built up their arms. Some even created new weapons, such as the hydrogen bomb. This new weapon is even more deadly than the atom bomb, which was first used during World War II.

Dwight had seen firsthand how hard it was to move troops and vehicles over the existing roads. He worried that if the country went to war, the roads could make it difficult to defend our giant country. For Dwight and many others, this was a good reason to support the idea of an interstate highway system.

## Highways for Growth

Dwight and others also believed that a highway system would help the country grow. After all, there were already a few highways in the nation. Cars began to travel on part of the Pennsylvania Turnpike by 1940. That year also saw part of California's Arroyo Seco Parkway open for business. In both cases, people soon began to settle in places along the highways' routes. This surely would happen with the highways in the interstate highway system, too.

In addition, the highways would connect the states as they had never been connected before. Dwight said that, together with communication, better ways to travel would help tie the states together. He said, "Together, the united forces of our communication and transportation systems are dynamic elements in the very name we bear—United States. Without them, we would be a mere alliance [group] of many separate parts."

## The Highway Act Passes

On June 29, 1956, President Dwight D. Eisenhower saw his dream of an interstate highway system begin to

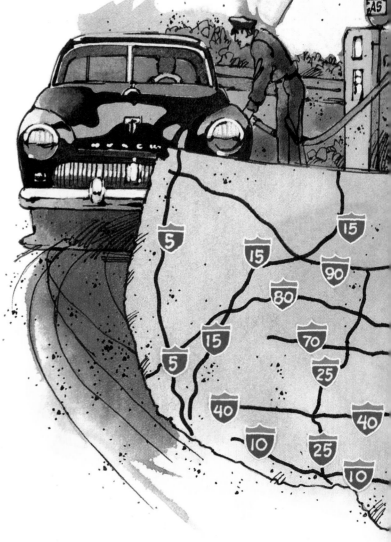

come true. On that day the Highway Act of 1956 became law. The law stated that the national government would pay $32 billion to help build the interstate system. The government figured that would be about 90 percent of the cost of building the system. The states would have to pay the rest of the cost.

The act also explained where the national government would get that money. Most would come from a new tax on gasoline. The act also predicted that it would take over 20 years to build the system's 42,500 miles of highways. It actually took 40 years to finish the interstate highway system. The final cost was over $128 billion.

## The Interstate Highway System Gets a New Name

After he retired, President Eisenhower wrote the story of his life. In that book, he explained why he thought the interstate highway system was so important:

*More than any single action by the government since the end of the war, this one would change the face of America. . . . Its impact on the American economy—the jobs it would produce in manufacturing and construction, the rural areas it would open up—was beyond calculation [measure].*

President Eisenhower would have been happy to know that, not long ago, the interstate highway system was renamed in his honor. Today, it is called the Dwight D. Eisenhower System of Interstate and Defense Highways.

## Show What You Know

In 1939, a designer named Norman Bel Geddes created an exhibit for the World's Fair in New York. In his exhibit, he showed what he thought roads would be like 21 years from then—in 1960, to be exact. He said that highways would be up to 14 lanes wide. Cars would go up to 100 miles per hour, and they would send out radio beams that would keep them a certain distance from other cars on the highway.

Norman's exhibit showed that city highways would have several levels. You would go to the bottom level to exit or to park. You would stay on the top level if you wanted to go past the city without stopping.

Get a piece of paper. On that paper, draw Norman Bel Geddes's dream of the future of highways. Or, think about what highways might be like 20 years from now and draw your own dream of the future of transportation.

*Norman Bel Geddes designed this exhibit of what he thought future transportation networks would look like. His exhibit was shown at the 1939 New York World's Fair.*

Now, use the map of the interstate highway system on page 314–315 to answer the following questions. Write the number of the interstate.

What interstate would a driver most likely travel . . .

from Chicago to Seattle?_____

from Michigan to Florida? _____

from Texas to Minnesota? _____

# Cesar Chavez Organizes Workers

The Chavez family came to the United States because their own country, Mexico, was in the middle of a revolution. When they arrived in their new homeland, they settled near Yuma, Arizona. They worked hard, and they saved their money. Eventually, they bought a little farm. In 1927, Cesar Estrada Chavez was born on that farm.

## Who Are America's Hispanics?

*Hispanics are people who come from a Spanish-speaking country to live in the United States. Most Hispanics come from Mexico, our neighbor to the south. Many others come from Spanish-speaking countries in Central America and in South America. They also come from the islands of Puerto Rico and Cuba, in the Caribbean Sea.*

*Hispanics, like all other immigrants, come to the United States for many reasons. For example, many who lived in El Salvador and Nicaragua escaped their homelands when wars broke out. Cubans came by the thousands because they disagreed with the politics of Cuba's leader, Fidel Castro.*

Soon after Cesar was born, the United States was hit with the Great Depression. The Chavez family struggled to hold onto their land. However, like thousands of other farmers during that time, the Chavez family lost their farm. Cesar was only 10 years old when this happened. To keep from starving, the Chavezes went to California and became migrant workers.

## The Life of a Migrant Worker

Migrant workers are workers who harvest crops on other people's farms. Their work means they must regularly move from farm to farm, and even from state to state, as each crop is harvested and the next crop ripens.

Migrant workers live a difficult life. The pay is poor, and the housing various farmers provide is often dirty and miserable. Migrant workers usually can't stay in one place long enough to receive food stamps or any other kind of government help that is offered to people who live in the same place all the time. In fact, the government doesn't even know how many migrant workers there are!

This wandering way of life also makes it very difficult for migrant children to receive an education. For example, young Cesar went to over 30 elementary schools. He dropped out of school in seventh grade to help support his family. This lack of education makes it difficult for migrant workers to get another kind of job. So, many migrant workers are caught in a cruel circle: They work as migrant workers, so they are not able to go to school. They have no regular education, so they aren't able to get another job. They can't get another job, so they remain migrant workers. And on and on.

## Cesar Chavez Starts a Farmers' Union

When Cesar grew up, he decided to help migrant workers improve their lives. In 1962, he started the first union for farm workers. A union is a group of workers who work together for the good of the union's members. Cesar named his union the National Farm Workers Association. In 1966, it joined together with another union, and its name changed—first to the United Farm Workers Organizing Committee, then to the United Farm Workers of America, the name it still uses today.

Cesar, like Martin Luther King, Jr., did not believe in violence. Union members used strikes, sit-ins, and boycotts against the farmers. For example, California table-grape growers didn't want to even talk to the union. So, Cesar organized a nationwide boycott of California grapes. That is, Cesar asked all Americans to stop buying grapes grown in California. Many Americans supported the boycott. Eventually, the grape growers gave in.

For the rest of his life, Cesar Chavez worked to make the lives of migrant workers better. This is what he was doing when he died.

He had gone to San Luis, Arizona, to testify in court on behalf of some farm workers. On April 23, 1993, he died there in his sleep. Cesar was 66 years old.

On April 29, over 20,000 people gathered in Delano, California. They all came for one reason—to attend Cesar's funeral. Some were famous people and government and religious leaders. Most, though, were just ordinary folks, whose lives had been touched by the work of Cesar Chavez.

*Cesar Chavez gives a speech.*

## Show What You Know

Hispanics are one of the fastest-growing groups in the United States. To help Hispanic children learn, some schools offer classes in two languages— English and Spanish. The method of teaching that uses two languages is called bilingual education. In U.S. schools, the second language may be Spanish. Or, it may be any other language that a school finds is spoken by many of its children.

Ask family members or friends whether they speak a language other than English. *(You yourself may be able to answer yes!)* Then, ask the person to write down the words for numbers in a second language. Or, go to the library or check on the Internet for the number words. Practice saying each number in the second language. Now, you're on your way to becoming bilingual!

1 = ONE = _____

2 = TWO = _____

3 = THREE = _____

4 = FOUR = _____

5 = FIVE = _____

# MAYA LIN DESIGNS A MEMORIAL

Involvement between the United States and Vietnam began in the late 1950s. The United States joined with South Vietnam to try to prevent communist North Vietnam from uniting the country. At first, the United States sent only military advisors. Later, in the mid 1960s, the U.S. became involved in combat. After years of fighting, many people on both sides were killed or wounded. In the end, South Vietnam fell to the communists of North Vietnam in 1975.

In 1979, some Vietnam veterans of the United States got together and created the Vietnam Veterans Memorial Fund. Its purpose was to pay for building a monument that would honor the Americans who died during the Vietnam War.

The Memorial Fund needed a design for the memorial. So, it held a nationwide competition.

*Maya Lin, shown in this photograph, designed the Vietnam Wall, a monument to Vietnam veterans, in Washington, D.C.*

Any adult American could enter a design in this competition. Over 1,400 entries were received by the group. Among those entries was one by a 21-year-old college student named Maya Ying Lin.

## Maya Ying Lin Enters the Contest

Maya's parents came from China to live in the United States. Her father was an artist. Her mother was a poet. They both taught at Ohio University, in Athens, Ohio, where Maya grew up. Maya was a student at Yale University when the Memorial Fund announced its contest. She was studying to become an architect—a person who designs buildings.

Maya decided to enter the competition. Before she started to draw, however, she did a lot of studying. She read about other war memorials that had been built around the world. She also went to the place where the Vietnam Memorial would be built and studied the shape of the land there.

Many memorials include statues of people. Maya's memorial did not. Instead, Maya designed a very unusual memorial. It would be two big, black, polished stone walls that meet in a kind of "V." On the walls would be carved the names of all the American men and women who had died in Vietnam, as well as the names of those whose fates are unknown. In all, over 58,000 names would be carved on the walls.

Maya had to draw her design to show the judges. She also had to write about it. Here is part of what she wrote when she sent in her idea. These sentences describe where the two walls meet:

"At the intersection of these walls, on the right side, is carved the date of the first death. It is followed by the names of those who died in the war, in chronological order [the order in which they died]. These names continue on this wall appearing to recede [fall back] into the earth at the wall's end. The names resume on the left wall as the wall emerges [comes out] from the earth, continuing back to the origin [beginning] where the date of the last death is carved."

## Maya Wins the Competition

In the end, every judge chose Maya's design. Then, trouble started. Some people were not happy with Maya's unusual idea. One veteran called her design "a black gash of shame." Another said it was like a "giant tombstone."

Members of the Vietnam Veterans Memorial Fund did not want the monument to divide the people. After all, that is what the Vietnam War had done—divide the American people into those who thought the war was right and those who thought the war was wrong.

*Far Left: This photograph shows vistors at the Vietnam Wall that Maya Lin designed.*
*Near Left: The second monument to Vietnam veterans, these three bronze soldiers, was created in 1984.*

So, the members decided on a compromise. Maya's wall was built. It opened for visitors in 1982. Then, in 1984, a second monument was added. It was designed by another artist named Frederick Hart. It stands near the entrance to the wall and shows three fighting Americans. The way the bronze figures are placed, it almost seems as if the three are forever looking at Maya's wall.

In 1993, a third monument was added to the existing two. This one was designed by Glenna Goodacre.

It honors the American women veterans who served in Vietnam.

## Maya, the Architect

Maya felt bad that her design upset some people. However, she began to feel better when she realized that the American people were very moved by her monument. Millions have walked by the names. Many have reached out to touch the wall. Many others have made rubbings of some of the names on the wall.

*Visitors to the Vietnam wall make rubbings of names to keep as a remembrance.*

Maya continues to design things. For example, she created a memorial for civil rights that you can see in Montgomery, Alabama. She also designed a garden with 40 tons of crushed, recycled, green glass for the Wexner Center for the Arts on the campus of Ohio State University in Columbus, Ohio. She has even designed some private homes.

## Offerings Left at the Wall

Many of the people who come to visit Maya Lin's Vietnam Veterans Memorial leave little things in memory of those they knew and lost. Sometimes, they leave a piece of a soldier's uniform, like boots or a helmet. Sometimes, they leave army medals or family photographs or flowers. Other times, they leave little notes. Here is one of the notes left at the wall:

*"I came down today to pay respect to two good friends of mine. Go down and visit them sometime. They are on panel 42E, lines 22 and 26. I think you will like them."*

And, here is another:

*"Just wanted you to know I love you, brother.*

*Still talk to Cathy and your babies. They're grown and proud of you. . . . I'll always watch over them for you.*

*I'll see you soon. Just thought I'd let you know everything is ok."*

Each night, park rangers from the National Park Service collect the objects left at the wall. These objects are cataloged and put into storage. They become a part of a museum collection. The Smithsonian Institution in Washington, D.C., has an exhibit for the public to view many of these objects.

## Show What You Know

In this section, you read about three different monuments. Each monument was created to honor Vietnam veterans.

You have recently read about several important Americans—John F. Kennedy, Martin Luther King, Jr., and Cesar Chavez. Imagine you have been asked to design a monument for one of these men. Choose one of the men and consider what you have learned about him. What kind of monument would do him honor? Use a blank sheet of paper to draw your design.

# THE WRECK OF THE EXXON VALDEZ

For thousands and thousands of years, humans didn't have to worry about whether they were hurting their environment. The environment is the world around you. After all, there were so few people and so much land. If you wanted to kill an animal for dinner, you would drive a whole herd over a cliff. If you wanted to clear some farmland, you would set fire to the forest. And, if you used up the land, you would just move to somewhere new. There would always be more animals, more trees, and more unused land. At least, that's what the early people in America thought.

*This beautiful waterfall is located in Yellowstone National Park.*

Decades passed, and America became more crowded. Then, came the Industrial Revolution. The Industrial Revolution not only brought new ideas and new inventions. It also brought factories, wastes, and pollution. More Americans—and the American government, too—began to see the need to conserve, or protect, the nation's natural resources.

## Conservation and Our National Parks

Creating national parks is one way our government helps protect our resources. In 1872, Congress established Yellowstone National Park. Yellowstone became the United States' first national park. In fact, Yellowstone was the first national park in the entire world!

Today, the United States has over 350 national parks. Some of these parks preserve what is special about our geography. Yellowstone is an example of that kind of site. So are parks that protect seashores, deserts, mountain regions, and certain rivers. Other national parks preserve what is special about our history.

For example, a national park protects Abraham Lincoln's Kentucky birthplace. Another protects the missions of early San Antonio, Texas.

## Conservation and the CCC

Do you remember reading about the Civilian Conservation Corps? That was one of the groups President Franklin Roosevelt created to help put Americans to work during the Great Depression. The two million young men who went to work for the CCC did many jobs that helped take care of the environment. For example, they planted trees. They built dams. They even fought forest fires!

## Conservation and the EPA

In 1970, a new government agency was formed. It was named the Environmental Protection Agency, or EPA. Its job was to fight pollution. Ten years later, a Superfund was created. That fund gave the EPA over $1 billion to help it clean up polluted sites around the country.

## The Tragedy of the Exxon Valdez

Despite the hard work of people trying to protect the environment, accidents do happen. In 1989, the southeastern shore of Alaska was the scene of one such accident.

It was only a few minutes after midnight on March 24, 1989. The Coast Guard received a call. The call was from an oil tanker, the Exxon Valdez. "We've fetched up, uh, hard aground," the ship's captain said. In other words, the Exxon Valdez had wrecked.

Even as the Coast Guard started toward the wreck, oil was spilling out of the Exxon Valdez. The ship had torn open its hull on the rocks of Prince William Sound. The almost 11 million gallons of oil it carried were pouring into the sea.

Volunteers hurried to Prince William Sound. They hoped to stop the oil from spreading. They also hoped to save some of the oil-drenched animals that were dying in the sound. However, there weren't enough people to stop the spill. By then, it was on its way to becoming one of the worst environmental disasters in U.S. history. Ocean currents carried the oil out of the sound and deposited it along Alaska's coast. The oil polluted over 1,200 miles of shoreline.

Biologist Terrie Williams was one of the volunteers who tried to help the animal victims of the Exxon Valdez spill. Terrie and others set up a hospital for injured sea otters. The first otter to come to the hospital was covered in oil. He also was sick from swallowing the oil as he tried to lick his fur clean. Terrie and others washed him with soap and water for two hours before they got all the oil off his fur. Still they couldn't save him. In all, the oil from the Exxon Valdez killed nearly 3,000 otters. It also killed hundreds of seals and bald eagles, thousands of seabirds, and millions of fish.

*This photograph shows Prince William Sound as it looks today, years after the Exxon Valdez oil spill.*

It has been over ten years now since the Exxon Valdez ran aground at Prince William Sound. Much of the shoreline is clean again, although oil still hides in cracks and crevices along the coast. Some kinds of animals, like bald eagles and river otters, have recovered. Others, though, have not come back to their pre-oil-spill numbers. Scientists think that the salmon and clams and some other species of the region will recover sometime in the future. They worry, though, about other animals in the area, like killer whales and harbor seals, whose numbers haven't begun to recover.

## Show What You Know

On April 22, 1970, the United States celebrated its first Earth Day. Since then, every year, that day is set aside for Americans to think about how to take care of their environment. Some people use Earth Day to study about Earth's environmental problems. Others plant trees or clean up roadsides or do some other activity that helps protect our Earth.

Imagine that Earth Day is coming up soon—you don't really have to wait for Earth Day to do something good for the environment! Look around your own house or your own neighborhood, and find one way in which you can improve your environment. Then, plan the steps you will need to take to complete your Earth Day project. See if you can convince others to help you finish the job.

Safety Note: Make sure you have permission from an adult in your family before you begin any Earth Day project. You need to be sure that what you would like to do is safe.

# THE INFORMATION SUPERHIGHWAY

You have already read about how the Cold War helped in building our interstate highway system. Now, read about how the same Cold War helped in creating the Internet.

## First Came Computers

Computers have been around for a while. In fact, the government used a simple kind of computer to figure out the results of the 1890 census. A census is an official government count of its people and their property.

The first, real electronic computer that could do several things was called the ENIAC. ENIAC stands for Electronic Numerical Integrator and Computer. It was built in 1946 by two engineers who worked for the University of Pennsylvania.

ENIAC was the first electronic computer. It was built in 1946.

## The Language of the Internet

The Internet has added many words to our dictionaries. Here are some you may have heard:

**download:** to take information from the Internet and store it on your own computer, so you can use the informatin later

**e-mail:** a message sent electronically to someone over the Internet

**home page:** the first page on a Web site

**HTML:** stands for Hypertext Markup Language, the programming language used by the World Wide Web

**software:** computer programs

**spam:** junk e-mail

**World Wide Web:** allows the Internet to use pictures, videos, animation, and sound

This computer was so big it could have filled a regular house. It also used a lot of energy to make its calculations.

During the 1950s and 1960s, scientists figured out how to store information in smaller and smaller spaces. That meant that computers became smaller and smaller. By the middle of the 1970s, the information that used to take a roomful of equipment to store could be put onto a bunch of tiny chips. Computers that used to be as big as a house could now fit on the top of a desk.

## Then, Came ARPANet

It was the 1950s, and the Cold War was raging. For a while, it looked like the Soviet Union was taking the upper hand. After all, in 1957, the Soviets sent the first satellite into space. Their satellite, called Sputnik, went around the Earth once every 96 minutes for three months before falling to Earth again.

To catch up with the Soviets, the United States government began spending more money on training scientists. The government did this by making loans to students who promised to study science in college.

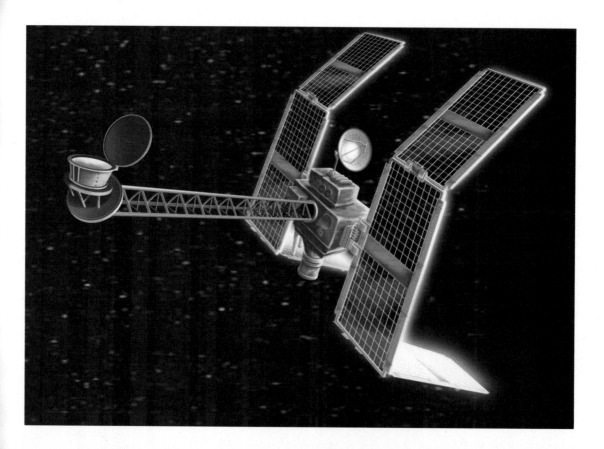

The United States also began spending more money on scientific research. Some of this scientific research was done by a new government agency, called Advanced Research Projects Agency, or ARPA. It was created by President Dwight Eisenhower in 1958.

It was ARPA that first decided to hook its computers together, so the computers could speak directly to each other. In 1969, this mini-computer network linked four computers together. By 1971, 24 ARPA computers made up the ARPANet.

### And Now, the Internet

ARPANet grew slowly. One reason was that it was very difficult to use. Its users practically had to be computer programmers themselves just to figure out how to get to the information they needed.

In 1991, something happened that turned ARPANet into the Internet. That something was the World Wide Web. Before the World Wide Web, the Internet carried only words. The World Wide Web enabled the Internet to have pictures, sound, and animation. Plus, the Web allowed a user to connect directly to a Web site, without having to know a lot of computer language to get there. So, the World Wide Web made the Internet more fun and easier to use.

At the same time, computer prices were going down. That made it easier for businesses and schools and families to buy computers. Also, computers kept getting smaller. Laptop computers became very popular. Now, even hand-held computers are available. In addition, the amount of information available on the Internet has significantly gone up.

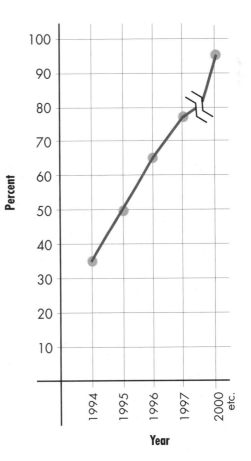

### PERCENT OF U.S. SCHOOLS WITH ACCESS TO THE INTERNET

The number of things you can do on the Internet, such as shopping and playing games, has also increased.

So, in the last ten years, computers have become smaller and less expensive, and the Internet has offered more information and more things to do. All these things together have increased the number of people hooked up to the Internet. In 1981, about 200 computers were linked together on ARPANet. Today, tens of millions of computers all over the world can speak to each other over the Internet.

## Show What You Know

In this unit, you have learned about the people and events from the last half of the twentieth century. Here is a list of the names of the readings in this unit, just to remind you of what you have read:

Linda Brown Goes to School

John F. Kennedy's Legacy

Martin Luther King, Jr.

The Interstate Highway System

Cesar Chavez Organizes Workers

Maya Lin Designs a Memorial

The Wreck of the Exxon Valdez

The Information Superhighway

Choose the reading in this unit that interested you the most. Then, ask a family member to help you with this assignment.

Your job is to get on the Internet, using your own computer or one at the library. Go to a search engine, like Yahoo or HotBot. Type in two or three key words or important terms from the reading you have chosen. The search engine will bring back several articles about your topic. Click on an article that sounds interesting. Then, read the article. Every time you come to a fact that was not presented in the reading in this book, write that fact down on a piece of paper.

When you have finished the article, look at the list of facts you have created. Write one or two paragraphs using the new information you learned about the topic.

# COMPLETE BOOK OF UNITED STATES HISTORY
# REFERENCE SECTION

- The Declaration of Independence
- The Constitution of the United States
  - The Preamble
  - The Articles
  - The Bill of Rights
  - Additional Amendments
- The Three Branches of Government
  - Legislative Branch
  - Executive Branch
  - Judicial Branch
- Making Laws:
  - How a Bill Becomes a Law
- The President
  - Requirements for President
  - Term
  - Members of the President's Cabinet
  - Order of Power
- U.S. Presidents
- The United States, Capitals, and Dates of Statehood

# THE DECLARATION OF INDEPENDENCE

The Declaration of Independence was written to declare the freedom of the American colonies from British rule. The idea that the colonies should be free and independent of Britain was brought up at the Second Continental Congress. This meeting of representatives from all the colonies was held in Philadelphia, Pennsylvania, in May 1776. The Revolutionary War had begun a year earlier, on April 19, 1775.

At the Second Continental Congress, a committee of five men was appointed to write the Declaration of Independence. Those men were Thomas Jefferson, John Adams, Benjamin Franklin, Robert Livingston, and Roger Sherman. Thomas Jefferson wrote the first draft. After making changes, the committee presented the document to the congress. After more changes, Jefferson's work was approved. Church bells rang out on July 4, 1776, the day the Declaration of Independence was adopted. That day, our nation was officially born.

The Declaration of Independence has five parts. They are the preamble, the statement of human rights, charges against the king and parliament, the declaration of freedom for the American colonies from British rule, and the signatures. The main purpose of this document was to announce the colonies' separation from Britain. In doing so, the colonists also expressed the ideals they held that caused them to seek independence.

The Declaration of Independence states "that all men are created equal" and are entitled to certain rights, including "life, liberty, and the pursuit of happiness." These same ideas form the basis of our beliefs in our government's role in our lives today.

# THE CONSTITUTION OF THE UNITED STATES

After the American colonies won their freedom from Britain, they had to set up a government. The first American government was based on the Articles of Confederation. This document was written by the Continental Congress during the Revolutionary War. However, under the Articles of Confederation, each of the thirteen states acted alone, in its own best interest. In just a few years, American leaders agreed that the Articles of Confederation had to be changed to provide for a stronger central government.

In May 1787, delegates from every state except Rhode Island met in Philadelphia for the Constitutional Convention. George Washington served as president of the convention, and James Madison took detailed notes. For four months, the delegates worked behind closed doors to draft a new constitution.

On September 17, 1787, the Constitution of the United States was signed by the convention delegates. Then, it had to be approved by at least nine of the thirteen states. By the summer of 1788, eleven states had approved the Constitution, and it became the foundation of the U.S. government that still exists today.

The parts of the Constitution are the Preamble, the Articles, the Bill of Rights, and additional amendments. These parts are explained below.

## The Preamble

The Preamble is the short introduction to the Constitution. It states:

"We the people of the United States, in order to form a more perfect union, establish justice, insure domestic tranquility, provide for the common defense, promote the general welfare, and secure the blessings of liberty to ourselves and our posterity, do ordain and establish this Constitution for the United States of America."

The Preamble explains that U.S. citizens have set up their own government to keep law and order at home, to defend the United States against other countries, and to ensure the freedom of everyone.

## The Articles

The Articles make up the longest part of the Constitution. The Articles explain how the government is set up and establish how power is shared between the national government and state governments. The national government is divided into three branches: the legislative branch, which includes the Senate and the House of Representatives; the executive branch, headed by the president; and the judicial branch, including the Supreme Court. The three branches of government are explained in more detail on page 339.

## The Bill of Rights

When the Constitution was sent to the states for approval, some states would not approve it until it included a bill of rights listing the individual rights of every citizen. So, the convention promised a bill of rights would be attached to the final version. When the first Congress met in 1789, it immediately considered several amendments, or additions. James Madison wrote twelve of them, which were presented to the states for final approval. Ten were approved. Those ten make up the Bill of Rights. They are also the first ten amendments to the Constitution. Following is a brief explanation of each amendment in the Bill of Rights.

1. Prohibits a national religion and guarantees the freedoms of speech, of the press, to meet peaceably together in groups, and to go to the government to solve problems.

2. Gives citizens the right to own guns so that states can maintain militias.

3. Prohibits the government from forcing citizens to house soldiers in their homes.

4. Limits the government's right to search or take personal belongings.

5. Guarantees fair treatment for people charged with committing crimes.

6. Gives a person accused of a crime the right to know what the crime is, to have a lawyer, and to have a speedy trial.

7. Guarantees a jury trial for disputes in which people sue for damages.

8. Forbids bail and fines that are too high as well as cruel and unusual punishment of prisoners.

9. Says that the rights listed in the Constitution are not the only rights of the people.

10. Gives any powers not given to the national government by the Constitution to the states or the people.

## Additional Amendments

An amendment can be added to the Constitution when enough members of Congress and citizens agree to it. So far, seventeen additional amendments have been added to the Constitution. Some famous amendments include the following.

13. Passed in 1865, making slavery illegal

16. Passed in 1913, allowing Congress to collect personal income tax

19. Passed in 1920, giving women the right to vote

26. Passed in 1971, allowing 18-year-olds to vote

# THE THREE BRANCHES OF GOVERNMENT

Delegates to the Constitutional Convention wanted to make sure that the U.S. government would never be controlled by one person or group alone. The delegates feared that if any person or group was given too much power, the country could once again be under the rule of a tyrant, as when Britain ruled the American Colonies. To avoid this, the Constitution divides the government into three branches: legislative, executive, and judicial.

## UNITED STATES GOVERNMENT

**Legislative Branch:** Headed by Congress, which is made up of the House of Representatives and the Senate. The main task of these two bodies is to make the laws by which our government operates. Its powers include passing laws, originating spending bills (House), impeaching, or charging officials with misconduct, (Senate) and approving treaties (Senate).

**Executive Branch:** Headed by the president. The president carries out federal laws and recommends new ones, directs national defense and foreign policy, and performs ceremonial duties. Powers include administering government, commanding the Armed Forces, dealing with international powers, acting as chief law enforcement office, and vetoing laws.

**Judicial Branch:** Headed by the Supreme Court, its powers include interpreting the Constitution, reviewing laws, and deciding cases involving states' rights.

By having the three branches of government, the Constitution built in a "checks-and-balances" system. No one branch of our government can become too powerful, because each branch is controlled by the other two in several ways. For example, the president may veto, or turn down, a law passed by Congress. Congress, however, can override that veto with a vote of two-thirds of both houses. Another example is that the Supreme Court may check Congress by declaring a law unconstitutional. This power is balanced by the power of the president to appoint members of the Supreme Court. The president's appointments, though, have to be approved by Congress. Look at the diagram below to see how this system of "checks and balances" works.

# MAKING LAWS

When a member of Congress decides to create a new law, he or she introduces a "bill." Any member of Congress can introduce a bill, but only members of the House of Representatives may introduce bills that deal with taxes or spending. Both houses of Congress must pass identical versions of a bill before it can become law.

Once a bill is introduced in either house, it goes through almost the same process. Follow this process below.

## HOW A BILL BECOMES A LAW

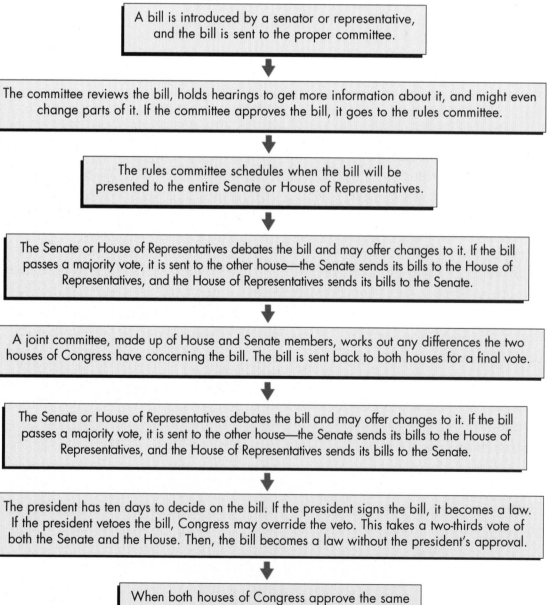

A bill is introduced by a senator or representative, and the bill is sent to the proper committee.

The committee reviews the bill, holds hearings to get more information about it, and might even change parts of it. If the committee approves the bill, it goes to the rules committee.

The rules committee schedules when the bill will be presented to the entire Senate or House of Representatives.

The Senate or House of Representatives debates the bill and may offer changes to it. If the bill passes a majority vote, it is sent to the other house—the Senate sends its bills to the House of Representatives, and the House of Representatives sends its bills to the Senate.

A joint committee, made up of House and Senate members, works out any differences the two houses of Congress have concerning the bill. The bill is sent back to both houses for a final vote.

The Senate or House of Representatives debates the bill and may offer changes to it. If the bill passes a majority vote, it is sent to the other house—the Senate sends its bills to the House of Representatives, and the House of Representatives sends its bills to the Senate.

The president has ten days to decide on the bill. If the president signs the bill, it becomes a law. If the president vetoes the bill, Congress may override the veto. This takes a two-thirds vote of both the Senate and the House. Then, the bill becomes a law without the president's approval.

When both houses of Congress approve the same version of the bill, it is sent to the president.

# THE PRESIDENT

## Requirements for President

1. Must be at least thirty-five years old.
2. Must be a natural citizen—born in the United States.
3. Must have lived in the United States for fourteen consecutive years.

## Term

Four years. May be re-elected once.

## Members of the President's Cabinet

Attorney General
Secretary of Agriculture
Secretary of Commerce
Secretary of Defense
Secretary of Education
Secretary of Energy
Secretary of Health and Human Services
Secretary of Housing and Urban Development
Secretary of the Interior
Secretary of Labor
Secretary of State (Foreign Affairs)
Secretary of Transportation
Secretary of the Treasury
Secretary of Veterans Affairs

## Order of Power

If a president is unable to serve out the full term, presidential power is passed along in the following order:

1. Vice President
2. Speaker of the House of Representatives
3. President pro tempore of the Senate
4. Secretary of State
5. Secretary of the Treasury
6. Secretary of Defense
7. Attorney General
8. Secretary of the Interior
9. Secretary of Agriculture
10. Secretary of Commerce

# U.S. PRESIDENTS

| | Presidents | Vice Presidents | Term | First Lady |
|---|---|---|---|---|
| 1. | George Washington | John Adams | 1789–1797 | Martha Dandridge Custis |
| 2. | John Adams | Thomas Jefferson | 1797–1801 | Abigail Smith |
| 3. | Thomas Jefferson | Aaron Burr | 1801–1805 | Martha Wayles Skelton |
| | | George Clinton | 1805–1809 | |
| 4. | James Madison | George Clinton | 1809–1813 | Dolley Payne Todd |
| | | Elbridge Gerry | 1813–1817 | |
| 5. | James Monroe | Daniel D. Tompkins | 1817–1825 | Elizabeth Kortright |
| 6. | John Quincy Adams | John C. Calhoun | 1825–1829 | Louisa Johnson |
| 7. | Andrew Jackson | John C. Calhoun | 1829–1833 | Rachel Donelson |
| | | Martin Van Buren | 1833–1837 | |
| 8. | Martin Van Buren | Richard M. Johnson | 1837–1841 | Hannah Hoes |
| 9. | William H. Harrison | John Tyler | 3/1841–4/1841 | Anna Tuthill Symmes |
| 10. | John Tyler | [vacant] | 1841–1845 | Julia Gardiner |
| 11. | James K. Polk | George M. Dallas | 1845–1849 | Sarah Childress |
| 12. | Zachary Taylor | Millard Fillmore | 1849–1850 | Margaret Mackall Smith |
| 13. | Millard Fillmore | [vacant] | 1850–1853 | Abigail Powers |
| 14. | Franklin Pierce | William R. King | 1853–1857 | Jane Means Appleton |
| 15. | James Buchanan | John C. Breckinridge | 1857–1861 | |
| 16. | Abraham Lincoln | Hannibal Hamlin | 1861–1865 | Mary Todd |
| | | Andrew Johnson | 1865 | |
| 17. | Andrew Johnson | [vacant] | 1865–1869 | Eliza McCardle |
| 18. | Ulysses S. Grant | Schuyler Colfax | 1869–1873 | Julia Dent |
| | | Henry Wilson | 1873–1877 | |
| 19. | Rutherford B. Hayes | William A. Wheeler | 1877–1881 | Lucy Ware Webb Hayes |
| 20. | James Garfield | Chester A. Arthur | 4/1881–9/1881 | Lucretia Rudolph |
| 21. | Chester A. Arthur | [vacant] | 1881–1885 | Ellen Lewis Herndon |
| 22. | Grover Cleveland | Thomas A. Hendricks | 1885–1889 | Frances Folsom |
| 23. | Benjamin Harrison | Levi P. Morton | 1889–1893 | Caroline Lavinia Scott |
| 24. | Grover Cleveland | Adlai E. Stevenson | 1893–1897 | Frances Folsom |

# U.S. PRESIDENTS

| | Presidents | Vice Presidents | Term | First Lady |
|---|---|---|---|---|
| 25. | William McKinley | Garret A. Hobart | 1897–1901 | Ida Saxton |
| | | Theodore Roosevelt | 1901 | |
| 26. | Theodore Roosevelt | Charles W. Fairbanks | 1901–1909 | Edith Kermit Carow |
| 27. | William H. Taft | James S. Sherman | 1909–1913 | Helen Herron |
| 28. | Woodrow Wilson | Thomas R. Marshall | 1913–1917 | Ellen Louise Axson |
| | | | 1917–1921 | Edith Bolling Galt |
| 29. | Warren G. Harding | Calvin Coolidge | 1921–1923 | Florence Kling |
| 30. | Calvin Coolidge | [vacant] | 1923–1925 | Grace Goodhue |
| | | Charles G. Dawes | 1925–1929 | |
| 31. | Herbert C. Hoover | Charles Curtis | 1929–1933 | Lou Henry |
| 32. | Franklin D. Roosevelt | John N. Garner | 1933–1941 | Anna Eleanor Roosevelt |
| | | Henry A. Wallace | 1941–1945 | |
| | | Harry S. Truman | 1/1945–4/1945 | |
| 33. | Harry S. Truman | [vacant] | 1945–1949 | Elizabeth Wallace |
| | | Alben W. Barkley | 1949–1953 | |
| 34. | Dwight D. Eisenhower | Richard M. Nixon | 1953–1961 | Mamie Doud |
| 35. | John F. Kennedy | Lyndon B. Johnson | 1/1961–11/1963 | Jacqueline Bouvier |
| 36. | Lyndon B. Johnson | [vacant] | 1963–1965 | Claudia (Lady Bird) Taylor |
| | | Hubert H. Humphrey | 1965–1969 | |
| 37. | Richard M. Nixon | Spiro T. Agnew | 1969–1973 | Thelma (Pat) Ryan |
| | | Gerald R. Ford | 1/1973–8/1974 | |
| 38. | Gerald R. Ford | Nelson A. Rockefeller | 1974–1977 | Elizabeth Bloomer |
| 39. | James Earl Carter | Walter F. Mondale | 1977–1981 | Rosalynn Smith |
| 40. | Ronald Reagan | George H. Bush | 1981–1985 | Nancy Davis |
| | | | 1985–1989 | |
| 41. | George H. Bush | J. Danforth Quayle | 1989–1993 | Barbara Pierce |
| 42. | William J. Clinton | Albert Gore | 1993–2001 | Hillary Rodham |
| 43. | George W. Bush | Richard B. Cheney | 2000–present | Laura Welch |

# THE UNITED STATES, CAPITALS, AND DATES OF STATEHOOD

WASHINGTON
1889
★ Olympia

★ Helena

NORTH DAKOTA
1889
Bismarc

★ Salem

MONTANA
1889

OREGON
1859

★ Boise

IDAHO
1890

Pierre

SOUTH DAKOTA
1889

WYOMING
1890

CALIFORNIA
1850

★ Carson City

Salt Lake City ★

Cheyenne ★

NEBRASKA
1867

★ Sacramento

NEVADA
1864

UTAH
1896

Denver
★

COLORADO
1876

ARIZONA
1912

Santa Fe
★

★ Phoenix

NEW MEXICO
1912

ALASKA
1959

★ Honolulu

HAWAII
1959

★ Juneau

MINNESOTA
1858
★ St. Paul

WISCONSIN
1848
★ Madison

MAINE
1820
★ Augusta

NEW HAMPSHIRE
1788

VERMONT
1791
★ Montpelier
★ Concord

MASSACHUSETTS
1788

IOWA
1846
★ Des Moines

ILLINOIS
1818
★ Springfield

INDIANA
1816
★ Indianapolis

MICHIGAN
1837
★ Lansing

OHIO
1803
★ Columbus

NEW YORK
1788
★ Albany

★ Boston

Providence
RHODE ISLAND
1790

Hartford
CONNECTICUT
1788

PENNSYLVANIA
1787
★ Harrisburg

Trenton
NEW JERSEY
1787

Lincoln ★

MISSOURI
1821
★ Jefferson City

★ Topeka
KANSAS
1861

WEST
VIRGINIA
1863
★ Charleston

Dover
DELAWARE
1787

Annapolis
MARYLAND
1788

VIRGINIA
1788
★ Richmond

WASHINGTON, D.C.

KENTUCKY
1792
★ Frankfort

OKLAHOMA
1907
Oklahoma City

ARKANSAS
1836
★ Little Rock

TENNESSEE
1796
★ Nashville

NORTH CAROLINA
1789
★ Raleigh

SOUTH CAROLINA
1788
★ Columbia

MISSISSIPPI
1817
★ Jackson

ALABAMA
1819
★ Montgomery

GEORGIA
1788
★ Atlanta

LOUISIANA
1812
★ Baton Rouge

TEXAS
1845
★ Austin

★ Tallahassee

FLORIDA
1845

345

# ANSWER KEY

## Page 11

The three animals pictured are a woolly mammoth, a saber-toothed cat, and a ground sloth. All three of these animals lived in North America when the earliest Americans arrived. All three of these animals are now extinct, which means there are none left alive. Your report might contain information about the size of the animal you chose, as well as where it lived and what it ate.

## Page 15

The recipe you chose may be any recipe that includes corn as an ingredient. For example, you might have chosen corn chowder, corn pudding, succotash, or even corn bread, which is made from cornmeal.

## Page 18

Your petroglyph may be a simple, outline drawing of anything from your everyday life. For example, you might draw a petroglyph of you and a pet, of your family, or of some friends playing soccer.

## Page 22

Your completed table should look like this:

| Found in Mounds | Came From |
| --- | --- |
| copper | Great Lakes |
| seashells | Gulf of Mexico |
| silver | Canada |
| mica | Tennessee |
| shark's teeth | Florida |

## Page 26

The reasons why joining the federation of Five Nations would benefit an individual Indian nation might include the following:

- By being united, the Indian nations could better defend themselves.

- The government of the federation would decide when the Indian nations would go to war against other Indian groups.

- The government of the federation would try to settle differences among its members.

- The federation could provide a network for trade among its members and with others.

- The federation could provide a way to spread news and important information among its members.

## Page 29

The hand signals you created may include any words you think the Plains Indians might have needed to communicate with each other. For example you might have created signals for the words *come, go, wait, today, tomorrow,* or *enemy.*

## Page 34

Some of the errors you might have noticed on the 1490 world map when you compared it to a present-day world map include the following.

- The shape of Africa is wrong.

- The shape of Asia is wrong.

- The map does not show North and South America.

- The map does not show Australia.

- The map does not show Japan, the Philippines, or other islands in the Pacific Ocean.

- The map does not show Antarctica.

## Page 38

Your map should look like the one below to show correctly the route Juan Ponce de León followed on his 1513 voyage.

## Page 43

Your map key should look like the one below to show correctly the routes followed by Verrazzano and Hudson as they searched the New World.

| Route | Explorer |
| --- | --- |
| – – – – | Verrazzano (1523) |
| —— | Hudson (1609) |
| — · — · | Hudson (1610) |

## Page 47

Your completed figure-of-eight knot and square knot should look like the picture of each knot shown on page 49. If your knots do not look like the pictures, ask an older friend or relative to help you retie the knots.

## Page 53

You should have used the following Arabic numbers to replace the Roman numerals in the sentences.

1. 2    2. 23    3. 4    4. 17    5. 100

## Page 58

Your time line should look like the one below to show the correct order of events in the history of Roanoke.

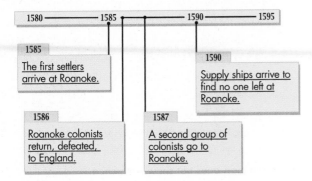

## Page 62

Your advertisement may include any words and pictures that would encourage people to come to an American colony in the 1600s. For example, you might say something like this: Great opportunity to seek your fortune in an exciting, new land!

## Page 66

You probably found it difficult to pack all the things you wanted to take to start a new life in a new country. Some items you might have packed could include rugged clothing and sturdy shoes, a cooking pot and skillet, a knife and a few cooking utensils, matches and candles, needle and thread, a fishing line and fishhooks, vegetable seeds and a garden trowel, a hatchet and nails, small saw, pencils and paper, first-aid supplies, and a book on wilderness survival.

## Page 71

You may have numbered the traits in various ways, depending on which traits you think are most important for a leader. For example, you might think the most important trait for a leader is to be *fair* or *honest* or *brave*. Other traits you may have thought of might include *decisive, generous,* or *kind.*

## Page 75

You could have chosen any modern machine, such as a washing machine, dishwasher, vacuum cleaner, or hair drier for your answer. Most likely, the machine you

chose is important because it makes life easier and allows you more time to do other things, such as sports, reading, and visiting with friends.

## Page 78

You should have numbered the sentences as shown below to put the events of Mary Johnson's life in the correct order.

7 Mary and Anthony move to Maryland.
2 Mary is kidnapped and taken to America.
8 Anthony dies.
4 Mary marries Anthony.
3 Mary goes to work on a Virginia farm.
1 Mary is born in Africa.
6 Mary and Anthony start a farm.
5 Mary and Anthony gain their freedom.
9 Mary dies.

Your storyboard of Mary Johnson's life should include all nine of the events above, placed in the correct order and each illustrated with a drawing.

## Page 82

Your completed word puzzle should look like this:

## Page 87

As you work, think about whether you would include windows in your house if you were really going to live there. Compare the amount of work involved in putting a window hole in the wall with the pleasure having a window will give you and your family.

## Page 92

1. b
2. b
3. c
4. Hardly a man is now alive

   (Who remembers that famous day and year.)

## Page 96

1. You may want to have someone read aloud the Baron's description. Ask the person to pause after each phrase to give you time physically to do what the words describe.

**Page 96** (continued)

2. Ask a friend or family member to read your instructions to make sure they are clear. Make revisions if you need to.

## Page 100

Check your picture to see if the woman you have drawn is wearing clothing like the clothing in the pictures for the readings in this unit.

## Page 103

Ship names usually are written in italic letters. To show that you are writing in italic, underline any ship's name that you use.

When you talk about what the battle meant to the United States, you might say that John Paul Jones was a lot like other American soldiers and sailors. He just wouldn't give up. The story of John Paul Jones and his success at sea probably inspired other Americans to keep fighting.

## Page 107

Each time you fold your "flag," stop and make sure that your fold looks like the fold in the illustration. You should end with a neat triangle.

## Page 111

Here are some of the streets you may have spotted: Pennsylvania Avenue, Massachusetts Avenue, Maryland Avenue, Delaware Avenue, Indiana Avenue, Louisiana Avenue, Virginia Avenue, and New Jersey Avenue.

## Page 117

If you decided that your life was better when you followed one of Thomas Jefferson's pieces of advice, choose another. Then, for the next week, try to live by that piece of advice, too. It might help to write the advice on a small piece of paper. Then, tape the paper to a mirror or to another place where you know you will see it every day. If you wish, circle three things Thomas said that you think you might tell your own grandchildren.

## Page 121

You may wish to set a timer or look at your watch and limit to two or three minutes the time you take to study the machine.

As you compare your drawing to the actual machine, identify the part that was most difficult for you to remember. Think about the problems Samuel Slater faced as he tried to memorize the parts of an English spinning machine.

## Page 125

1. c. In 1790 and 1795, the pictograph shows less than 1 bale of cotton. That means less than 25,000 bales of cotton actually were grown.

2. a. More cotton was grown. This is a good guess,

because in each five-year period on the pictograph, the amount of cotton grown in the U.S. went up.

3. Eli Whitney helped cotton growing increase dramatically. You can tell this from the pictograph. In 1800, after Eli had invented his cotton gin, there was a big increase in the amount of cotton being grown in the United States.

## Page 131

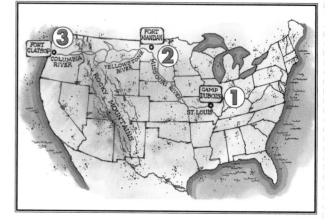

## Page 136

You probably realized quickly what difficult work it was to pole a keelboat against the current of a mighty river such as the Mississippi. In addition to the hard physical labor, your paragraph might describe the rhythm of the repeating motions of poling the keelboat.

## Page 141

Your epitaph could tell any of several things about Tecumseh, such as how he believed that the land belonged to all the Indians, how he tried to unite the Indian groups, or how he died in battle defending his beliefs.

## Page 145

Your poem or song can be about any event, such as a parade, a fireworks display, or a performance, or sight, such as a sunset, a mountain vista, or ocean scene, that impressed you. Your poem or song should be written so that others reading it can have a sense of how the event or sight was impressive.

## Page 150

You should have matched the pictures to the sentences as follows:
Picture 1: C; Picture 2: A; Picture 3: D; Picture 4: B.

## Page 155

If you used 2, 3, 4, 5, or 6 people in your figuring, you can find your answers on the following chart. First, locate the number of people you used. Then look down that column. Those are your answers!

## Page 155 (continued)

| | **People** | | | | |
|---|---|---|---|---|---|
| **Pounds of Food per Person** | **2** | **3** | **4** | **5** | **6** |
| 150 lbs. flour | 300 | 450 | 600 | 750 | 900 |
| 60 lbs. bacon | 120 | 180 | 240 | 300 | 360 |
| 50 lbs. lard | 100 | 150 | 200 | 250 | 300 |
| 25 lbs. sugar | 50 | 75 | 100 | 125 | 150 |
| 15 lbs. coffee | 30 | 45 | 60 | 75 | 90 |
| 10 lbs. salt | 20 | 30 | 40 | 50 | 60 |
| pounds of other items you could take | 1380 | 1070 | 760 | 450 | 140 |

## Page 159

You may want to check your work by first explaining your assignment to a relative or friend, then showing the relative or friend your poster. Ask whether your poster makes the person feel inspired. If the answer is yes, you have done a good job.

## Page 165

Make sure that you practice panning for gold outside or over a large bucket, since it is a messy process. It is tricky to pan for gold, so you may have to try it a couple of times.

## Page 169

The word is "HORSE."

When you make up your own secret message, make sure you leave space between the symbols for each letter, so the Morse code is easier to look up on the chart.

## Page 175

1. b. a little less than 1 million
2. b. in 1830
3. b. no
4. a. about 3 million more (3.9 million in 1860 minus .9 million in 1800 equals 3 million)

## Page 180

The compromise you used as your example should clearly show how you and another person settled a difference by each giving up something you wanted. In a true compromise, each would gain something and each would lose something.

You might have stated that a compromise is a good way to settle a difference because neither person is giving up everything. However, for a compromise to be fair, what both people are gaining should be about equal and what both are giving up should be about equal.

## Page 184

You may wish to draw or write about how happy the runaways felt when the slave catchers rode on by, fooled by the playing children. Or, you may wish to draw or write about how the runaways felt when they reached the North and gained their freedom.

## Page 188

Here are some sentences like those you might have written:

1. Actually, our democracy has worked well for over 200 years. Also, very few communist countries are left in the world, while more and more countries are becoming democracies.

2. Many ordinary citizens think it is very important to vote. Sometimes they choose the nation's leaders wisely. Sometimes they choose poorly. But in general, voters are the backbone of a democracy.

3. Many women enjoy voting and take the responsibility of voting very seriously. In fact, many women are now senators and representatives in our government.

## Page 193

Here are the places you should have marked on your map:

Gettysburg: C
Culp's Hill: U
Cemetery Ridge: U
Peach Orchard: U
Wheatfield: U
Devil's Den: U
Little Round Top: U

## Page 197

Here are how the fronts and backs match up:
**the penny:**
front: Abraham Lincoln
back: Lincoln Memorial, a building in Washington, D.C., honoring President Lincoln

**the nickel:**
front: Thomas Jefferson
back: Monticello, President Jefferson's home

**the dime:**
front: Franklin D. Roosevelt
back: the torch of liberty and branches of laurel and oak trees

**the quarter:**
front: George Washington
back: the eagle

**Page 197** (continued)
Help your friend or relative identify the presidents and their coins using the list above.

**Page 204**
1. a. 6:00 A.M.
2. c. Atlanta
3. a. mountainous land
4. Find where you live on the map. (Ask an adult to help you if you have trouble with this.) Then, look at the top of the map to find the name of the time zone in which you live.

**Page 209**
Since your problems are aimed at younger students, you should keep them pretty simple, just as they are in the chart. Instead of televisions, you can choose to use cars, toasters, computers, tennis shoes, or any other modern-day objects in your math problems.

**Page 214**
1. before
2. after
3. after

**Page 220**
You might want to use an encyclopedia or the Internet to find a picture of the animal you are going to draw. Then, you can use that picture as a guide. Your poster should be convincing as to why the animal should be saved. For example, you might explain why the animal is important to the environment and how it might disappear forever if it is not protected.

**Page 225**
**Sample Answers:**

| | |
|---|---|
| Printing Telegraph | 1869 |
| Stock Ticker | 1869 |
| Typewriter | 1871 |
| Automatic Telegraph | 1872 |
| Perforating Pens | 1877 |
| Incandescent Electric Lamp | 1879 |
| Electric Meter | 1881 |
| Electric Motor | 1881 |
| Phonograph Recorder | 1888 |
| Kinetograph | 1888 |

**Page 230**
1. c. Philadelphia's population was the highest in 1870. It had nearly 700,000 people, while Detroit and Los Angeles had under 100,000 people.
2. b. The population of Detroit grew from about 90,000 in 1870 to nearly 300,000 in 1900.
3. c. It makes sense to think that the cities settled first would be larger than the cities settled later, and according to the bar graph, Philadelphia had the largest population of the three cities in 1870 and in 1900.

**Page 235**
1. You may have named three of the following things that are the same: students, a teacher, a U.S. flag, electric lights, writing on the chalkboard, presidents' pictures hung on the wall.
2. You may have chosen these for your answers: Girls today usually don't wear long skirts; most girls today don't wear their hair in a bun; boys usually don't have to wear ties to school; classrooms don't usually have benches.
3. You may have chosen facts about Booker T. Washington, George Washington Carver, or Tuskegee Institute. For example, you might say that Booker T. Washington was born a slave; he worked hard to educate himself; he started the Tuskegee Institute to educate African Americans.

**Page 241**
Your welcome message should be different from the examples given, but could include any friendly words of welcome for newcomers to the United States.

**Page 246**
You could choose some of your answers based on how you yourself might use a car. Grocery shopping, food shopping, taking the dog to the vet's, and going on vacation all might appear on your list.

**Page 250**
If you find your average is less than the average of the first plane's flights, get another piece of paper and try changing another part of the airplane. You might also try flying one of your planes five times. Then, figure an average, and see if the average is the same as the average you figured on fewer flights.

**Page 255**
The reasons you listed might include the following.
• The distance over land is shortest.
• There is a river (or lake) that can be used as part of the canal.
• There are no mountains that have to be crossed.

**Page 259**
Your map should support the statement, because many of the states in the West are colored to represent the earliest time period through 1896.

**Page 264**
It is said that the artist who drew the Uncle Sam in the poster used himself as a model. You may want to create a character with your face for your own poster. Your poster should use drawings and words to make people want to join the Army.

## Page 268

Your map should look pretty much like this:

Use the ruler to measure the length of the line you have drawn. Then multiply the number of inches you get by the number of miles per inch, according to the map scale. Your answer should be around 3,600 miles.

## Page 274

1. a. You can find the current price under the heading, "Last."

2. b. The stock dropped by $.25.

3. b. The high for the past year was $28.88, $10 higher than the current price. The low for the past year was $14.00, $4.88 lower than the current price.

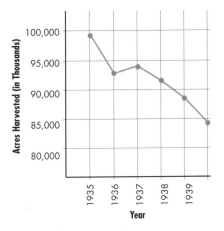

## Page 278

For your mural, you may choose to draw any scene of everyday American life, such as Americans working, Americans playing, Americans at home, or Americans on vacation.

## Page 284

Your line graph should look like this:
1. 1935
2. 1940
3. The number of acres of corn harvested decreased during the Dust Bowl years.

## Page 287

If you ran less than 100 yards in 10 seconds, subtract how far you ran from 100. The answer tells you how much farther Jesse could run than you. If you ran more than 100 yards, subtract 100 from the distance you ran. The answer tells you how much farther you could run than Jesse.

## Page 293

You probably found it difficult to plan an appetizing menu without the rationed foods. Your menu might include fresh vegetables and fruits plus foods such as pasta, rice, and beans.

People sometimes gave their dishes names that reminded them of the war they were helping to fight through rationing. "Military Meatballs," "Home Front Vegetable Plate," and "Wartime Cake" all are examples of food nicknames created during World War II. You might wish to make up a World-War-II-type nickname for your soup or salad, main dish, or dessert.

## Page 297

Your bar graph should look like this:

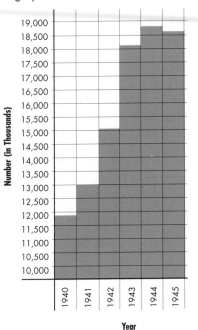

## Page 302

Here are the words hidden in the word search:

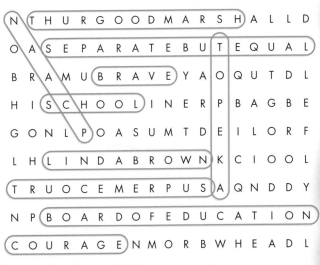

Make sure your sentence includes three of the terms hidden in the word search. Maybe your sentence will read something like this sentence:
Linda Brown's father took the Topeka Board of Education to the Supreme Court.

## Page 307

Your drawing or collage may show any example of people doing things that help our country. For example, you might show people working to clean up a highway, a river, or a beach. You could show doctors and nurses caring for the sick or a teacher helping students to learn. You could show firefighters or police officers keeping a community safe. You could show a farmer planting crops that feed the nation.

## Page 311

There are no right and wrong answers for this activity. Our country's founding fathers thought all these rights were important. In fact, they felt these rights are so important that they put all of them in the very first amendment to the Constitution.

## Page 316

If you decide to draw Norman Bel Geddes's dream of the future of transportation, you might want to start by rereading the first two paragraphs of the activity before you begin drawing. A drawing of Geddes's plan would show highways up to 14 lanes wide and several levels high. The bottom levels should have exits and parking areas. The top levels should be for through traffic.

If you decide to create your own transportation future, you may decide not to include cars at all. If you wish, you can create a whole new way to travel in your drawing.
Chicago to Seattle: I-90
Michigan to Florida: I-75
Texas to Minnesota I-35

## Page 320

The words for the numbers may be in any language. In Spanish, the words are: uno (1), dos (2), tres (3), cuatro (4), cinco (5). Be sure to ask your friend or relative how to pronounce the words.

## Page 325

You may choose to use an unusual design for your monument, in the same way that Maya Lin chose her wall. Or, you may choose to create a statue that looks like the man you are honoring.

Before you begin your design, you may want to do some additional studying about the man you have chosen. Then, you can use what you have learned to make sure your monument reflects something that was important to that man.

## Page 330

Your project may be anything that will help improve your environment. For example, you might volunteer to clean up a park or a vacant lot. You might decide to plant some flowers, shrubs, or trees in your own yard. Even picking up litter on the sidewalk is a way to help your environment.

If you belong to a group, such as Boy Scouts, Girl Scouts, or 4-H, you may wish to ask if the group's members would like to join you in planning and carrying out an Earth Day project.

If you have a camera, you may want to take a "before" picture of the area on which you're going to work and an "after" picture when you have finished. These pictures will remind you that one person or one group really can make a difference to Earth.

## Page 334

Here are some key words you might use to help you find articles about your topic:

Reading 1: Linda Brown Goes to School: Linda Brown, segregation, Brown v. Board of Education of Topeka.

Reading 2: John F. Kennedy's Legacy: John F. Kennedy, Peace Corps, space race, Neil A. Armstrong

Reading 3: Martin Luther King, Jr.: Martin Luther King, Jr., civil rights, Rosa Parks, Montgomery bus boycott

Reading 4: The Interstate Highway System: Cold War, Dwight D. Eisenhower, Pennsylvania Turnpike, Dwight D. Eisenhower System of Interstate and Defense Highways

Reading 5: Cesar Chavez Organizes Workers: Cesar Chavez, migrant worker, United Farm Workers of America

Reading 6: Maya Lin Designs a Memorial: Maya Lin, Vietnam Veterans Memorial, Vietnam War

Reading 7: The Wreck of the Exxon Valdez: conservation, Yellowstone National Park, Exxon Valdez, Prince William Sound

Reading 8: The Information Superhighway: ENIAC, ARPANet, Internet, World Wide Web